HAWAII

BY BIKE ™

20 TOURS GEARED FOR DISCOVERY

Rainbows sparkle in Akaka Falls

HAWAII
BY BIKE™
20 TOURS GEARED FOR DISCOVERY

Nadine Slavinski

THE
MOUNTAINEERS

To my Mom, who's still the best

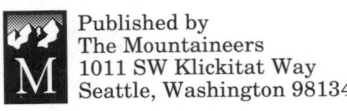 Published by
The Mountaineers
1011 SW Klickitat Way
Seattle, Washington 98134

9 8 7 6 5
5 4 3 2 1

Published simultaneously in Canada by Douglas & McIntyre, Ltd., 1615 Venables Street, Vancouver, B.C. V5L 2H1

Published simultaneously in Great Britain by Cordee, 3a DeMontfort Street, Leicester, England, LE1 7HD

Manufactured in the United States of America

Edited by Heath Silberfeld
Maps by Barbara Dow
All photographs by the author
Cover design by Watson Graphics
Book design and typesetting by The Mountaineers Books
Book layout by Michelle Taverniti

Cover photograph: lush growth along the road to Hana, Maui, Hawaii © James Randkley/Allstock; *inset*, author cycling on Maui

Library of Congress Cataloging–in–Publication Data
Slavinski, Nadine, 1968–
    Hawaii by bike : 20 tours geared for discovery / Nadine Slavinski.
        p.   cm.
    Includes index.
    ISBN 0-89886-432-1 (pbk.)
    1. Bicycle touring—Hawaii—Guidebooks.   2. Hawaii—Guidebooks.
3. Hawaii—Description and travel. I. Title.
GV1045.5.H3S53   1995
796.6'4'09969—dc20   94–48634
                                            CIP

CONTENTS

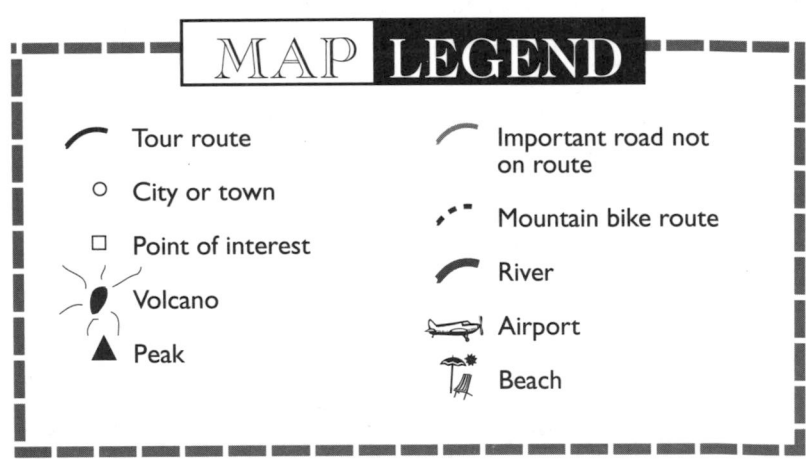

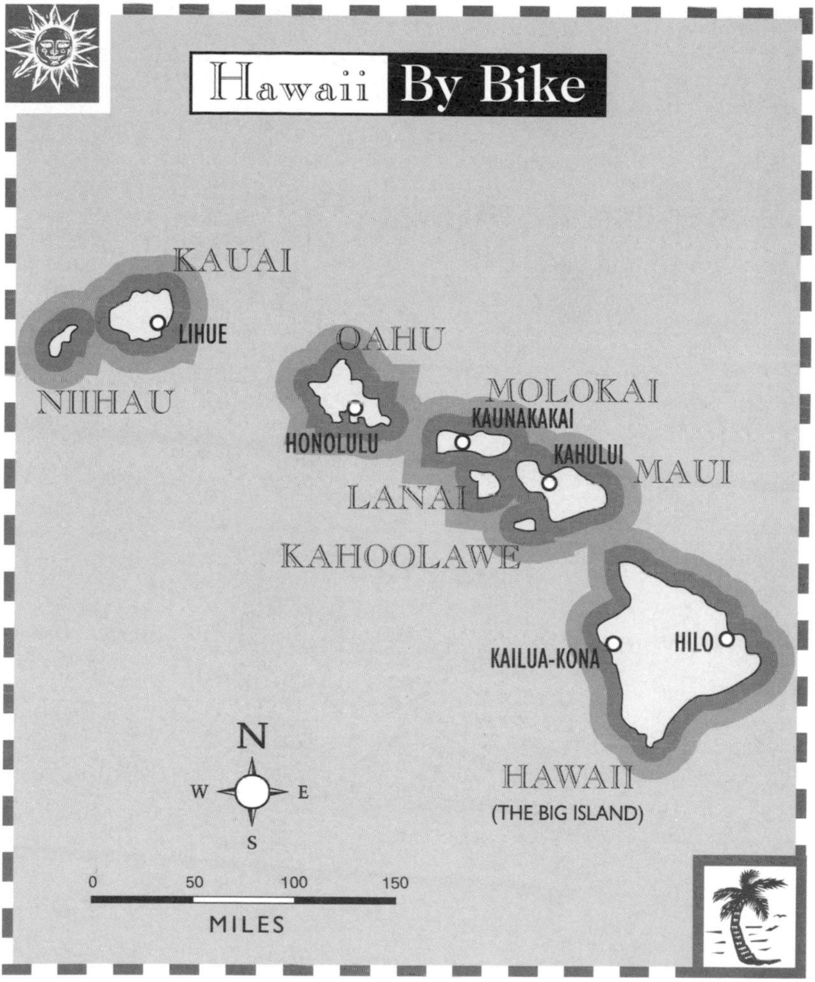

Hawaii By Bike

KAUAI

LIHUE

NIIHAU

OAHU

HONOLULU

MOLOKAI

KAUNAKAKAI

KAHULUI

LANAI

MAUI

KAHOOLAWE

KAILUA-KONA   HILO

HAWAII
(THE BIG ISLAND)

N
W • E
S

| 0 | 50 | 100 | 150 |

MILES

Hula display entertains visitors to Honolulu.

PREFACE

In travel, the memories you keep longest and most vividly are the journey's extremes, its highs and lows. At its most perfect, Hawaii leaves images of rainbows streaming over pounding waterfalls and mesmerizing lines of surf rolling over perfect white beaches. A cyclist's Hawaiian highs might include a sight as magnificent as whales breaching on a perfect tropical day or an image as fine as the newest leaves of a fern, curled into tight rolls, or simply the memory of a stranger's kindness to a weary traveler in an unfamiliar place. These are the good times, when Hawaii does indeed seem to be (in Mark Twain's words) "the loveliest fleet of islands that lies anchored in any ocean."

Hawaiian lows? They certainly occur. You can count on having an exhausting day when your legs cannot manage even one more rotation, when every bump stretches into an endless mountain. There will be times when winds seem to counter your forward motion, or when the picture-perfect vista you were promised is obscured by a blanket of clouds.

The most common cyclist's low, no matter where one travels, must be the flat tire. Punctures interrupt your progress, delay your lunch break, and spoil your mood. Instead of flying along gracefully, you find yourself sitting in the dirt trying to find the needle-thin hole in your tube. It could happen anywhere, but many wondrous and delightful things occur in Hawaii alongside the challenges. As I cursed and fumbled with one flat tire in Hawaii, I caught sight of two whales playing offshore. Racing and splashing, the two were joined by a third whale, the trio flipping their tails before diving and sending up fountains of spray upon resurfacing. Long after the flat was fixed and ready to go, I remained to watch their offshore antics.

The point is that Hawaii, even at its worst, is not bad at all. Part of cycling is gaining a complete experience, balancing both the good and the not-so-good. For every black cloud that promises to soak you to the bone, a crisp white missionary church stands out before lush green hills and blue ocean waters. For every tiring, endless ascent, there comes a thrilling downhill cruise. Bicycle touring in Hawaii promises both challenge and rewards, as well as memories rich with pleasant images like these.

PART I

GENERAL INFORMATION

Tropical sunset brings another day of touring to a close.

WHY HAWAII BY BIKE?

Some things can only be seen in Hawaii, and some things can only be appreciated by bike. With that in mind, think of what a combination of the two can offer. Roll together Hawaii's stunning tropical scenery, multiethnic culture, and prime natural attractions, then add them to all the advantages of bicycle travel: the flexibility to travel in the direction and pace of your choice, freedom from restrictive schedules and high costs of conventional travel, and a close understanding of your host land.

The reasons for choosing Hawaii as a travel destination are many. Hawaii offers the best of two worlds as a Pacific island that is also a part of the United States. Visitors need not deal with money, language, or border confusions, or worry about mysterious tropical diseases. At the same time, they can experience the most exciting aspects of an exotic island destination by cycling remote coasts, hiking volcanic ridgelines, or simply relaxing by turquoise waters on a white sand beach.

Hawaii is a fascinating blend of native culture, immigrant influences, and modern movements. In a single bicycle tour, one can explore historic village ruins, step inside a pristine missionary church, and watch the children of a small town fly colorful kites in a brisk seaside breeze. Cyclists can pedal miles along scenic, unpopulated coastlines, then stop to sample Hawaiian wine and spend the night at a beachside campsite.

Bicycling is a fitting means by which to travel Hawaii for several reasons. First, the slower pace of a bicycle approximates the pace and mellow attitude typical of Hawaii. Instead of being another frantic mainlander speeding to cram sights into a short vacation, you can linger over each newfound treasure or view. Your bicycle immediately sets you apart as a motivated, interesting visitor who demonstrates a true interest in Hawaii. Many locals approached me on their own initiative, offering advice, help, cold drinks, or directions to a secret local spot simply because of my wheels. Cyclists who set out to discover the "real" Hawaii will find it more easily than they ever imagined.

Unlike motorized travel, cycling emphasizes the journey, not just the destination. Cyclists are better equipped to see, learn, and experience throughout their travels because they move in such close contact with the land. Bicycle travel delivers more subtlety of detail than does a blur framed by a car window. Along with the most spectacular scenery, cyclists notice the most modest: children at play, dogs snoozing in the shade, or roadside fruit stands that operate on an honesty system.

The islands teem with life and hidden delights, offering limitless opportunities for outdoor enthusiasts with open minds and strong legs. Invest just a small effort in exploring Hawaii and you will be pleasantly surprised at the numerous rewards. Meeting kind people, seeing beautiful scenery, and collecting lasting memories are just the most obvious prizes of a Hawaiian bicycle tour.

Other reasons for traveling Hawaii by bike have as much to do with how much the islands offer off two wheels as on. Cyclists do not have to pedal marathon distances before coming across a tempting opportunity

Shopping for snacks at an honor-system fruit stand

to hike, kayak, snorkel, or just relax on the beach. For this reason, Hawaii is not simply a good choice for cycling enthusiasts, but for any lovers of the outdoors who wish to challenge themselves, enjoy Hawaii's air and waters, and go to bed pleasantly weary from the day's adventures.

Having said that, it is time for a warning: Do not fool yourself into believing that bicycling Hawaii will be an idyllic endeavor. There is plenty to challenge—and perhaps even discourage—the traveler in Hawaii. Towering volcanoes have a nasty habit of putting thousand-foot ascents between you and your chosen destination, setting up a battle of wills: Cyclist vs. the Mountain. When a fair tropical breeze blows, all is well, but full-scale ocean storms can also roar by, blowing a fierce headwind in your face or turning trails into swamps.

While Hawaii makes a good cycling destination, the sport has yet to sweep fanatically through the islands. Therefore facilities like repair shops and lack of alternative means of transportation leave gaping holes in your support network. Some islands, for example, do not have a single bicycle shop, leaving cyclists to their own devices. Many roads are in poor condition and prices are inflated. Finally, cycling can be a tiring and uncomfortable exercise at times. Many cyclists can sympathize with Mark Twain's complaint after spending the day in another type of saddle: ". . . to tell the honest truth, I have a certain delicacy about sitting down at all."

No place is perfect, and for all its disadvantages Hawaii can come surprisingly close to the ideal if your attitude allows it. While many tours in this book are extremely challenging, a number of shorter, easier tours give beginners a chance to meet Hawaii as well. Recognize your limits and set reasonable goals, but trust in your capabilities— and a little bit of luck as well. With that in mind and this guidebook in hand, you are ready for an exciting tour.

SAFETY FIRST!

Lazy days of pedaling past swaying palms, tropical scenery alive with color, steady lines of surf rolling over wide white beaches . . . ready for Hawaii by bike? But first things first—safety first! Any travel venture, no matter how modest or grand, carries some inherent risks. Before letting loose your dreams of touring Hawaii by bicycle, take a moment to consider safety issues.

Small, everyday risks of cycling are compounded when one spends hours a day, every day, on two wheels. You will be sharing the road with cars and traveling an unfamiliar land. Many tours visit remote areas where you can rely only on yourself for help in whatever situation may arise. To counter potential hazards, take the following advice to heart:

Always wear a helmet and use hand signals before turning or stopping. Wear highly visible colors and use bright panniers. Be careful not to let Hawaii's beautiful scenery distract your attention from the road—just pull over for a moment to take in a view instead of rushing by. Consider weather and road conditions carefully before moving ahead and prepare yourself with information on your route. Cycling Hawaii offers many opportunities to challenge yourself, but do not stretch your limits too far. Before making a quick turn, before starting off each morning, before deciding on a route, put safety first.

The following sections of Part I cover many aspects of bicycle touring, from pre-trip preparation to on-site advice. Together with these basic safety considerations they will help you enjoy a safe and richly rewarding bicycle tour of one of the world's most beautiful areas.

Now then, back to thoughts of picnicking under shady palms, breezing down a spectacular mountain road, gazing at a sky aglow with stars and new constellations. . . .

PLANNING A BICYCLE TOUR OF HAWAII

Preparation makes the key difference between an average trip and a memorable voyage. Many people have limited vacation time and waste much of it because they are uninformed. Know what you can see, what you want to see, and how to find it. Even those who like to take things as they come should have an inkling of what lies ahead before it rushes up and delivers a nasty surprise.

Preparation does not imply making inflexible plans, but merely serves as a flexible groundwork for a safe and successful trip. Neither does it imply a need to check off an exhausting list of sights in your guidebook. It simply means that to gain full enjoyment of Hawaii— whether that means exploring for hidden ruins or relaxing on a beach— you should know all your options and make decisions accordingly.

INFORMATION SOURCES. As a well-established tourist destination, Hawaii offers visitors many sources of information and assistance. First, contact the Hawaii Visitor's Bureau (H.V.B.) by telephoning (800) 257-2999 or writing to Waikiki Business Plaza, Suite 801, 2270 Kalakaua Avenue, Honolulu, HI 96815. To make the most of H.V.B., request specific information on cycling, camping, bed & breakfasts, and the like. Upon arrival on each island, pick up the free magazines *Guide to the Big Island, Guide to Maui, Guide to Oahu,* or *Guide to Kauai,* found in airports or tourist areas. These magazines are full of area maps, coupons for activities such as whale watching, and schedules of events like farmer's markets and hula exhibitions.

Supplement the information in this book with a good, general-purpose guidebook that provides further contacts and information on sights. Choose a reasonably sized book that includes tips for independent travel matched to your budget. *Hawaii,* a book in the respected Lonely Planet series, offers oodles of information for independent travelers of all budget levels, including good coverage of lower-end accommodations. For detailed information on one island at a time, look for the Handbook series by Moon Publications. *Country Roads of Hawaii* by Robert Wenkam offers a nice alternative to traditional guidebooks with a chatty, not encyclopedic, approach.

Bookstores in Hawaii also sell guidebooks specific to beaches, scuba diving, nature areas, hiking, Hawaii with kids, and so on. In addition to guides, look for works of fiction or travelogues. Such books add flesh and character to places listed in guidebooks, bringing history to life. For starters, try Michener's *Hawaii* or, for a lighter touch, Mark Twain's *Letters from Hawaii.*

Beyond general tourist information, you can also tap cyclists' resources such as the Hawaii Bicycling League (H.B.L.), whose bimonthly newsletter is available in many bicycle shops. The newsletter lists free group rides (on Oahu only). Contact H.B.L. at P.O. Box 4403, Honolulu, HI 96812-4403 (telephone 735-5756). Bicycle shops are still another valuable resource, since shopkeepers are happy to offer local insight on local rides or mountain-biking spots.

Bicycle tour operators offer another source of guidance and information. Even if you are not interested in a guided tour, you can gather ideas for your own trip by looking over their offerings. Locally, you will discover a booming business in downhill tours, especially on Maui and the Big Island. Bicycle shops that offer tours are noted in the Appendix, and many tour operators advertise on leaflets at airports or in outdoor/cycling magazines.

PAPERWORK AND MONEY. Hawaii is an exotic tropical getaway that is also part of the United States. Therefore, travelers need not worry about complicated paperwork, health problems, or other annoyances that sometimes restrict travel in other parts of the world. Canadian and British citizens, for example, do not need visas to enter the United States (British: for up to three months; Canadians: unlimited entry). Hawaii is an easygoing place where very little paperwork is necessary. Since few student and youth discounts are offered in Hawaii, do not bother obtaining an official international student identity card or an International Youth Hostel card.

The Food, Lodging, and Supplies section will give you an idea of how much money you can expect to spend in Hawaii depending on your style of travel (or lack thereof). Try to estimate a reasonable budget, but be prepared for costs to run higher. For security, bring money in the form of traveler's checks. Credit cards are readily accepted throughout Hawaii, useful both for making purchases and as a source of emergency cash. You might also choose to withdraw money from your home account by using automatic-teller machines (ATM) along the way. Before leaving home, ask your bank for an updated list of compatible ATM locations in Hawaii. If your home bank is not part of a major network, you may encounter difficulties finding a partner site in Hawaii.

TELEPHONES. Hawaii is 5 hours behind Eastern Standard Time (6 hours during Daylight Saving Time), and 3 (4) hours behind America's west coast. Subtract 10 (11) hours from Greenwich Mean Time to calculate Hawaii time.

The area code for Hawaii is 808 (all local phone numbers listed in this guide omit this area code). While public telephones abound in Hawaii's main towns, one can pedal for miles in remote areas without passing basics like telephones and mailboxes.

A phone call to a location on the same island is considered a local call, while interisland calls are considered long distance and are more expensive. Big businesses such as airlines often have different phone numbers for offices on each island, so be sure to dial the local office to save money.

TRAVEL TO AND BETWEEN THE ISLANDS. Hawaii is unique as a state composed of an island group. In the words of Dan Quayle, "Hawaii is a unique state. It is a small state. It is a state that is by it-self. It is a—well, all states are different, but it's got a particularly unique situation." However, there is no need to deploy flotation devices or barter for passage on a steamer. Today Hawaii's six principal is-lands are united with reasonably priced and easy flights, convenient even to cyclists.

Every island has at least one main airport for large planes, often supplemented by one or more small airfields serviced by eighteen-seater planes. Visitors flying to Hawaii from the mainland or abroad usually arrive in Honolulu (Oahu). The two main interisland airlines are Aloha Air (with subsidiary Aloha Island Air) and Hawaiian Air-lines. Interisland flights are short hops of only fifteen to thirty min-utes, but few flights directly link islands that are not neighbors. For example, to fly from Kauai to Maui you will probably stop over (but not change aircraft) in Oahu. Specific seat reservations are not made for interisland flights, so board early to secure a good seat. Ask the flight crew which side of the plane will offer the best views, as Hawaii from the air can be a spectacular sight.

Since air travel is common between Hawaii's islands, it is not neces-sary to book a seat far in advance. However, popular flight times do fill up quickly, so try to reserve a few days ahead. Thanks to the regularity with which passengers ship bulky baggage such as surfboards and scuba gear, transporting your bicycle between islands is a breeze. You need only remove panniers from your bicycle and pay a fee (see Shipping Your Bicycle below). However, small aircraft that serve secondary airfields may not accept or may severely restrict bicycle transportation (check with both the airline and the airport beforehand).

All interisland flights are the same price, no matter which islands you fly between. However, most travel agents sell flight coupons. These coupons, specific to one airline, are valid for any flight between any islands on any day until the expiration date. Coupons are sold individually or in sets of six, the latter a good bargain for two people visiting several islands.

Alternatively, only a few ferries provide interisland service, a fun and convenient option at about half the cost of air travel. For detailed information on these ferries, see the introductory sections of Maui, Molokai, or Lanai.

SHIPPING YOUR BICYCLE. Ironically, most airlines charge a fee for bicycles on domestic flights, although they demand no bicycle fee on international flights. Members of the League of American Wheelmen (L.A.W.) can ship their bikes for free on certain airlines if they book travel through the club's agent (L.A.W., 6707 Whitestone Road, Suite 209, Baltimore, MD 21207).

Before flying, buy a bicycle box at the airport and pack there. These huge boxes require only that you remove pedals and turn the handlebars, avoiding having to squeeze a completely disassembled bicycle into a cramped manufacturer's box. However, you may run into trouble if the airline runs out of boxes. To avoid trouble, try to obtain one of these boxes the day before and always bring extra tape to the airport. The scenario is much less complicated on interisland flights. You are not required to box your bicycle, only to remove panniers and accessories. Baggage handlers may ask you to remove the pedals and turn the handlebars, so keep the appropriate tools handy.

There are two schools of thought on the "to box or not to box" issue. Some people always box their bicycle for protection, while others maintain that baggage handlers are less likely to toss around an unpacked bicycle. I have had my bike abused both when boxed and unboxed, defying attempts to establish order in the chaotic world of airline travel.

Officially, airlines will not accept any responsibility for damage they cause by stacking suitcases and surfboards on top of your bicycle. I seem to average minor damage every third flight or so—ranging from rips in the saddle to a bent derailleur. Try to fly into a town with a bicycle shop and do not schedule any substantial cycling for the day of arrival or the next in case you require a time-consuming repair.

Finally, clean your bicycle frame and tires of dirt and mud before flying between islands. Non-native species pose a terrible threat to Hawaii's indigenous flora and fauna, and this measure can prevent spreading the problem species. Moreover, your luggage must pass agricultural inspection before leaving the state, so clean with particular care the day before departure.

EQUIPMENT

In bicycle touring, you depend entirely upon yourself and your equipment. A day or even an entire vacation can be spoiled by anything from a broken pocket knife to an unreliable bicycle. Bring quality, durable gear and take care of it. Keep track of your belongings and keep them clean and functioning efficiently. A few moments invested in basic prevention can save hours of frustration later.

Seasoned bicycle tourists know the value of versatile and dependable equipment, in terms of everything from clothing to panniers. Only so much gear can be packed on a bicycle, so multipurpose items can make a great difference in the load you carry. You will bear the full burden of caring for and pedaling around your gear, so choose carefully.

HELMET USE. Again, always wear a helmet. There is no excuse for cycling without a helmet when light, comfortable, and well-ventilated models are available at reasonable prices. Remember, fit is as essential as the helmet itself, as poorly fitted helmets offer little protection. Although chances of a serious accident are slim, the risk is compounded when one spends hours a day pedaling unfamiliar roads.

YOUR BICYCLE. Choosing a bicycle for riding in Hawaii is an important decision. Logic dictates that a specialized touring bicycle is best for touring, since they are efficient, comfortable, and sturdy, with features tailored for a loaded trip. However, a mountain bike may also be appropriate in Hawaii because many roads are bumpy or unpaved. On the other hand, mountain bikes are not ideal for road riding. Their frames are designed for off-road performance, not comfort, and features such as wide, knobby tires double your work load on pavement.

Therefore cycling Hawaii creates a perplexing situation. If you equip yourself with a touring bike, you risk suffering over bumps and occasionally restricting your range. On the other hand, you can prepare for rough riding with a mountain bike and pay the consequences in comfort and efficiency over long stretches of paved road that constitute the majority of most rides.

One possible resolution to the problem is compromise. Hybrid bicycles, a popular choice these days, are exactly that—a compromise. They are not terrific for touring, nor are they ideal for off-roading, but they are pretty good at both. Cyclists must decide what is best for themselves. Read tour descriptions thoroughly to decide what routes are most appealing to you and therefore what type of equipment is most appropriate. Those who want to do a little of everything will have to compromise to some degree, but they will also enjoy a well-rounded Hawaiian experience.

Tire selection is one quick way to adapt your bicycle to different road conditions. Hybrid tires with knobs that line up along a smooth central tread create less friction on the road but still offer good traction on trails. Like hybrid bikes, these tires are fairly good for everything but not ideal for anything. The only other option is to switch between two sets of tires, one narrower and smooth for the road, another knobby for off-road. If you elect this approach, use foldable tires. Although this may seem tiresome, it offers something closer to the ideal, and you will quickly hone the changing skills of an Indy 500 pit crew. Most tours that offer chances to ride both on- and off-road divide themselves conveniently enough for tire changing. Of course, you needn't bother to change tires at all for short stretches.

Off the beaten track on Lanai

BICYCLE RENTAL. Rental presents a practical alternative to shipping a bicycle from home, particularly for shorter trips. Bicycle and outdoor shops throughout Hawaii offer rentals, usually high-quality mountain bikes, as well as helmets, locks, and water bottles. Some shops lend panniers and car racks as well. For details, check the list of rental shops in the Appendix, and call ahead to check on availability.

PANNIERS. Panniers for your gear can be fitted on both front and rear racks. Although rear panniers alone should offer enough capacity for a short tour, the most stable combination consists of rear panniers together with low front panniers. This creates more even weight distribution and avoids overloading your already strained rear (rear wheel, that is).

Name-brand gear proves to hold up over time to accompany you on tour after tour, while generic products tend to develop zipper problems, rips, clamp breaks, and so on. A front handlebar bag with a plastic map case is essential for either road or mountain bikes, holding small items for quick access (snacks, sunblock, sunglasses, camera, wallet). Look for easy on/off pannier design and try to find a set that works well for day use (bags that convert or can be used in halves).

ACCESSORIES. Some accessories are practical, others are simply fun. First, always carry a frame-fit pump that matches the Schrader or Presta valves on your tubes (many pumps can be converted to either type). Mount two water bottles and a rear-view mirror on your bicycle as well. Optional items include a bell, a light, and fenders to block muddy spray. Cyclists riding mountain or hybrid bikes should attach handlebar extenders to their bar ends and pad them well. Finally, cyclometers prove to be both handy and fun. Measuring your progress and speed can be rewarding (at times disheartening) and helps track your position.

TOOLS. Tools are another category that divides cyclists into two camps: be-prepared roadside mechanics and minimalists. After thousands of miles of hauling around tools I never used, I have converted to conservative minimalism. Cyclists are not exempt from the basic principles of Murphy's Law; if you carry special tools in anticipation of one problem, any breakdown that does occur will certainly affect a completely unrelated part of the bicycle.

On one hand, the Hawaiian Islands are quite compact and developed, so that you are rarely far from a town with a bicycle shop. On the other hand, many suggested tours reach fairly remote areas that will seem even more remote when you encounter a problem. In any case, most problems that arise can be tackled with a few basic tools, ingenuity, and a positive attitude.

Pack along at least the basics: a patch kit, tire levers, oil, and any tools needed to reassemble your bicycle after shipping. Other basic tools include small pliers, hex or allen wrenches, and duct tape, that king of makeshift repairs. In order to decide what else you need, read tour descriptions to judge where you will be within range of professional help and where you will be on your own.

CAMPING GEAR. With the correct gear, camping can be as comfortable as any other accommodations. Basic camping gear includes a tent, sleeping bag, and pad; candle, matches, and flashlight; stove, cooking gear, and perhaps an extra water container for convenience. When selecting camping gear, it pays to invest in top-name brands, then care for your investment by keeping equipment clean and storing it properly.

Within reason, do not fret over the bulk of items as much as weight since a front/rear pannier combination provides plenty of space. Neither should you trade comfort for weight, or you will quickly discover that squeezing into a tiny tent each night is no fun. Although you must pedal your load over hill and dale, remember that the bicycle frame supports the weight, not your back as in hiking. It is better to carry a spacier tent, for example, and save weight elsewhere.

For Hawaii, dual-fuel backpacker stoves (using either unleaded gas or white gas) are best because fuel is always available at the nearest gas station. Special fuel cartridges or white gas can be difficult to obtain in Hawaii. Coleman-type fuel is also impractical because only gallon-size containers are sold in Hawaii. Remember to empty your stove of fuel before a flight and keep camping gear free of dirt that might transport spores of invasive species from one island to another.

Tap water is always drinkable in Hawaii, although some remote campgrounds do not supply drinking water (noted in text). If you will be camping in undeveloped areas, a small pack of water-purification tablets may come in handy. The need does not arise often enough to justify carrying a water filter, however.

CLOTHING. Panniers should not bulge with clothes that you could just not stand to leave at home. Bring a few useful, versatile items and wash them often. Try showering and immediately hand washing your biking clothes upon arrival at the day's destination and waiting for a more thorough machine wash every week or so when a good opportunity arises. If in doubt, bring too little rather than too much.

In spite of Hawaii's reputation for sun and warmth, at times you may need more than the bare minimum. Cyclists who find themselves at higher elevations on the wet side of an island will find warmer clothing welcome, so bring a few items that store compactly.

Although some prefer stiff cycling shoes, bicycle tourists should opt for comfortable sneakers ("tennies") that are as useful for hikes or around town as for cycling. After all, your aim is not to grind at the crankarms for hours but rather to see and enjoy Hawaii by bike or on foot.

Items on the following list will prepare you for most of your needs:

> bathing suit
> 2 to 3 pairs of socks
> 2 to 3 sets of underwear
> 2 T-shirts or tank tops
> long-sleeved shirt
> biking shorts
> casual shorts
> lightweight pants
> sweater
> waterproof jacket
> long underwear (or running tights/turtleneck)

OTHER GEAR. In addition to the gear mentioned above, a number of odds and ends should accompany you on your tour. Choose items carefully and resist the temptation to throw in unneeded extras at the last minute. To save space, bring multipurpose items such as soap that serves as a cleanser for body, clothes, and dishes. The following list will help you plan your packing:

Essentials:	Optional:
pocket knife	padded camera case
flashlight and batteries	compact day pack
first-aid kit and sunblock	snorkel and mask
matches in waterproof container	book or deck of cards
money belt	star map
highlighter for marking route	field binoculars
multipurpose soap	

PACKING. First, identify how often each item will be used or how quickly you may need access to it. Tools and a first-aid kit should be readily available, while small items like a pocket knife, pen, money, and extra roll of film can be on hand in your front handlebar bag. Include a good selection of plastic bags, from small ziplocks to large garbage bags. No panniers are waterproof, and simply lining each bag with one layer of plastic will not do. For maximum protection, wrap all gear in two plastic bags, and do not put more than a few items in each bag. Use garbage bags to protect bulky items like tents and sleeping bags.

Aim for equal distribution when packing your panniers, heaviest items low and near the center. Load front panniers carefully since they play an essential role in bicycle stability and handling. Strap camping gear atop your rear rack with web straps or bungee cords (a handy place to stick in extra items such as sandals or wet clothes). Once you establish a set routine for packing your gear, daily moves will be a breeze.

SECURITY

People traveling in unfamiliar areas put themselves at some risk. This is particularly true of popular tourist areas such as Hawaii where visitors stand out as easy targets. However, with a few basic precautions you can effectively counteract many potential risks. Always keep track of your valuables and assess every situation for security. If you do not feel comfortable in a certain area or undertaking a certain activity, avoid it.

Problems occur with far more frequency in large tourist centers than small towns where an old-fashioned, leave-your-door-unlocked atmosphere prevails. Crime on the islands generally falls into the category of petty theft. However, so many careless visitors offer such easy targets that a person who uses common sense is at little risk. Never leave your valuables unsecured, not even for a moment, and never leave a wallet "hidden" under a towel on the beach.

Your singlemost valuable item besides your wallet is your bicycle, so bring a good lock and use it whenever leaving your bicycle, even if only for a moment. While U-shaped bar locks are among the strongest options, it also pays to carry a cable to secure your bicycle to a tree or fence. Do not lock your bicycle just anywhere; leave it in view of yourself or others.

Beyond petty theft, there is a very slight risk of more serious problems. Before heading to a remote area, ask locals what to expect there. Respect people's privacy and NO TRESPASSING signs. Mountain bikers in particular should ask around before exploring trails blindly. Marijuana is illegally cultivated in some upslope areas, and farmers may not take kindly to unexpected visitors. Ask locals about an area before you pedal in; most often you will be assured that an area is safe, but it pays to be sure.

Cyclists who travel alone must exercise special caution. You will not have the advantage of calling on a companion to watch gear in turns or provide safety in numbers. Take extra care in locking your bicycle, choosing a place to leave your belongings, and in daily explorations. Simply accept these as the compromises that come with the advantages of solo travel.

Women must also keep security in mind at all times, whether traveling alone or with company. The key is to assess every situation carefully to prevent potential problems long before they can threaten. Women should not be afraid to chat or be friendly. On the other hand, be careful to present yourself as a capable and thinking person and do not divulge too many particulars (where you are staying, where you are heading). Solo women should not explore remote beaches or similar areas, either.

Solo women should not prioritize budget considerations over issues of safety. For example, camping in many public sites is not recommended. Be resourceful as well. Twice I found myself in tricky situations in which the nearest campsite was unsuitable and all B&Bs within range had no vacancies. Both times I called B&Bs run by women or couples and explained my situation, and both proprietors allowed me to pitch my tent on their lawns at no charge. Of course, you should not put people on the spot or expect special treatment, but as a last resort this is a good bet.

Unfortunately, security is an important consideration in the modern world. If you read this section and gulp, don't worry. In order to counter any potential risks, you must first identify them, as this section does. The more you keep security in mind, the less likely your chances of actually encountering trouble.

FOOD, LODGING, AND SUPPLIES

In practical terms, Hawaii is very much part of modern America, with supermarkets, convenient shopping hours, and a familiar system of organization. At the same time, however, Hawaii's physical and cultural landscape sets the islands apart as effectively as the Pacific Ocean. Whether you prefer a tour based on cozy B&Bs with dinners out or a more simple, camping-under-the stars approach, Hawaii offers numerous options.

Due to Hawaii's location and high rate of tourism, the cost of living is very high. You can expect everything from groceries to accommodations to cost 10 to 25 percent more than average mainland prices. However, with careful planning and restraint, even a budget cyclist can manage Hawaii quite reasonably.

FOOD. As a cyclist, you decide where you want to go, when, and at what pace. However, if you do not fuel your engine—that is, your body—correctly, you may be unable to keep pace with your wishes. Emphasize carbohydrates and steer away from fats in your diet. Consider yourself an athlete and take care of your body accordingly.

Food intake has a tremendous impact on your physical ability and mood, especially when your body is stressed by the demands of touring. When you anticipate a particularly long or difficult day, prepare an extra snack both for energy and a mental lift. Recognize that your body naturally swings through highs and lows during the day. Once you get to know the pattern, you can prevent a mild, natural dip from turning into a major abyss.

Make a conscious effort to drink throughout the day, emptying your water bottles several times. Tour descriptions include tips on water-refilling sources or warn of remote areas in which a third water bottle is essential. Ideally, fill one water bottle with fruit juice or punch for extra energy. Although tap water is fit for drinking, many locals prefer filtered or bottled water. Tap water on the dry side of an island usually tastes awful, having been piped in and heavily treated, while tap water on the wet side has a fresh, clear taste.

Remember to calculate the high cost of living in Hawaii into your budget. Visitors are often surprised to learn that most fruits and vegetables sold in Hawaii are shipped from the mainland or abroad. Even pasta, that staple of the budget biker, is considerably more expensive than on the mainland. Those on a tight budget can make up for high prices by preparing their own meals on a camping stove and shopping carefully in discount supermarkets.

Hawaii offers every type of accommodation for cyclists of all budget levels, from fancy hotels to family-run bed and breakfasts (B&Bs), hostels, and campgrounds. The only catch is that the type of accommodation you desire may not be within bicycling range. Some tours are easily covered from all camping or all B&B bases, for example, but others demand more flexibility.

ROOMS. Hotels crowd Hawaii's most popular towns, and resorts crop up in remote areas. However, hotels tend to be too inconvenient or pricey for independent travelers, catering to package tourists with whom cyclists have little in common. In addition, a statewide 10-percent tax is levied on hotel stays. A far better choice for independent travelers are B&B accommodations. Hawaii's B&B business has boomed in recent years, with countless inns and many central offices that offer booking services. B&Bs are usually cheaper than hotels (or the same price as cheap hotels) and offer a much nicer atmosphere.

B&B accommodations range from a bedroom in a private home to a separate area or detached cottage/studio unit. B&Bs usually charge about $50 to $60 per night, although some are as cheap as $30 to $40 and others run $100 or more. Many B&Bs require a three-night minimum stay. However, many of these B&Bs will accept cyclists for shorter stays on short notice to fill a vacancy.

Unless a particular B&B appeals to you, take advantage of a booking service to make arrangements for you. Shop around for a good service; some charge a flat rate, while others are free. Although large, multi-island offices can be convenient, they often do not want to bother with one pesky biker. I had better luck with small offices that specialize in one island; they were friendly and knew their area of concentration intimately. A woman at one such office even began calling her friends when she could find no vacancy for me.

Although reservations take away some flexibility of travel, they do provide the security of definite accommodations each night. If your trip is still some time away, call soon to ask when you should begin making reservations for particular areas. Most B&B owners know others in their area and are happy to recommend them if no rooms are available at their own homes.

YOUTH HOSTELS. Hostels in Hawaii are not the reliable resource they can be in other parts of the world. No Hawaiian island has two hostels within cycling range of each other, making it impossible to base a tour exclusively on hostels. Most are independent hostels, not members of an international association. Therefore these are free of restrictive rules but are also free of the cleanliness and order of official hostels. A rate of about $15 a night is the standard for a bunk in a common room, with private rooms available at higher prices.

Many independent hostels are officially limited to international guests, partly to discourage locals from moving in permanently. This can be frustrating to legitimate travelers from the United States who become dependent on hostel staffs' laxity in enforcing that rule.

CABINS. For an indoor option between hotels and camping in both comfort and price, look into cabin rental. A few state and national parks rent simple cabins from about $10 a night. Cabins may come to your rescue in remote areas where no other indoor accommodations are available. They range from tiny A-frames to full cottages with varying facilities. Some of these cabins are booked far in advance, although cancellations may create last-minute openings. Locals often reserve cabins for weekends and holidays, making weekdays your best chance for a vacancy on short notice.

CAMPING. Camping requires one to carry bulky gear, an inconvenience easily outweighed by flexibility gained and money saved. In addition, by camping in your own familiar little den each night, you gain a sense of comfort in a world of constant variables. But camping in Hawaii is a mixed bag. Campers will often revel in their idyllic locations, convenience, and affordability. On the other hand, some campsites are uncomfortable or even unsafe. On some islands, you can easily tour the entire island staying only in campsites, while others do not have enough sites within cycling range of each other.

Hawaiian campgrounds fall into three categories: state parks, county parks, and private sites (the last being few in number). Most of these are directly on the beach in quiet areas. County and state parks require that campers secure a permit for each night in each campsite. State parks charge no fee for camping but require a permit, while county parks charge a few dollars per night (free to residents).

Permits can be obtained by mail or in person at the appropriate office. The mail-in process is complicated, and so few visitors bother camping that it is rarely difficult to secure a site. Usually, it is possible to make reservations on a weekly or island-by-island basis. The trickiest times are holidays when locals may reserve sites, as camping is very popular in Hawaii as a means of getting out in the fresh air.

Few sites are supervised so you must secure a permit at a central office before camping. Park employees make rounds to check for permits, but rangers are generally understanding if you arrive on an island when offices are closed. Plan to stop by the appropriate office during permit-issuing hours (usually 9:00 A.M. to 4:00 P.M. weekdays). State offices will make reservations for state parks on all islands, while county offices issue permits only for sites on their island.

Because many homeless people live in campsites, officials warn against using some sites. Although homelessness is an unfortunate state and not a criminal act, this can create an uncomfortable situation. In some public campsites, you should not leave your gear unattended but otherwise risk little. Other sites are not recommended, period (noted in text).

Some people feel comfortable free camping outside established sites. In some places, free camping is readily tolerated, while it is strictly forbidden in others. If you wish to free camp, be sure to ask locals for advice, but decide what is reasonable for yourself.

SUPPLIES. Supplies and services normally found on the mainland are readily available in Hawaii, plus many native and imported elements. To aid in planning, locations of stores, gas stations, and other services are described in each tour. Large supermarkets are usually open from 8:00 A.M. to 9:00 or 10:00 P.M. daily, while smaller shops may keep a more strict 9:00 A.M. to 5:00 P.M. schedule.

TIPS FOR TOURING HAWAII

Novice and experienced bicycle tourists alike will quickly adapt to cycling in Hawaii. Many standard techniques useful for cycling anywhere are applicable to Hawaii, although a few tips for touring are specific to these unique islands.

MAPS. Shop for a good, clear road map that indicates important landmarks, points of interest, and secondary roads. An extremely detailed contour map is not a must, but be sure that your map at least indicates topographical features with shadowing. Typically, the islands of Hawaii have good paved roads along the coast, a few alternate offshoots, and an extensive network of dirt roads (often private "cane roads"). An up-to-date map is critical for touring in Hawaii. Development brings rapid change to some areas, quickly rendering old road patterns obsolete. On the Big Island, mapmakers face a unique challenge as lava from the active volcano obliterates some roads and cuts off others.

There are no special cyclists' maps available for Hawaii. Several map series offer sufficiently detailed treatment, with one map per island (Lanai and Molokai usually share one sheet). The *Reference Maps of the Islands of Hawai'i* by the University of Hawaii Press is one reliable series. These and other suitable maps are easy to find in airport shops, bookstores, bicycle shops, and tourist stands.

ROUTE FINDING. Whether you plan to follow the suggested tours strictly or branch out on your own, a few basic tips will help you choose and follow routes through unfamiliar territory. Hawaii's relatively small islands offer a natural aid in route finding, with the visual aids of ocean and inland mountains. Moreover, the islands offer only limited number of roads to follow and, consequently, few to get lost on. On the other hand, the network of small dirt roads can be tricky to navigate once off the main track.

Keep a few basics in mind when planning a tour. As a general rule of thumb, roads circling island perimeters are usually flat coastal routes, while those cutting straight overland probably involve a climb. A road that bends away from but continues to parallel the coast probably means a steady climb. Furthermore, northeast trade winds prevail in Hawaii, adding an extra challenge to the windward legs of some rides.

Paved roads are generally well signed, although towns are rarely marked with signs at their boundaries. When asking for directions, remember that locals use road names (like Kamehameha Highway) more often than numbers (Highway 99). Cyclists eager to explore off the beaten track may find themselves frustrated by areas of restricted access. However, many NO TRESPASSING signs are actually posted for the sake of liability rather than concern about encroachment. On the other hand, many should be respected because there is no telling what is growing behind the bushes (such as illegal marijuana). Also consider that heavy farm machinery flies along private back roads not expecting to encounter cyclists.

TOURING APPROACHES. There are two basic approaches to bicycle touring, each suited to a particular situation. First, the "daily progress" approach moves you gradually along a point-to-point route, such as a circle tour around an entire island. This approach is ideal for covering long stretches and always seeing something new.

In a few cases, a "base camp" approach is more practical: you establish a base in a convenient spot and make day trips from that point. This approach works best in compact areas such as the small island of Lanai. Rather than repacking your gear every morning, you can establish one comfortable base and cover the island's tours in a few day trips. Each day you can see new sights yet return to a familiar and comfortable place.

CONDITIONS. Road conditions vary greatly in Hawaii, from smooth asphalt with good shoulders to terribly potholed back roads. Do not be intimidated by "highways" suggested in many tours as the term is definitely a misnomer. There are simply fewer cars and fewer people rushing to get somewhere in Hawaii, especially outside town centers. Traffic also tends to be relatively slow on these winding roads.

As for hills, some tours require long climbs to over 1,000 feet—up to 10,000 feet in the most extreme case. Tackling big climbs with a loaded bicycle is a challenge best met with basic conditioning. Even if you cycle or work out at home, ease into touring with a less challenging tour before undertaking a major climb.

Kiawe thorns are a cyclist's worst enemy.

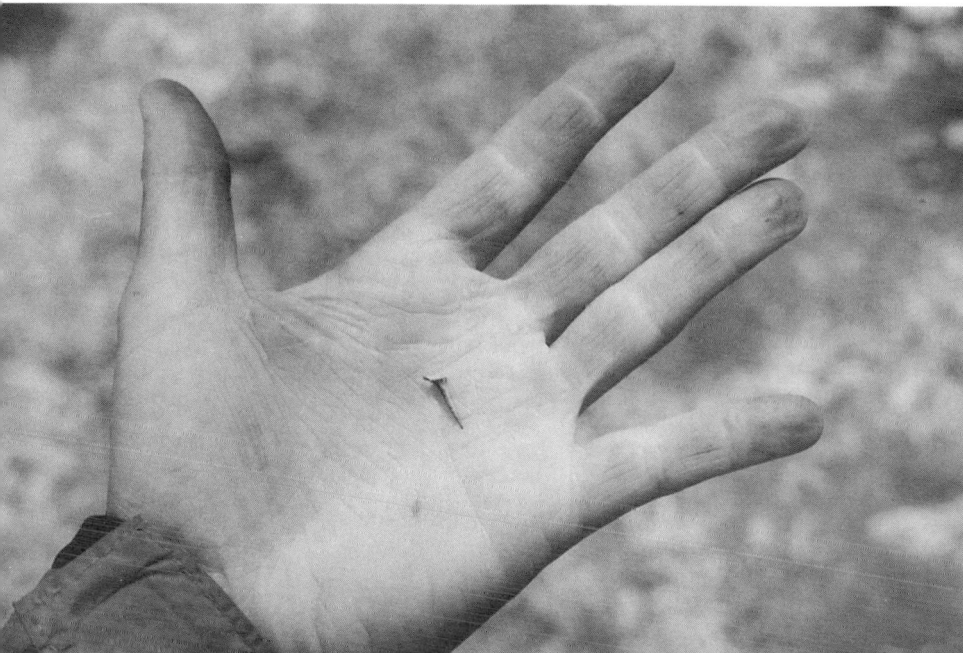

Ideally, plan your tour(s) with an eye on the weather and recent conditions. Don't delay a hike or mountain-bike ride during an unusually dry spell, as conditions may worsen with mud and rain that could disrupt your plans.

Two types of rain shower occur in Hawaii: passing tropical storms that sweep in, drench everything, then sweep out again, and rain that clings tenaciously to windward slopes for hours or even days. In the first case, you can find shelter while the storm passes, and in the second, well, there is little you can do but grit through (safety considerations permitting). In high, cool elevations, getting wet is of more concern. Happily, relief in the form of lower elevations or indoor accommodations is never too far away.

Although weather systems can be unpredictable, the Hawaiian Islands do exhibit a few reliable patterns. As a rule of thumb, windward (northeast) coasts tend to bear the brunt of most storms, while sheltered leeward shores remain drier and calmer. Mountains like Mauna Kea or Haleakala create their own weather, trapping a layer of clouds in the day and clearing through inversion at night. Therefore weather is more a function of your location than passing systems.

Remember that wet rims are slower to brake and roads more slick in rain. Once a shower passes, do not let down your guard. After a day of rain, I was so happy to find no mud along a trail that I ignored slick clay that soon sent me flying off my bicycle—another lesson learned the hard way.

In addition to rain, another potential obstacle to consider is wind. Be especially careful on exposed shoreline roads where an unexpected gust can knock you off balance. Instead of coasting, pedal steadily to improve control. Very high winds may bring branches down or destabilize your bicycle. If an especially strong wind storm blows through, hole up until it passes rather than risking injury and enduring miserable conditions.

Unlike many Pacific islands, Hawaii concerns visitors with only a few health hazards. You may hear warnings of leptospirosis, a bacterial disease that is actually extremely rare (carried by livestock and often contaminating still water). Avoid contact with still water that may have been in contact with infected animals, especially if you have an open cut. There are no dangerous snakes or animals in Hawaii. As in most places around the world, the most dangerous animal is yourself. Push yourself to achieve, but do not be afraid to recognize your limits and back off from too great a challenge.

SEASONS. Hawaii basks in a mild climate year-round, with coastal temperatures in the high seventies to mid-eighties. Of course, temperatures on barren lava can rise to over 100 degrees, while the summit of Mauna Kea is often covered with snow. Seasonal variations are more noticeable in terms of precipitation than temperature, winter and spring being wetter and slightly cooler than summer and fall. However, where you are on an island is more relevant than when you are there.

Although longer periods of bad weather are more likely in winter, those months are still an attractive time to visit Hawaii. Other mammals also find Hawaii an attractive winter destination: humpback whales migrate to Hawaii at that time. There is nothing better than seeing a whale spout offshore as you pedal along the coast—other than the spectacular sight of a breeching whale. Winter disadvantages are more crowds and higher peak-season prices. Occasionally, the windward/leeward pattern shifts during unpredictable *kona* weather, which brings storms from the south. The futility of trying to predict such factors is reflected in official weather reports; you will notice that few forecast more than one day at a time!

MOUNTAIN BIKING

There are mountain-bike destinations in Hawaii suitable for riders of any experience level, although some require advanced technical skills. No matter what level rider you are, take a moment to remember some important issues in mountain biking: safety, impact, and sensitivity. The Hawaiian Islands are small, highly sensitive lands that undergo constant pressure from development and multiple use. All visitors have a responsibility to protect and preserve the beauty that makes Hawaii so special.

Unfortunately, mountain biking in Hawaii is restricted by issues of access. Most coastal land (that is, level land) is locked up in development or private holdings with restricted access, although local mountain bikers often ride there anyway. Unless otherwise marked, all dirt roads on public lands are open to vehicles of any type, including mountain bikes.

Guidelines of the State Division of Forestry summarize the rules for mountain biking: "Always yield to hikers, and do not slide around corners or slide down the trail—this damages the trail and causes erosion. If accidents are reported or damage to the trail is extreme, the trail will be closed to mountain bikes." Heed the warning, enjoy your rides, preserve the area for the future, and let others enjoy their recreation at the same time.

LANGUAGE TIPS

Language in Hawaii today reflects the varied cultural history of the islands, from the first Polynesian settlers to later waves of immigrants from Europe and Asia. Native Hawaiian language, although not widely used, remains an obvious influence on the English spoken throughout the islands today.

Missionaries were the first to put the melodious Hawaiian language into writing, using a phonetic system of only twelve letters. Keep the vowels soft and distinct: a=ah, e=ay, i=ee, o=oh, u=oo. An apostrophe is often used to indicate a glottal stop or verbal break between letters (Kamaaina = Kama'aina). Keep an eye out for compounds like the double "meha" in Kamehameha, and sound words out slowly: Kah-me-ha-me-ha. The Big Island's famous City of Refuge, Puuhonua O Honaunau, seems impossible to say until you roll it over your tongue a few times, letter by letter. Long words are often shortened to a single syllable, especially in place or road names. For example, Kamehameha Highway is often called "Kam" Highway for short.

Familiarity with basic words and their origins can clue you in to the character or background of a place. For example, *wai* indicates fresh water, while *kai* refers to sea water. Therefore you should not be surprised to find a place called Waimea along a river or other water source and a town named Kailua along the coast. *Honolulu* means sheltered bay, and *Kona* means leeward, place names befitting their locations.

Maps and signs frequently use Hawaiian terms, and many of the same words pepper the spoken language. Signs are as likely to read KAPU as NO TRESPASSING, or PLEASE KOKUA (help/cooperate in following rules). Start with *aloha* (hello/goodbye/welcome/love) and *mahalo* (thank you), and memorize *mauka* (inland) and *makai* (toward the sea), words frequently used in road directions. Then work on mastering other common terms like the ones below.

Alii—royalty, nobility (ali'i)
Hale—house
Haole—white/Christian/newcomer (How-lee)
Heiau—place of worship, temple (Hey-ee-ow)
Kamaaina—native born/long-term resident
Kapu—forbidden/taboo (no trespassing)
Kii—image, often a carving or artwork (ki'i)
Kii Pohaku—petroglyphs (rock art)
Kokua—help/cooperate
Lanai—veranda
Luau—traditional feast, party
Makai—toward the sea
Mauka—inland
Pali—cliff
Pupus—snacks, hors d'oeuvres
Puu—hill (pu'u)

Soon you will find it natural to slip some of these words into your own speech and roll out tongue-twisters without hesitation. Before you become overconfident, however, listen to someone speaking pidgin English. The dominance of slang and Hawaiian words in pidgin makes it nearly impossible for anyone but a long-time resident to understand.

ALTERNATIVES TO BICYCLING

Although you are planning a bicycle tour, for reasons of practicality or enjoyment you may choose another means of travel in Hawaii at times. Bicycle touring offers a unique experience and up-close view of the land, but no single form of travel is ideal in all situations. If time restrictions prevent you from covering every area you wish by pedal power, or if you simply need to get out of the saddle for a time, consider the available alternatives.

Unfortunately, few means of public transportation service the Hawaiian Islands, offering no practical back-up to cycling. The only extensive public system of note is Oahu's handy and inexpensive bus service (The Bus). However, bicycles cannot be transported on The Bus system, making it useful only for non-biking day trips. Other islands do not even offer any bus service, and there are no trains to fall back on as in Europe. However, pickup trucks seem to be the vehicle of choice throughout Hawaii, making it fairly easy to catch a ride in times of dire need.

Too many cyclists allow themselves to become over-absorbed in their one chosen activity. For all its fun and convenience, cycling is not always the best way to visit a place. For the same reasons that you choose biking, you should choose to put your wheels aside and take a

An artist's work enlivens a Lahaina park.

hike. Who knows, a short side excursion may prompt you to plan another trip to Hawaii—Hawaii by kayak or Hawaii afoot! Try hiking, kayaking, snorkeling, scuba diving, stargazing, or whale watching to gain a different perspective on the islands.

In Hawaii, "flightseeing" helicopter rides are another popular means to view remote natural areas or cliffy coastlines. However, you should think twice before signing up for a helicopter trip. Although helicopter trips offer spectacular views, they are an extremely selfish means of seeing an area. The obnoxious buzz of helicopters drowns sounds of waterfalls and birdcalls, ruining a hiker's solitude. For the pleasure of a few high-paying passengers in the air, dozens of visitors on the ground have their experiences disrupted. Put responsibility and consideration first whenever planning alternative activities.

A NOTE ABOUT SAFETY

Safety is an important concern in all outdoor activities. No guidebook can alert you to every hazard or anticipate the limitations of every reader. Therefore, the descriptions of roads, trails, routes, and natural features in this book are not representations that a particular place or excursion will be safe for your party. When you follow any of the routes described in this book, you assume responsibility for your own safety. Under normal conditions, such excursions require the usual attention to traffic, road and trail conditions, weather, terrain, the capabilities of your party, and other factors. Keeping informed on current conditions and exercising common sense are the keys to a safe, enjoyable outing.

The Mountaineers

PART II

BICYCLE TOURS IN HAWAII

Viewpoint overlooking the stunning Na Pali cliffs

Steam rises where lava meets the sea (Volcanoes National Park)

Twenty suggested tours throughout the Hawaiian Islands follow in an order that proceeds along the island chain from the Big Island of Hawaii (the newest and largest island) to Maui, Molokai, Lanai, Oahu, and finally Kauai. Each island is introduced in turn, with practical island-wide information regarding airports, gateway towns, accommodations, and so on, followed by self-guiding tours. Most tours connect into others on the same island, allowing cyclists to link lengthier rides. Tours that branch off at the midpoint along one route are described under their own tour heading for easier reference. Mix and match these options for a trip of your own design by using suggested tips on how and where to connect separate tours. Alternative activities such as hiking, sightseeing, and beachgoing are also suggested within the text of each tour. The information block at the beginning of each tour includes a rating for difficulty (*moderate, challenging,* or *most challenging*) to enable you to choose a tour that fits your needs.

All distances are in miles (1 mi = 1 mile = 1.6 kilometers). Tour summaries include total tour distance, giving a mileage range if detours are suggested but not vital elements of the ride. Any day ride with its own heading is included in the total mileage of the tour. Daily distances indicated are point-to-point or one way for dead-end rides. For example, on Tour No. 5, cyclists have no choice but to pedal the same 11-mile road to and from South Point. Therefore the distance given (11 mi) measures a one-way trip although cyclists not spending the night there will cover twice that distance. Some sections are designated as day rides, which indicates a ride that can be covered from a single base (starting and ending at the same point). A 1-day ride, on the other hand, begins at one point and ends at another after a day on the road.

As you follow the tours, keep in mind that all "highways" are suitable for cycling except those prefixed by an H (for example, Oahu's H1, H2, H3). Locals usually refer to roads by their names (such as Kamehameha Highway), not their numbers (for example, 99), so keep both in mind. Unless a particular map is suggested for a tour, use any suitable map (see Part I: Tips for Touring).

HAWAII
The Big Island

Hawaii, better known as the Big Island, is the newest and biggest of all the islands—and still growing. Its active volcano, highlighted in Hawaii Volcanoes National Park, still erupts periodically, mercilessly pouring lava toward the coast. However, Hawaiian volcanoes are generous enough to erupt slowly, letting bystanders move out of the way. Soon after, however, when the goddess Pele's patience runs thin, lava rolls over roads and entire towns, the most recent example being the 1990 destruction of the village of Kalapana.

The Big Island is actually a conglomeration of five volcanoes (Kohala, Hualalai, Mauna Kea, Mauna Loa, and Kilauea), three of which have been active in historic times. Mauna Loa is the largest single land mass and the largest volcano in the world, while Mauna Kea is the highest mountain on earth when measured from the sea floor. On the Big Island, big really means BIG! The newest volcano of all is Loihi, still a half mile below sea level but growing fast off Hawaii's southern shores.

For bicycle tourists, the island's sheer size and incredible variety offer more cycling opportunities than any other island. However, the island's ever-rolling slopes demand a high level of fitness, with long, steady climbs of thousands of feet. Visitors arriving from any of the other islands will immediately discover that the Big Island is a whole new story in terms of size and environment. Offshore waters quickly drop off to tremendous depths, the reason why Hawaii is better known for deep sea fishing than whale watching.

The sharp division between wet and dry sides typical of the Hawaiian Islands is especially obvious here on the Big Island, each day of a tour delivering drastically different landscapes. Legends assign responsibility for this division to bickering gods. When Madame Pele scorned her lover Kamapuaa, he responded to Pele's assault of fire with rain. In the end, the two gods each claimed half the island, Pele controlling the dry, volcanic districts of Puna, Kau, and Kona, while Kamapuaa claimed the windward side. Thus the west, Kona side of the island is hot and dry, a blistered volcanic moonscape. The Hilo side, on the other hand, is lush and green, its cliffs brimming with waterfalls and colorful blooms.

Practical Information

The island of Hawaii is commonly called the Big Island, avoiding confusion between the island and the state. Although the Big Island is larger than the rest of the islands combined, its population is only a fraction of Oahu's or Maui's. Stretches between towns loom long and lonely, with few conveniences along the road. The Big Island is composed of five volcanoes, of which Kilauea is still active, putting on pyrotechnic displays in Hawaii Volcanoes National Park in the south. The island's north end (Kohala) is the oldest, most eroded region and an area of rapid development. Most tourists flock to the sun-drenched Kona Coast, while Waimea (Kamuela) offers refreshing views of green ranchlands. The Hilo side of the island receives the most rain, fueling trickling waterfalls and lush forests. Finally, windswept South Point in the Kau District is the southernmost point in the United States.

For information specific to the Big Island, write or call Big, Box 5900, Kamuela, HI 96743, or telephone (800) 648-2441. Interisland airlines pass out free, cartoon-style maps of the Big Island that provide a good overview of topography and attractions, but for route finding you will need a detailed road map such as the *Reference Maps of the Islands of Hawai'i* series. For up-to-date information on current events, pick up a free copy of *Guide to the Big Island* magazine at the airport or around town.

Tips for Touring

The two sides of the Big Island are at such extremes that neither is perfectly suited for cycling, but both offer compelling scenery and memorable cycling experiences. The Kona side can be uncomfortably hot as you cycle through barren lava fields, and the Hilo side can be very wet, with almost daily rain showers. However, the fascinating contrast and exotic landscapes on both sides make up for any inconvenience. Running from west to east is the high Saddle Road between Mauna Loa and Mauna Kea, one of the island's most rewarding bicycle destinations. All that together with Waimea's verdant ranchlands and North Kohala's remote vistas make the Big Island unique even within the extraordinary Hawaiian chain.

Although Belt Highway circles the Big Island parallel to the shoreline, the road is not level. Only the section from Kawaihae south to Kona is relatively low. South of Kona the road ascends to over 1,000 feet, and the section from South Point to Volcanoes National Park climbs steadily to 4,000 feet. Therefore short detours to the coast usually turn into major undertakings, a point to remember before zooming off on a side trip.

Thanks to the high profile of the Ironman Triathalon, the sport of cycling on the Big Island is widely recognized and respected. The Ironman bicycle course begins at Kailua Pier, runs north along the Queen "K" Highway (Road 19), then backtracks south to the Kona Surf Hotel where the marathon portion begins. However, Queen "K" Highway does not cater to cyclists other than by posting signs to warn drivers of their presence. Most of the shoulder is poorly paved (racers use the road on the race day), and traffic is not particularly polite. Aside from this main road, however, few cars crowd most other roads on the Big Island, where cyclists often have long stretches of "highway" to themselves.

Airports

The Big Island offers two main airports with one small, local field as well. The two principal airports in Kailua-Kona and Hilo are on the west and east sides of the island, both within easily cycling range of the town centers. Only small commuter planes service the airfield in Kamuela (Waimea). Small planes may not accept bicycles as baggage, but Waimea is a good option for those planning to rent a bicycle upon arrival.

Large planes service Lyman Airport, only 3 mi and an easy ride from Hilo center. Although most tourists fly to Kailua-Kona, Hilo is a convenient starting point since government offices are located there (camping permits issued). From Lyman Airport, exit to Road 11 and pedal past shopping centers to the intersection of Roads 11 and 19. Turn left there to reach the town center via Kamehameha Avenue, or turn right on Kalanianaole Avenue to reach budget accommodations and the campground.

Kailua-Kona (officially Keahole Airport) handles most flights to the Big Island, including a few direct flights from the mainland, although connections via Oahu are more common. The airport is 9 mi from the center of Kona. Follow signs out the driveway to Road 19 (Queen "K" Highway) and pedal along a wide shoulder all the way into town. Those who arrive from tours of other Hawaiian islands will immediately take notice of mile markers numbering in the hundreds, a rare sight on these compact islands.

Accommodations

The Big Island offers accommodations of all types, but options are not always closely situated due to the sheer size of the island. All tours can be covered exclusively with indoor accommodations but not by camping at official sites.

ROOMS. Perhaps the best way to tour the Big Island is with bed-and-breakfast (B&B) accommodations. B&Bs are scattered throughout all parts of the island, and many booking services are based here on the Big Island. In a few places, in fact, a B&B may be your only option. Rather than fussing with endless phone calls, use a booking agency, preferably a local one like My Island B&B (see Appendix). On the Big Island you may stay one night in a small B&B overlooking South Point, another with a fireplace in Waimea's ranch country, or a studio apartment where you can stretch out. The many B&Bs will each introduce you to the character of the island's distinct regions.

The Kona Coast is the Big Island's prime hotel/resort area, where prices run high. Basic, cheap hotels in Kailua-Kona, Hilo, Waimea, and Honokaa help ease tight budgets. There are also two youth hostels on the Big Island, both open to any travelers, not just foreigners (see town sections below).

CABINS. State parks offer cabins at reasonable rates in two key locations on the Big Island. First, A-frame cabins at gorgeous Hapuna Beach make a good overnight point that conveniently divides a long cycling leg. These must be reserved through the park's concessionaire (see Tour No. 1). Second, cabins at Mauna Kea State Recreation Area offer the only overnight point along the entire length of the Saddle Road. They may be reserved through any state park office for one to six people (see Tour No. 4). Make reservations for the cabins at least several weeks in advance, as they are in high demand, especially on weekdays. With luck, you might chance upon a last-minute cancellation or an off-peak or weekday opening.

CAMPING. Unfortunately, it is impossible to cover all of the Big Island by camping in official sites alone, although free campers will find plenty of open spaces that may suffice. Many county and state parks offer camping, but distances between sites are often too great to cover in one day's ride.

For a summary of county sites, facilities, and a locator map, write or call the Hawaii County Department of Parks and Recreation (telephone 961-8311; 25 Aupuni Street, Hilo, HI 96720). All vital information is summarized in a few handy sheets. Only two state parks permit camping: MacKenzie State Recreation Area in the Puna District and Manuka State Wayside Park near South Point. State officials may not encourage camping at Manuka, although it is a safe site. Hawaii Volcanoes National Park offers several free sites, the most convenient being Namakani Paio near the Visitor's Center (no permit required; 7-night limit).

The county and state park offices that issue permits are both in Hilo. The county office (address above) issues permits from 7:45 A.M. to 4:30 P.M. for a small fee. Call there to ask if other permit pickup locations on the island are open. The state office is located at 75 Aupuni Street (mailing address: Box 936, Hilo, HI 96720; telephone 933-4200). Camping at state and national park sites is free.

Hilo

Hilo is often called the most Hawaiian city of the Big Island because it remains largely unchanged by development and tourism. Visitors generally bypass the town, preferring the sunny Kona side of the island. As a result, Hilo is left to its quiet, traditional ways, with fishermen auctioning their daily catch and merchants tending small shops. In spite of—or because of—almost daily rain showers, Hilo is a wonderful place to visit for its vivid rainbows and rushing streams. Best of all, parting clouds open above to reveal panoramic views of Hawaii's interior and the gently sloping Saddle area that separates the 14,000-foot volcanic peaks of Mauna Loa and Mauna Kea.

FOOD AND ACCOMMODATIONS. Visitors arriving by plane or from the direction of Volcano will pass two supermarkets in the Kuhio Shopping Center along Road 11. There are also supermarkets near the state and county buildings on Aupuni Street and another under McDonald's on Haili Street in the town center. Hilo's compact business center is dotted with small restaurants and cafes as well. The local Hawaiian Visitor's Bureau is located at 180 Kinoole Street, in the center of town.

A number of small hotels and B&Bs fill out indoor options both in Hilo and the surrounding area. An excellent choice for budget cyclists is Arnott's Lodge, an independent hostel that offers dorm and private rooms, kitchen facilities, and a covered patio (telephone 800-953-7773 or 969-7097 locally). To reach the lodge, follow Kalanianaole Avenue east from the intersection of Roads 11 and 19. Pass the port, industrial zone, and a long beach park before turning left on Keokea Road at the

ARNOTT'S sign. The lodge is 1.5 mi from the highway intersection.

Arnott's Lodge also offers excursions at bargain rates, a perfect alternative for those who don't have the time or energy to reach all parts of the island by pedal power alone. The stargazing excursion to Mauna Kea's summit is a steal, considering that Kona-based tours charge much more for the same ride.

To obtain state and county camping permits, follow Pauahi Street *mauka* from Kamehameha Avenue (midway between Waiakea Peninsula and the town center), then turn left on Aupuni Street where both offices are located. The campground nearest Hilo is Onekahakaha Beach County Park, an uncomfortable place to stay due to both the large number of homeless and the damp weather (located 0.5 mi past Arnott's Lodge).

SIGHTS. Hilo's principal sights are all within walking distance of each other, perfect for short dashes between afternoon showers. Most points of interest are not simply sights to see but tell stories as well. For example, outside Hilo Library stand the Pinao and Naha stones that both come from one *heiau*. Stories say that a person who could move the Naha stone would have the power to conquer all the Hawaiian Islands, which is just what Kamehameha did (on both counts). From there walk over to the Wailuku River bridge and overlook a rock formation known as Maui's Canoe. Legend has it that when the god Maui paddled over from the neighboring island to rescue his mother from a monster, his canoe turned to stone upon landing.

Downtown Hilo has small shops and cafes but can hardly be called touristy. Note that street lamps are shielded to reduce light pollution affecting Mauna Kea's observatories (although by now, many new observatories operate outside the visible light spectrum). Above town on Haili Street stands Hilo's top sight, the Lyman Museum. The museum is compact and concise, offering a full run through Hawaiian history without the excessively cluttered displays that exhaust visitors at other museums. Museum admission includes a guided tour of the missionary home next door, offering perspective into early missionary life. Overall, Lyman Museum makes a fun, dependable activity for a rainy afternoon, a reliable occurrence in itself (open 9:00 A.M. to 5:00 P.M., 1:00 to 4:00 P.M. Sundays).

The entire waterfront area of Hilo is carpeted with broad green parks because tsunamis destroyed the original waterfront buildings. Peaceful, Japanese-style Liliuokalani Gardens lie near stately Banyan Drive and little Coconut Island. Each vine-laced banyan tree of the drive is marked with a plaque bearing the name of the person who planted it, creating a very Hollywood-esque effect. Be careful to keep one eye on the road while checking out the trees, however!

While in Hilo, do not miss the Suisan Fish Auction at the western junction of Banyan Drive and Kamehameha Road where the catch of the day—tuna, mahimahi, and others—is auctioned (8:00 A.M. Monday to Saturday). Buyers walk around stacks of fish prodding and poking, then nod bids to the shouting auctioneer. The atmosphere is very good-natured and friendly, and fishermen are not above explaining the auction to tourists.

FESTIVALS. Hilo's Merrie Monarch Festival, held annually over

Japanese-style gardens grace Hilo's waterfront.

the first week in April, delights locals and visitors alike. This huge hula festival features competition and exhibitions in two types of hula, *Kahiko* (the traditional, ritual style) and *Auwana* (modern dance). The festival is named for King David Kalakaua (1874–1891) who reversed a longtime ban imposed by missionaries and restored the tradition of hula by sponsoring a *halau* (hula school). Tickets and accommodations should be reserved well in advance, however, because B&Bs and hotels within 30 mi of Hilo are chock full during the festival.

Kailua-Kona (Kona)

An early visitor called Kailua-Kona "one of the least lovely spots in all Hawaii. . . . Barren, dry, its black lava desolation appears at first ghostly beyond words. . . ." Yet today Kailua-Kona (or simply Kona) is the destination of countless tourists from all over the world, thanks to the area's reliable sunshine and warmth. Kona is also a popular center for deep sea fishing because steep offshore slopes drop off to tremendous depths within a very short distance of land. Thousand-pound marlins have been caught off the Kona Coast; some of them are on view around town.

PRACTICAL INFORMATION. Kona's center has been spoiled by shopping centers and fast-food chains, so stop for supplies and then escape to the more soothing sight of the old Kailua harbor area. Bicycle shops and rentals are available in several locations, and several Kona-based companies offer downhill bicycle tours.

ACCOMMODATIONS. Hotels and condominiums practically outnumber palm trees in the Kona area, but few cater to cyclists of any budget level. Ideally, book a B&B in the area instead. Patey's Place is the only budget accommodation in town. The independent hostel offers co-ed dorms and private rooms (75-195 Ala-Ona Ona, Kailua-Kona, HI 96740; telephone 326-7018). There are no campgrounds near Kailua-Kona; locals recommend free camping in undeveloped beach areas to the north near Old Airport Park and Natural Energy Lab.

SIGHTS. Originally Kailua was a site favored by Hawaiian nobility (*alii*), as evidenced by King Kamehameha's residence. The original site now stands on the grounds of the Hotel King Kamehameha. Of the reconstructed buildings, the most notable is Ahuena Heiau, occupying a spit of land that shelters the calm swimming cove. While in the area, visitors should stroll through the hotel lobby, where featherwork capes and headdresses as well as prize marlin are displayed.

In Kailua harbor you will see swinging six-person crews in outrigger canoes, swimmers training for the Ironman race, and the *Tamure*, a 150-foot "replica" of a Polynesian war canoe (although you can bet the Polynesians didn't bring a steel-drum band along). Kailua Pier acts as both start and finish line of Hawaii's Ironman Triathalon held every October, in which competitors endure a 2.4-mi swim, a 112-mi bicycle leg, and finally a full marathon. Any time of year, you can see the catch of the day being weighed in on Kailua Pier as sport fishers return. During the Bullfish Tournament held each August, prize winners are photographed with their fish hanging between themselves and "Miss Bullfish" beauty queen. Fishing can hardly get more glamorous than that!

Mokuaikaua Church graces the harbor area with its white walls and traditional spire. Mokuaikaua was the first church built on the Hawai-

Placing bids at Hilo's Suisan Fish Auction

Historic Kailua harbor hosts a variety of activities.

ian Islands, site of the first missionary landing. The building's principal attraction is a small but fascinating display on early missionaries at the north end of the church. Opposite the church, Hulihee Palace occupies an ideal position on the waterfront, a stately mansion that once served as the governor's residence.

For excursions from Kona, try snorkeling at Kahaluu, the best nearby site. Hotels and booths distribute brochures that list conditions and suitable activities for many Kona Coast beaches. Boat excursions are the easiest way to reach Kealakekua Bay, one of the island's best snorkeling destinations. The Hotel King Kamehameha rents open-shell kayaks by the hour, just enough time to paddle away from the busy harbor to beautiful, undeveloped sections of coast. Kayaking grants a unique perspective of Kona's volcanic slopes and high Hualalai, as well as the exhilaration of floating atop crystal-clear waters while watching steep underwater slopes drop deeper and deeper.

Along the Way

HIKING. In addition to the two day rides in Hawaii Volcanoes National Park described in Tour No. 2, visitors also have a number of good hiking options in Volcanoes National Park. Those with less time to spend in the park can do a little of everything by pedaling Crater Rim Road and stopping often to hike short trails that branch off the circular route. Depending on your pace, time should even permit a longer venture down in Kilauea Caldera, by descending Halemaumau Trail from Volcano House or Kilauea Iki Trail into a side crater (2–3 hours). These hikes connect with many other caldera trails, allowing for a walk of any duration.

Visitors with more grand visions will be tempted by Napau Trail, an exciting 14-mi venture. This hike leads through rainforest, past lava trees, and ends with views of Puu Oo, an active cinder cone. Naulu and Kalapana trails turn down to the coast from this path. Whatever your time frame or energy level, park rangers in the Visitor's Center can advise a suitable hike in Volcanoes National Park.

STARGAZING. Mauna Kea is the highest point in the state at 13,796 feet. From this lofty vantage point, 90 percent of the universe is visible. Where better, therefore, to spend an evening stargazing? For all your nights staring up at twinkling stars from seaside campsites, you will never get a finer view than that atop Mauna Kea.

Agents in tourist centers like Kona charge a whopping $100 for a stargazing tour of Mauna Kea, although the best bargain is Arnott's Lodge, which offers an identical sunset/stargazing excursion to Mauna Kea for only a quarter that rate (see Hilo Accommodations). Tours often stop to allow a hike to Lake Waiau, a small blue basin amid white patches of snow and red-hued boulders. From the summit, you can watch the sun slowly set over the Pacific, colors draining from other high peaks like Mauna Loa and Haleakala. This is an especially memorable trip as a counter to sunrise at Haleakala, making you feel as if you have come full circle with the universe.

The Onizuka Complex at the 9,000-foot level offers public programs at 7:00 P.M. every Friday and Saturday night, including a video presentation and stargazing led by knowledgeable and humorous staff. Using a powerful telescope, you can marvel at the craters of the moon, the rings of Jupiter, and distant stars like the Orion Nebula. You will learn and laugh a great deal during the program, during which down-to-earth scientists distribute star maps and hot chocolate. Those curious to learn more about astronomy should look for Will Kyselka's book, *The Hawaiian Sky*.

NORTH HAWAII
Hilo to Kona via North Kohala

Distance: 164 to 172 miles
Riding time: 5 days
Difficulty: Challenging
Terrain: Rolling hills and two long ascents over 1,500 feet
Roads: Paved; moderate to heavy traffic
Connecting tours: Tour Nos. 2, 4

The Big Island's sheer size notwithstanding, this tour covers almost every major zone in a week-long ride, a remarkable achievement. Beginning in Hilo on the lush windward side, this tour curves over the island's northern half in a counterclockwise direction. The first day includes detours to the plunging waters of Akaka Falls and cascade-lined Waipio Valley, considered one of the island's most beautiful vistas. Another day's ride climbs to Waimea in the ranchlands below Mauna Kea's snow-rimmed peak. Another climb over the island's oldest volcanic rise brings cyclists to North Kohala, a coast of stunning views.

Finally, a long, hot ride south leaves cyclists with a hard-earned impression of the lava-covered Kona Coast, bypassing the ancient village of Lapakahi and beautiful Hapuna Beach before finishing in Kona. In fact, the only Big Island highlights not covered in this route are the City of Refuge and Hawaii Volcanoes National Park. Never fear—those sights are saved for Tour No. 2, which completes a full circle from Kona back to Hilo.

B&Bs are a cyclist's best choice for this tour, the only accommodations available at every overnight point. Campers must either free camp or pay for indoor lodgings at several stops along the tour, as the Big Island does not offer visitors a good selection of closely spaced sites. This tour is arranged with one overnight at state park cabins at Hapuna Beach, which should be reserved as far in advance as possible. Other, less convenient options in the area are also listed.

Hilo to Honokaa: 52 miles via Akaka Falls

The tour begins with a long and scenic stretch over the lush windward side of the Big Island. To divide the challenge of both distance and terrain, stop halfway along the ride at a B&B or camp at Laupahoehoe Beach County Park. As a last resort, shorten the ride by subtracting the challenging 8-mi detour to Akaka Falls. Akaka Falls is a worthwhile side trip, but Waipio Valley waterfalls are more spectacular if you must choose between the two. Organize the next few

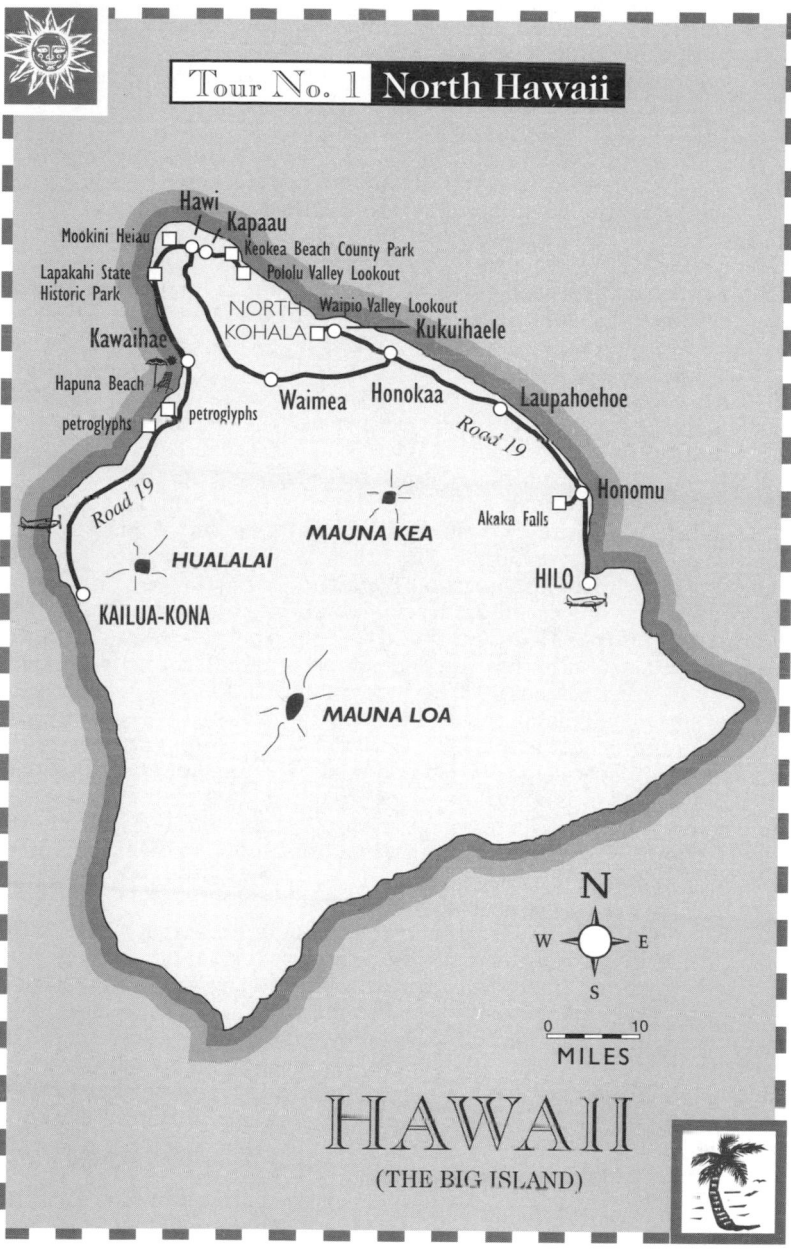

Tour No. 1 **North Hawaii**

Hawi
Kapaau
Mookini Heiau
Keokea Beach County Park
Lapakahi State
Historic Park
Pololu Valley Lookout
Waipio Valley Lookout
NORTH
KOHALA
Kukuihaele
Kawaihae
Hapuna Beach
Waimea
Honokaa
Laupahoehoe
petroglyphs
petroglyphs
Road 19
Road 19
MAUNA KEA
Akaka Falls
Honomu
HUALALAI
HILO
KAILUA-KONA
MAUNA LOA
N
W   E
S
0   10
MILES
HAWAII
(THE BIG ISLAND)

days' rides to your taste: you may choose to drop off gear in Honokaa and proceed immediately on to Waipio Valley, or save the 18-mi round trip for the next morning. The next two rides are each short and may also be combined in a single day to reorganize the route (Honokaa to Waimea and on to Hawi for a total of 39 mi).

With luck, winds along this coast will blow crosswise rather than pestering cyclists from straight ahead. Only a few small stores dot the route, so bring the day's supplies from Hilo. Cyclists share the Belt Highway (Road 19) with steady but not constant traffic, taking advantage of shoulders all the way except for a few miles north of Laupahoehoe.

As you leave Hilo on **Road 19**, heed the sign to walk your bicycle over a **bridge** with an uneven metal grid surface. After 4 mi, leave the highway to follow a **scenic drive** for a quieter alternative. The spectacular drive winds down, up, and around a tangled rainforest where streams cascade and bird calls pierce the thick vegetation. A highlight of the drive is the viewpoint over picture-perfect Onomea Bay with its protected rainforest "gardens." When the 4-mi scenic drive ends, **return to Road 19** by making a sharp **left** turn.

The **turnoff** for Akaka Falls and Honomu lies to the **left** after the 13-mi mark. It is quite a **climb** up to the **falls** (almost 4 mi each way), but two beautiful waterfalls reward those who sweat it out. Do not be put off by the initial steep climb from the exit to town, which is far steeper than the long road up. Even if you are not up to the entire ride, at least detour up to **Honomu** town (0.75 mi from the exit). The town's main street is lined with rows of shops with false fronts, a scene straight out of the Old West (the very far West). Ishigo's general store and bakery is as much a museum as a shop, its walls decorated with photos and mementos that chronicle the trials and successes of the Japanese immigrant family who opened the store in 1910. One wall displays photos of tsunami damage, including one wild shot that actually shows people fleeing from a rogue wave. Ishigo's documents part of Hawaii's immigrant history in an extremely personal manner, bringing history alive more than the best-organized exhibit at the Bishop Museum.

In less than 4 mi, you will reach the parking area for Akaka Falls State Park. Lock your wheels there and cover the short loop hike through stands of bamboo to **Kahuna** and then **Akaka Falls**, the latter a 400-foot drop with rainbows glittering in its spray. Then move on to an even better reward—an effortless cruise downhill **back to Road 19**!

Continuing **north** along Belt Road, you may be further delayed by a succession of views as the road crosses several long **bridges** across lush green valleys. Each view seems more beautiful than the last, so take your time at each by pulling over rather than wobbling along the road trying to take it all in on the roll.

Next, cyclists are challenged by a series of **three broad gulches** where the road sweeps down, around, and up again. Near the 18-mi mark, you will reach a **scenic pullout** with views of the rocky coast below, a good place for a break unless you plan to bike down to nearby **Laupahoehoe Beach**. Laupahoehoe is both a sad and beautiful spot where a tsunami claimed the lives of teachers and students in a seaside schoolhouse. The area is now a county park with a memorial.

Camping with permits is also permitted at Laupahoehoe, the last campsite along the tour until North Kohala. The final 16 mi from Laupahoehoe to Honokaa are marked by a drier landscape and sugar-cane fields. Few fields are still tended as the industry fails and plantations subdivide and develop properties instead. This is a common story throughout the Hawaiian Islands as the traditional, agricultural economy gives way to development and the big bucks of tourism. The highway's shoulder becomes too narrow or bumpy to ride for a few miles, but traffic is more sporadic so far away from town centers. Again, you will pedal over **bridges** and a series of long **ups and downs** parallel to the coastline.

Bear **right** off the highway after the 43-mi mark to reach the center of **Honokaa** and its main drag, Mamane Street. Head for the west end of town to find the large supermarket and a handful of eateries, and to pass a cheap, plain hotel (Club Honokaa, telephone 775-0678). Once in Honokaa, you can drop off your gear and continue straight into the Waipio Valley ride, or relax in town and put it off for the next morning. Weary cyclists might be tempted to stay in town, soaking in afternoon rays and watching the local kids play ball as life rolls by sleepy Honokaa.

Waipio Valley Ride: 9 miles each way

This side trip is a quick 9-mi trip from Honokaa, quicker still with an unloaded bicycle. The dead-end road (240) to the lookout is clearly signed from both the Belt Road and Honokaa center. The ride to Waipio is mostly downhill (and mostly uphill on the return), but, mysteriously, cyclists are likely to enjoy a helpful crosswind push in both directions. The road passes fields of sugarcane and a few flumes that lead to the now inactive seaside mill. Early along the ride, you will enjoy outstanding views of Maui's Hana Coast poking out behind Kohala slopes in the foreground.

The **main road** comes to an end at **Waipio Valley Lookout**, one of the most dramatic coastal views on the Hawaiian Islands. There, *pali* (cliffs) sheer 2,000 feet vertically into the sea and lush valley. Waterfalls cascade in long leaps, some spraying off seaside cliffs into the ocean, others needling into the deep cleft of Waipio Valley. Only a winding foot trail marks this rugged coast between Waipio and Pololu, the windward landscape severely eroded by time and the elements.

Although your vantage point provides amazing views, do not content yourself with passively "looking out" at the lookout. Instead, **descend on foot** into the valley itself for a new angle on the waterfalls. Only a narrow, 25-percent-grade road drops into the valley; it is not advisable to bicycle down the road due to the dangerously steep and winding descent compounded by the extra distraction of beautiful views. Besides, it is hard enough to walk back up this road, let alone push a bicycle up. Instead, lock your bicycle securely in the overlook park and hoof it down.

At the base of the road, turn **left** for views of Hiilawe Falls' pencil-thin sliver in its own amphitheater cleft (at 1,000 feet, it is Hawaii's highest free-fall waterfall). Several more cascades leap down the valley's northern walls. The **dirt road** through the valley is a public

Waipio Valley Lookout offers a panorama of cliffs and waterfalls.

road; PRIVATE ROAD signs are often misleadingly placed, referring only to side roads and drives. Continue **across two streams** to round a corner and gain a full view down the length of the valley, which ends at an equally steep bluff. Wading through these valley waters might not be a good idea, on the other hand, due to the threat of leptospirosis.

Alternatively, head for the sandy beach at the mouth of the valley by turning **right** at the base of the hill. A switchback trail climbs the opposite wall of the valley, leading to uninhabited Waimanu Valley. Adventurous visitors may be tempted by the 9-mi hike to Waimanu and beyond, although that venture, perhaps, should be saved for a Hawaiian hiking trip on another occasion.

On the **return** ride to Honokaa, zoom through nearby **Kukuihaele**, a small coastal town. To do so, turn **left** down a hill instead of immediately rejoining the main road back to Honokaa. This interesting detour through the sleepy town passes an ice cream shop, small houses, and ocean vistas. Cross a **bridge**, pass the Last Chance store, and then **rejoin** Road 240 to Honokaa just 2 mi farther on.

Honokaa to Waimea: 17 miles

The short stretch of road between Honokaa at 1,000 feet and to Waimea at 2,500 feet climbs constantly but gradually. Cyclists can choose between an easier, less interesting ride directly on noisy Road 19, or opt to follow Mamalahoa Highway, a neglected side road. Mamalahoa adds two bumpy, twisting miles to the ride but subtracts all sounds of traffic with close-up views of ranches and Mauna Kea's upland slopes.

To reach **Mamalahoa Highway**, pedal from lower Honokaa to meet **Road 19** at Tex Drive Inn near the 43-mi mark. Instead of turning onto the highway, continue **straight** across and up a small street. At the **first right**, look for the Mamalahoa sign to begin your journey along the twisting country road. This "highway" **rejoins** the main road 5 mi east of Waimea. By that point, cyclists attain more level terrain and enjoy the help of powerful tailwinds to sail into town.

Waimea looks the part of a traditional ranching town nestled in the rich green saddle spreading between **Kohala** and **Mauna Kea**. Kohala's eroded, hilly landscape to the north contrasts with Mauna Kea's smooth, high slopes on the opposite side. Morning is the best time to catch a clear view of the snow-topped mountain ridge dotted by white observatory domes, as afternoon clouds move in to obscure the view.

On the way to Waimea center, you will pass sources of spiritual and mechanical aid, that is, Church Row, where Waimea's churches form an orderly line, and a bicycle shop. Waimea serves as headquarters of Parker Ranch, which claims to be the largest ranch in the United States (a statement qualified by footnotes; it is the largest single-owner private ranch, with 2,000 acres and 50,000 cattle). Not by chance, Waimea is a good place for a steak dinner and hosts an annual summer rodeo.

Rather than confuse it with other towns of the same name on other islands, Waimea is officially known as Kamuela. Of course, that system has only created more confusion, but so it goes. Phone books and post offices use the name Kamuela, while locals say Waimea. In any case, the town has two large supermarkets and several B&Bs, inns, and restaurants. Although a traditional ranch town in appearance, Waimea is also quite cosmopolitan, with frozen yogurt and health food shops as well as a number of international restaurants.

Campers must pay for indoor lodgings in town or push on to the Hawi area to reach Keokea Beach County Park. Those in a rush may shorten the tour by riding directly to Kona on Road 190 (Belt Road) or due west to Kawaihae Bay via Road 19 (Kawaihae Road). Either option cuts off the interesting Kohala portion of the tour and covers uncomfortably busy roads.

Waimea to Hawi: 22 miles

These 22 mi constitute one of Hawaii's most scenic rides. You will pedal out of Waimea at 2,500 feet and climb to 3,500 feet in Kohala's heights for an incredible perspective over all the major regions of the Big Island. One view encompasses pure white snow atop Mauna Kea, Waimea's green pastures, Kona's dry black coast, and small red-ash cinder cones along the island's center. Cresting Kohala's rise, you will be treated to views of Maui's Haleakala, purple-blue in the distance. Cyclists will be tempted to stop often to catch their breath on this ride—if not from the exertion of the climb, then from the incredible views.

Leave **Waimea** by riding **west** with signs for North Kohala and Hawi (**Road 250**, Kohala Mountain Road). After 3 mi the road begins a steady 5-mi rise, with little to no shoulder but only occasional traffic.

The incline slacks after 5 mi, although bikers must conquer one more short hill before reaching the **crest** at 3,564 feet (near the 9-mi mark). Then begin a well-deserved **descent** to Hawi, breezing down the full 3,500 feet. An avenue of ironwood trees shelters the road from winds near the top. Note Kohala Ranch on the way, a new subdivision of residential units that may foreshadow the future of Hawaii's agricultural lands.

When the **main road forks** above Hawi, bear **left** to cruise 2 mi into **Hawi** town (22 mi total), or keep right for **Kapaau** if you are heading for camping at Keokea or accommodations on the way to Pololu Valley Lookout (29 mi total). North Kohala has several B&Bs but no hotels. The cheapest indoor option is a room at the private school on Kapaau's Bond Estate (phone 889-5028 or 889-5217).

For camping, pedal 4 mi past Kapaau's Kamehameha statue and turn left at the sign for Keokea Beach County Park, 1 twisting mi downhill. There is no beach at Keokea, but tired cyclists can dip in a nearby stream. The county park fills with day users on weekends, while weekdays are quieter. Facilities at Keokea include outdoor showers, drinking water, and large shelters for day use. One disadvantage of the site, however, is the climb back up to the main road.

There are grocery stores in Hawi, Kapaau, and another 1 mi east of the Kamehameha statue in Kapaau. This is the original statue that was lost at sea and therefore never delivered to Honolulu, its intended site. Only after a copy was erected in Honolulu was the original statue recovered and placed here, near the king's birthplace. Many believe that supernatural forces were at work in ultimately bringing the statue to its rightful home—and given its unusual fate, who can argue?

Hawi and Kapaau each offer a few small eateries. Hawi is a small town with a unique character and a good sense of humor. In a hometown approach to things, one store is called "As Hawi Turns," and bumper stickers may read "Give Peas a Chance" or "Work for Whirled Peas." Many cyclists pass through the area, a popular destination for day trips with local tour companies.

Once you settle into your accommodations, head off to **Pololu Valley Lookout**. With a full layover day, on the other hand, you can ride to the lookout, hike, and squeeze in side rides. The main road (270)

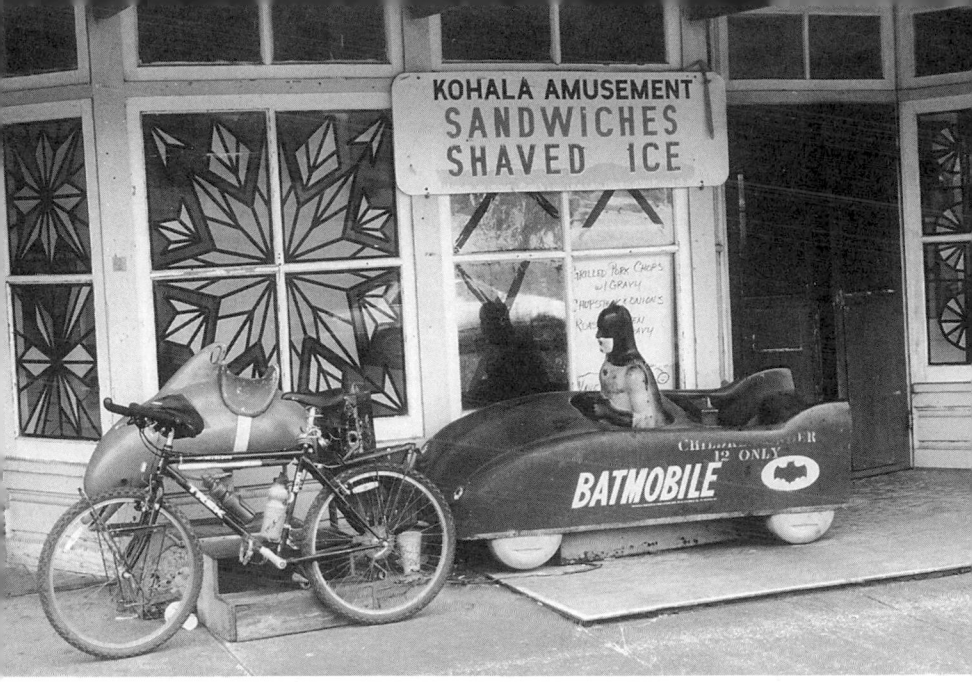

Bike-mobile meets Batmobile in friendly Hawi

ends at Pololu Valley Lookout, where views rival those of Waipio Valley Lookout at the opposite end of this undeveloped shoreline. It is a real roller-coaster ride to the lookout, 4 mi past the Kamehameha statue.

Rather than snapping a few photos and moving on, consider a hike down into the beautiful valley and its beach. A trail leads from Pololu into the next valley, **Honokea,** another tempting but strenuous option.

Another local ride not to be missed is the detour to Mookini Heiau, 5 mi southeast of Hawi near Upolu Airport. Mookini is the oldest *heiau* in Hawaii, dating back to A.D. 480. The temple is impressive in size, in its good state of preservation, and in its scenic setting. Mookini is especially interesting as a designated *luakini*, or place of human sacrifice.

Hawi to Hapuna: 22 miles

Although it is possible to ride on to Kailua-Kona in 1 day (55 mi/65 mi with detours), the long ride would not allow time for all of the Kona Coast's worthwhile sights. Unless you love marathon days or are short of time, break up the ride into two shorter legs as suggested. This day is organized around a stop at state park cabins at beautiful Hapuna Beach. Other accommodations include a few B&Bs, hotels, and camping at Spencer Beach County Park near Kawaihae. The only places to buy food along this ride are Hawi, Kawaihae, and a refreshment stand at Hapuna Beach.

Begin by riding **west** from Hawi on **Road 270** (Akoni Pulo Highway) to circle **North Kohala** toward Kawaihae. A shoulder begins only at the 15-mi mark of this road, where passing cars are fast but infrequent. Within 7 mi, you will reach the first and most interesting sight of the day, **Lapakahi State Historic Park**. Lapakahi was a village settled 600 years ago; admission to the park and an informative brochure that describes a walking tour are free (estimate 45 minutes for the walk). This is perhaps the best archaeological site in Hawaii in terms of its easy access, good state of preservation, and excellent interpretive materials.

The brochure points out house ruins, burial platforms, fishing shrines, and canoe shed. Best of all, the hike has been designed to show not only ruins and artifacts but also to bring it all to life. In the games section, implements and rules are explained so that visitors can play. This is a wonderful, hands-on site as well as a beautiful picnic and swimming spot with its coral beach, protected cove, and views of Maui on the horizon.

Next, pedal the remaining 13 mi from Hawi to **Kawaihae**, a rather unexciting harbor sheltering a fishing fleet. As you approach the harbor, turn **left** for Waimea and push on to **Puukohola Heiau**. Look for the *heiau*'s fortresslike walls 1 mi ahead, a **national historic park** marked to the right atop a hill. *Puukohola* means Hill of Whales, a name given to the temple built by Kamehameha the Great. The king was advised that he would conquer all the islands if he dedicated a temple, which he did in due course (on both counts). Below the hill lies Spencer Beach County Park, an alternative rest or overnight spot.

From Kawaihae, ride **south** on **Road 19** (Queen Kaanumanu—Queen "K"—Highway). In some ways this final stretch of the tour to Kailua-Kona represents the worst biking on the Big Island as the Queen "K" Highway seems to bear the most, the fastest, and the least cautious cars around. Either rattle along the terrible shoulder or follow the road's far right edge and turn onto the shoulder when cars pass (having a rear-view mirror is essential here). If you stay to the side, the ride is unpleasant but at least safe. For some compensation, the ride south reveals good views of three volcanoes—Mauna Kea, Mauna Loa, and Hualalai, with tail- and crosswinds prevailing along the way.

At the 69-mi mark, **turn off** Road 19 for **Hapuna** to rate the beach for yourself. Hapuna has been called the best beach in Hawaii and even the world, a claim not hard to believe. Weary cyclists will marvel at this oasis of turquoise water, white sand, and purple flowers, dotted with small rocky outcrops and ringed by swaying palms. Shaded picnic tables, toilet facilities, a refreshment stand, and equipment rental round out the attractions.

Hapuna Beach State Recreation Area also rents simple A-frame cabins for up to four people. Reserve as far in advance as possible to ensure a spot by contacting Hapuna Beach Service (P.O. Box 44318, Kamuela, HI 96743; telephone 882-1095). Otherwise, cyclists must turn to expensive hotels or cycle on to Kona. Unless you can make do with burger-type fare, bring food from Hawi or Kawaihae.

Those staying at Hapuna can pedal a short distance **south** to **Puako** over a terribly bumpy side road. The quiet little settlement stretches along a palm-tree–lined coast with interesting tidal pools. To get there, either follow the bumpy side road along the coast or take the smoother highway to the Puako exit.

Hapuna to Kailua-Kona: 33 miles (41 miles with detours)

The only points to buy supplies along this route are shops in hotel resorts that line this coast. Simply follow Queen "K" Highway all the way to Kona, with a few detours as relief from the busy road. Cyclists will rejoice at the sight of a smooth, **wide shoulder** at the 73-mi mark. Shortly past this point, an incongruous clump of palms and flowers amid aa lava fields marks the entrance to **Mauna Lani Resort**. This is a good place for a worthwhile **detour** that will add 5 to 6 mi to the day. The resort grounds contain an extensive petroglyph site as well as small ruins and unusually interesting fishponds.

To see the petroglyphs, ride down **Mauna Lani Drive** and turn **right** at the traffic circle, following signs for the petroglyphs. The 0.75-mi **trail** to the petroglyph field begins at **Holoholokai Beach** parking area, 2.5 mi from the highway. Just watch out for kiawe thorns when you lock your bicycle at the trailhead.

The trail leads to the greatest concentration of petroglyphs in all Hawaii, a large, flat lava area covered with ranks of stick figures, all pointing to Mauna Kea (estimated to date from A.D. 1000 to 1800). Damage from selfish visitors who tread beyond the protective fence is evident, so appreciate the site from a distance. Those with sharp eyes can look for other carvings scattered around the trail as well. Back at the trailhead, take a moment to enjoy the coral beach of Holoholokai and refill water bottles at the restroom fountain.

Once in the area, you can also cover a short **historic hike** marked by informative plaques. To walk the 15-minute trail, return to the traffic circle and turn **right** for Mauna Lani Hotel, then follow HISTORIC PARK signs **left**. The walk passes a once-inhabited lava tube, small ruins, and ends at the fishpond, an appealing oasis in this black lava desert. As far as fishponds go, these are by far the most interesting along the tour.

Then **return** to the highway, a short but nasty ride into a strong headwind until the turn **south** on the highway itself. After the 75-mi mark, you will reach **Waikoloa Resort** entrance, one of the most extravagant developments of the Kona Coast. Another **detour** there (barely 0.75 mi) brings cyclists to more petroglyphs and a portion of the **King's Trail**. Even if the last side trip satisfied your appetite for petroglyphs (or detours), this ride is worthwhile because several historic features are visible in one place. To reach them, **stop at a corner** before the King's Shops and follow a **white sidewalk** to its end, where a short **trail** begins.

King's Highway was the name given to ancient footpaths that were eventually upgraded to horse and mule lanes with a "curb" to keep pack animals on track. This section is part of the same islandwide system still visible in other areas (see Tour No. 3). Rough, C-shaped shelters built by travelers along the historic trail also remain visible.

Back on the highway, you must negotiate another stretch of bouncy pavement. The **coastal ride** is now characterized by long gradual inclines and declines where tail- or crosswinds provide an extra push. Temperatures on this road can top 100 degrees with the effect of black asphalt and barren lava fields. As part of the Ironman course and a popular training ground, the highway is marked with bicycle signs to alert drivers. Pedaling the Queen "K" Highway may not be a joy ride, but it is a good place to dream about a glorious Ironman finish, so let your imagination soar.

The 82-mi mark makes a good rest and lookout point with views back to Kawaihae, Kohala, and Kuhio Bay below. Just before the 91-mi mark, look left at the 55 miles-per-hour sign to glimpse a lava tube, a gaping cavity in the earth's surface. Soon after, you will reach Kona's **airport** and the last 9 mi stretch into town.

For a last stop, follow the marked **side road** to Natural Energy Lab, where a wave break provides entertainment in the form of surfers doing spectacular aerials both on and off the ends of their boards. Finally, pass the entrance to **Kaloko-Honakohau National Historic Park** (97-mi mark), with its fishponds, *heiau*, queen's bath, and a section of the King's Trail. Although the park makes a good getaway from Kona, most cyclists feel as though they have seen it all by now and are eager to reach town.

So they do! At mile-mark 100, turn right down **Palani Road** to pass the commercial area of **Kailua-Kona** and reach the historic harbor area. For tips on sights, accommodations, and other practical matters, refer to the Kailua-Kona section in the Big Island introduction.

TOUR NO. 2

VOLCANOES RIDE
Kona to Hilo via Volcanoes National Park

Distance: 197 miles
Riding time: 5 to 6 days
Difficulty: Challenging
Terrain: Long, steady elevation gains and losses
Roads: Paved and quiet
Connecting tours: Tour Nos. 1, 3, 4, 5

Completing a circle around the Big Island, this ride picks up where Tour No. 1 ended. From sunny Kona, the route visits sights along the Big Island's south coast before coming to an end in Hilo. First cyclists pedal south through the island's coffee belt to reach Kealakekua Bay, a top snorkeling destination and site of Captain Cook's last (ever) landing in 1779. A short ride then leads to a site representing another period in history, City of Refuge, before continuing to Painted Church, a relic of the missionary era.

Curving around the island's perimeter, the tour then passes South Point, the southernmost corner of the United States, with the option to detour there (Tour No. 5). Then only a long, steady climb of 4,000 feet stands between you and Hawaii Volcanoes National Park, a highlight of the Big Island. Steam vents and immense calderas make the national park a living laboratory where visitors witness land being destroyed and created before their very eyes. This sense of the awesome force of nature is often forgotten in the modern world, in which humans seem to have conquered nature. Here, you're not so sure. Finally, the tour swings around the Puna District with another optional extension into Tour No. 3 before rolling back into Hilo.

Cyclists undertaking this tour must be fit and flexible, ready to tackle gradual but endless climbs and cover vast tracts of remote land. As for accommodations, travelers with more forgiving budgets can count on indoor lodgings every step of the way, combining B&Bs with inexpensive hotels. Campers, on the other hand, cannot pitch camp in public sites at every overnight point. Those on strict budgets might get by with free camping, while others can turn to B&Bs for a nice change of pace.

Kailua-Kona to H.O.V.E.: 57 miles

For information on both Kona and Hilo, see the introduction to this chapter. H.O.V.E. stands for Hawaiian Ocean View Estates, a growing development near South Point, your goal for the first day of this tour.

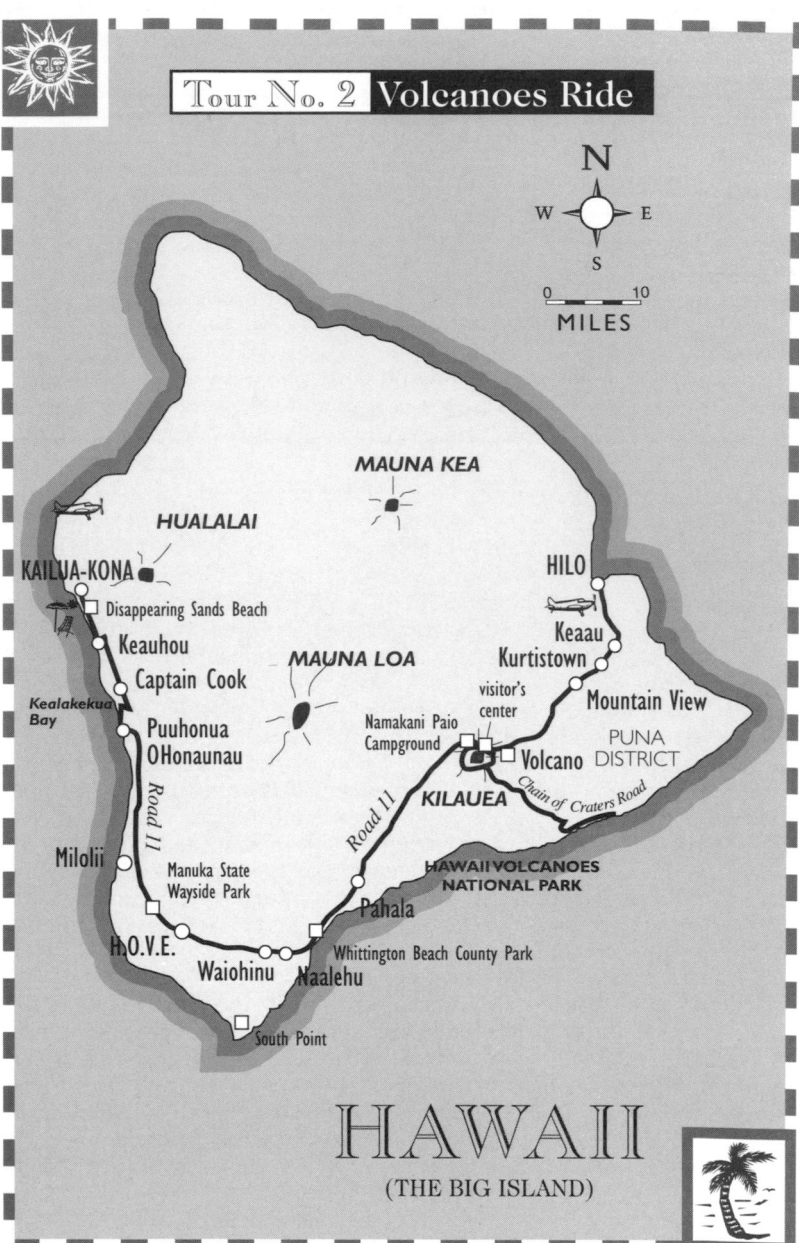

Tour No. 2 Volcanoes Ride

HAWAII
(THE BIG ISLAND)

Before setting off from Kona, be sure to pack enough food and supplies to last the full day, as there are few places to stock up during the ride. The day is also unbalanced in terms of sights, most of which cluster closely over the first half, leaving the second section feeling rather long and barren. Therefore, carry a special snack or energy bar to keep you perky later in the day. Alternate accommodations that help shorten the ride are B&Bs (a few cluster around Captain Cook and the City of Refuge) and county park campgrounds (Hookena and Milolii).

Throughout the day, the route passes miles of coffee plantations, so keep an eye open for sampling cafes in towns such as Captain Cook. Later, you will also pedal past macadamia nut orchards before reaching the stark lava landscape of southern Hawaii.

From Kailua harbor, head **south** on Alii Drive, where joggers outnumber cars in the early morning. Just 4 mi from town is the day's first point of interest, **Disappearing Sands Beach**. Also known as Magic Sands, wave action can steal the beach away overnight, only for it to reappear in pristine condition a short time later.

Just 1 mi farther is **St. Peter's Church**, a tiny white and blue church by the sea. The building's beautiful setting and vibrant colors practically shout "Kodak moment!" so have your camera ready. While there, walk 100 feet back north to a *heiau* beside the road. Exclusively devoted to surfing, the temple proves that ancient Hawaiians took their water sports very seriously, indeed. Look for the game board carved into a flat rock where *Konane,* a game similar to checkers, was played with pieces of white coral and black pebble.

Across the bay, several more historic sites dot the grounds of Keauhou Beach Hotel. These include several *heiaus*, a royal swimming pond, and fishponds. Ride another 0.5 mi down the road to reach the **main hotel entrance** and ask for a map of the grounds at the front desk. Nearby petroglyphs, for example, may be reached by crossing a small bridge to Kona Lagoon Hotel.

Then **continue north** on Alii Drive for a short distance until turning **left** at a turn marked to Road 11. Alii Drive continues another mile to pretty, compact **Keauhou Bay**, birthplace of King Kamehameha III, but dead-ends there. Unfortunately, that means it is time for a 2-mi **uphill** haul to Road 11 (Belt Road), which has a good wide shoulder. Road 11 continues to climb gradually all the way to Honalo. The shoulder comes and goes throughout the day, but traffic outside the resort area is far less constant.

Keep close track through the next few towns (none of which are marked) to avoid a confusing game called "where am I?" Honalo is a small, one-street town with a few shops. A short distance later, you will pass another cluster of shops before reaching **Kealakekua** town proper. Finally, you will reach the town of **Captain Cook** where Napoopoo Road branches down to the right, clearly marked for Kealakekua Bay. Captain Cook is the last place to buy lunch supplies before heading down to the bay or City of Refuge.

Whiz a quick 4 mi down **Napoopoo Road** to the bay. At an intersection nearly 3 mi down, turn **right** for the bay. Painted Church is marked to the left, but leave that sight for later. You will also pass the Royal Kona Coffee Mill and Museum on the way to the bay, where free samples and displays merit at least a quick look around.

The north side of **Kealakekua Bay** offers some of the best snorkeling on the Big Island, but you cannot reach the prime area except by swimming across from this southern approach. Otherwise, the north side can only be reached by hiking a trail off Napoopoo Road or by boat. Rougher waters on the south side of the bay make for variable snorkeling conditions. In a rare display, spinner dolphins often play close to the south shore, a protected conservation zone. Across the bay stands a white obelisk that marks the spot where Captain Cook was killed in a scuffle with native Hawaiians in 1779.

From the bay, bump 4 mi along a **coastal road** marked for **Puuhonua National Historic Park** (City of Refuge). *Puuhonua O Honaunau* means "Place of refuge at Honaunau." This represents one of the most interesting and best preserved historic sights in the islands. Hawaiian society was governed by a strict system of laws (*kapu*), and punishment for any infraction was the same: death. However, the rules came with one escape clause (literally). If offenders could reach one of several designated *puuhonua* (sacred places of refuge), they could avoid punishment and return home with a clean slate.

Pick up a brochure for a self-guiding walk around this magnificent seaside refuge. Huge jigsaw stones wall the city, the focal point of which is a *heiau* with remarkable *kii* (images or carved statues). Also on the grounds are gameboards, mystery petroglyphs (spot them if you can), and craftwork demonstrations. Rounding out the park's attractions are a water fountain with refreshingly cold water and friendly rangers with the patience of saints, especially with tourists who cannot

Huge kii *guard* Puuhonua O Honaunau *(City of Refuge)*

pronounce Puuhonua O Honaunau. A separate picnic area with shaded tables lies outside the park.

Moving right along, it is time to face a second long **climb** of nearly 4 mi back to **Road 11** (Belt Road). On the way up, botanical gardens are marked to the right, and Painted Church is marked on the left. The latter is an easy 0.75-mi round-trip detour, a must-see, clever variation on the typical tropical church theme. In 1899 a Belgian priest decorated the church interior with tromp-l'oeil artwork to create the illusion of vast space and a European cathedral background. St. Benedict's Painted Church features a colorful Hawaiian sky on the ceiling, Biblical scenes on the walls, and a bust of Father Damien outside.

Painted Church is the last of many sights along this trip, which now covers the remaining distance without interruption. Two small stores at the point where the route **rejoins** Road 11 are the last until H.O.V.E. Once you regain the main road's elevation, most of the ride is level or gradual in slope. Mile markers indicate remaining distance to Hilo, counting slowly down through 80s, 70s, 60s, and so on. With 10 mi still to go to H.O.V.E., the road may seem like a constant **series of small, tiring uphills**—time to see just how much pep your snack contains. The road's shoulder narrows, but traffic is so sparse here that it is rare for two cars to pass in opposite directions at once.

One interesting sight this route misses is the traditional fishing village of **Milolii**, 5 mi down from the highway on the coast (turn signed near the 89-mi mark). Unless you plan to camp at Milolii Beach County Park and pedal back up the hill the following day, there is no practical way to fit this detour into an already long ride.

The entrance to **Manuka State Wayside Park** lies just before mile marker 81, an isolated and drab site. The park has toilets, unpotable tap water, and a pay phone, but no showers to offer campers. To this point, the ride totals 53 mi. If possible, elect to stay in a B&B 4 mi farther in H.O.V.E., a far more comfortable choice.

The small but growing commercial center of **H.O.V.E.** has a gas station, grocery store, pizza place, and post office. One local happily anticipated, "We'll even have our own zip code soon!" The only B&B for miles is Bougainvillea B&B, located only a few blocks from the Texaco station that is also owned by the B&B couple, Martie and Don Nitsche. Bougainvilla has six guest rooms, creating a good chance for vacancies on short notice, although it is best to call in advance or book through an agency (P.O. Box 6045, Ocean View, HI 96704, telephone 929-9221).

H.O.V.E. to Waiohinu: 12 miles

This is a short little hop to the small town of Waiohinu, the most convenient place from which to base a day trip to South Point. The ride down to the point itself (the southernmost point in the United States) covers paved roads, and rough trails lead to Green Sand Beach beyond, rides described separately as Tour No. 5. Cyclists with little time or interest in the challenging detour can pass by South Point, resting for an afternoon or combining this day with the next.

From Manuka State Wayside Park and **H.O.V.E.** the road rolls constantly, seemingly more up than down until the turnoff for South Point Road (clearly marked 12 mi from Manuka, 8 mi from H.O.V.E.; 11 mi down to South Point). Instead of turning off, continue **straight** along **Road 11** to establish a **home base** in a nearby town before tackling the detour with an unloaded bicycle. After that point, you will enjoy breezy **downhill** runs to Waiohinu and Naalehu.

Accommodations define cyclists' tour arrangements in this area. Waiohinu's only lodging is the Shirakawa Motel (telephone 929-7462), a convenient place to safely leave your things and cover the South Point ride unburdened. Nearby, look for the monkeypod tree that Mark Twain planted during his travels in 1866, an interesting side sight for readers of his amusing *Letters from Hawaii*. **Waiohinu** is so small there is not even a pay phone or mailbox in town, although there is a small general store. Another 2 mi downhill is **Naalehu**, which offers bigger stores and more services. You can also remain at H.O.V.E. to avoid moving again, but that base is quite distant from your next day's destination, Hawaii Volcanoes National Park.

Last but not least, campers can head to Whittington Beach County Park, 5 mi past Waiohinu. To find the park, watch for a right turn after the 61-mi mark. The park is quite nice, quiet, and remote; facilities include outdoor showers by the pretty shoreline and drinking water.

Waiohinu to Volcano: 40 miles

This ride begins gently, with a long downhill from Waiohinu to Naalehu and beyond. After the 6-mi mark, however, Belt Road becomes a roller coaster and then begins a long, relentless ascent. The climb begins in earnest near Pahala at 800-foot elevation, with every 500-foot gain marked until the national park. Hawaii Volcanoes National Park Visitor's Center stands at 4,000 feet, so cyclists will have their work cut out for them. The quiet highway has a good shoulder until entering the park, where it narrows and then disappears entirely.

Macadamia nut orchards line the route, but not much else—there are no stores or even towns except **Naalehu**, **Pahala**, and finally the town of **Volcano** just beyond the national park. Procrastinators can make a **detour to Ninole** (sign for SEA MOUNTAIN) to visit a beach where turtles often swim close to shore. Back on the **main road**, hardworking cyclists will reach 2,000 feet at the 46-mi mark, 2,500 feet at 42 mi, the park boundary at the 41-mi mark (2,800 feet), and within another mile will attain 3,000 feet.

In clear weather, you will have good views of cinder cones dotting Mauna Loa shield volcano, its shape the result of steady volcanic pressure pushing the earth's surface up like a concave shield. For a break from pedaling, pull over past the 38-mi mark for a short walk on the marked **Kau Desert Trail**. A brisk 20-minute hike brings you to a series of badly eroded footprints left by a passing party of warriors in 1790. Gases from a volcanic explosion killed the men; their fresh footprints were preserved in a layer of mud and ash. The footprints are now protected by a shelter, although most are eroded enough to be a bit of a dud even to an archaeologist. Hey, at least it is a good introduction to the park, and the trail is also marked by interesting lava formations and prickly red blooms of desert scrubs.

Continuing along the road, you will reach 3,500 feet at the 35-mi mark, **climb** two hills past the 33-mi mark, and then reach two more hills past the 32-mi mark. Happily, the national park campground lies just before the latter two hills (whew!), for a total of 40 mi from Waiohinu. Namakani Paio Campground is the park's only drive-in (or pedal-in) site, a grassy meadow beside a grove of tall trees. The campsite offers drinking water, toilets, and covered picnic shelters. Renters of neighboring cabins have exclusive use of the nearby indoor showers. Cabins may be booked through Volcano House, a hotel near the Visitor's Center (Box 53, Hawaii Volcanoes National Park, HI 96713; telephone 967-7321).

The **park entrance** and Visitor's Center lie 3.5 mi from the campground (admission good for 7 days; keep your receipt). On the way, a sign provides another good introduction to the area: WARNING! RIFT ZONE! WATCH FOR CRACKS IN ROAD!

Volcano village lies another 1.5 mi beyond the park entrance on the road to Hilo. Volcano's general store, gas station, post office, and diner are all located under one roof (store open until 7:00 P.M. daily). The village also hosts scores of B&Bs with reasonable rates. A cafeteria in Volcano House serves the only prepared food available within the park, so stock up on food supplies in Volcano village.

Volcano's weather is difficult to predict because it borders both the dry and wet sides of the island. Days can be chilly at this elevation, especially if the atmosphere becomes damp. Extra layers and waterproof gear can make the difference between misery and fun during a poor weather hike, so come prepared.

Hawaii Volcanoes National Park

Schedule at least one full day in the park, or two or three in order to fit in both a day ride and a day hike. Far too many bikers who tour the Big Island limit themselves to cycling, excluding all other activities. Although the park does have a few paved roads, national parks are designed for best appreciation by foot. Ask at the Visitor's Center for more information on hikes with Kilauea Crater or a more remote hike to Puu Oo, an active cinder cone.

Free movies at the Visitor's Center explain aspects of volcanology and show recent eruption footage. Some park information is comic or even frightening, including handouts that issue ominous warnings such as "Plan your escape route!" To best appreciate the park, you must understand the forces at work there, so put in a little research time at the Visitor's Center before you head out and see it firsthand. For excellent views of Kilauea Caldera, simply cross the road to Volcano House and step onto its wide terrace, a perfect introduction to your stay in the park.

Kilauea's stark scenery and volcanic upheavals inevitably draw comparisons with hell—but a fascinating, thought-inspiring hell. As one visitor wrote in the Volcano House log, "When you are ready to shake the dust off this old Earth, go to Hawaii, for even at the worst, you must go through Paradise in order to get to hell" (signed: An Enthusiastic Visitor, 1920).

The volcano's current series of eruptions began in 1983 and continues along rift zones but not in the caldera itself. Molten lava sometimes flows on the surface near the end of Chain of Craters Road, where lava from the active cone Puu Oo rolls down to sea. However, lava is not always visible (flowing underground at times) and is accessible only for short times when rangers open a trail. All those movies that show spewing fountains of lava document the park's most spectacular, but not common, volcanic activity. Ask for a lava-flow update at the park entrance or Visitor's Center to judge your chances of spotting molten lava.

In addition to the day rides described below, a number of shorter excursions might also appeal to visitors who do not mind a hill or two. A short ride up Golf Course Road brings you to Volcano Winery, the only one on the Big Island. Bikers venturing up Mauna Loa Road will pass lava tree molds and Kipuka Puaulu, site of a mile-long loop trail through an "island" forest entirely surrounded by lava. Really insane bikers can ascend Mauna Loa Road to its endpoint at 6,600 feet, where the trailhead for a challenging hike to Mauna Loa's 13,679-foot summit begins. However, that grand hike may also be one for your future hiking trip in Hawaii.

Crater Rim Road Day Ride: 11 miles

This 11-mi circle makes a good introduction to Volcanoes National Park. Crater Rim Road completely encircles Kilauea Caldera, a bowl 2 mi wide and 400 feet deep. To offer a sense of the rate of change here, the caldera was 1,000 feet deep in the 1800s but has shallowed with lava fills. The magma reservoir that fuels eruptions lies only 2 mi below the surface, although these days most lava sloughs off to peripheral rift zones. This ride will bring you to several different volcanic features (lava tubes, rifts, side craters) while providing a grand overview of the main crater.

First, pick up a free handout sheet at the Visitor's Center—one side covers Crater Rim Road and the other depicts Chain of Craters Road, describing sights, latest conditions, and so on. Choose your own pace for this unique ride: some cyclists may circle the caldera quickly, while others stretch 11 mi into a half- or even full-day excursion.

Crater Rim Road rolls between 3,500 and 4,000 feet with equal climbs in either direction. A clockwise approach might prove better in case of a strong east wind, so that you feel a tailwind on the most exposed section near Halemaumau and pedal a more sheltered stretch when heading into the wind. A few picnic areas are marked along Rim Road, some with latrines and tables. A clockwise ride brings you to all the marked sights presented in the following paragraphs (in the order you will encounter them).

First you will reach **Kilauea Iki Overlook**, with open views into a side crater full of steaming vents, divided from the main caldera by Byron Ledge. Next, stop for an outstanding **walk** through **Thurston Lava Tube** (dimly lit) and a beautiful tree fern/ohia forest. Take a close look at early shoots of the giant ferns, all curled in tight locks, down to the tiniest leaves.

Continuing past the lava tube, **detour** to **Puu Puai Overlook** and

Devastation Trail for a different angle on Kilauea Iki crater. Devastation Trail winds through a barren landscape of charred trees and ash incongruous with the road's lush surroundings. After **passing the turnoff** of Chain of Craters Road, the drive comes to **Keanakakoi Overlook** for a view of the otherwise hidden side crater.

Crater Rim Road then crosses the 1982 lava flows to reach the Halemaumau **turnoff**. Even today, offerings and dedications to the goddess of fire are left at Halemaumau, a crater within the crater (look for piles of fruit, notes, and other items at the rim). Halemaumau was a spectacular lake of boiling lava until 1924, when the whole shebang blew up. The fiery sight prompted one turn-of-the-century visitor to observe, "It is like sitting in the front row of heaven watching hell boil over." Today the crater still steams moodily, but otherwise most activity has slowed.

When you pass over a 1974 flow, pause at Kilauea's southwest rift. The gaping crack is another visual reminder of how intense natural forces manifest themselves on the surface of the earth. With that proof to fuel your thoughts, just imagine what's going on below the surface.

Climb gradually uphill through an area frequented by endangered nenes, rising to the **Jaggar Museum and Observatory**. Among more scientific displays in the museum, visitors find a funny photo of Mr. Jaggar himself (Thomas, not Mick) in his boat-mobile, and black-and-white movie clips that document the Keystone Kops antics of early lava-sampling efforts. One fascinating exhibit focuses on Loihi, 25 mi offshore. This young volcano will rise above the ocean's surface and form the next island (or merge with Hawaii, itself a conglomeration of five volcanoes) in the next 10,000 to 100,000 years—a mere tick of the clock in geological terms.

To complement the museum's exhibits, stop at the next **pullout**, **Kilauea Overlook**. There, a diagram illustrates how the caldera has changed with contrasting profile drawings of 1823 and today. The next sight is impossible to miss for all its hot air. **Steaming Bluff** is literally that, a cliff of blowing gases that seem to foreshadow the entire cliff breaking off and slipping into the caldera. Contrary to appearances, however, the bluff is apparently stable—for now. Finally, the **last stop** of the ride before coming full circle back to the Visitor's Center is **Sulphur Banks**, a detour north of the road. More steam breaks the surface there, emitting a strong smell and leaving yellow sulphur deposits around the vents.

Chain of Craters Day Ride: 27 miles each way

Cyclists may also follow Chain of Craters Road for another spectacular excursion in Volcanoes National Park, albeit a more challenging one. The road lives up to its name, as for 23 mi (27 mi from the Visitor's Center) it descends past a series of craters, each a geology lesson in itself. Flattening near the coast, the road passes a remarkable collection of petroglyphs and ends—well, at the end of the road. This road once extended to the Puna corner of the Big Island, although Madame Pele obliterated the offending section with an all-consuming lava flow in 1988. Not exactly ancient history, these lava flows!

Before setting off, remember that there are no toilets or water sources along Chain of Craters Road, and beware of cattle grids on the way down. The ride is entirely **downhill on the way out** and therefore all uphill on the return, but a helpful tailwind should pick up on the return trip. The only serious climbing occurs over one steep, cliffy rise, but even that grade is manageable with an unloaded bicycle.

Several **pullovers** line the route; those who do their homework in the Visitor's Center will recognize different types of craters and other volcanic features. Information boards on the way describe Mauna Ulu, a recently formed lava shield visible upslope. Nearby, scarred trees lie across the lava landscape like bleached bones, victims of another Kilauea attack. In contrast, you will be amazed by hardy plants that manage to subsist on seemingly bare lava, the first signs of renewal on newly formed land.

Ke Ala Komo makes a perfect break point, with a covered picnic area and beautiful views to the coast. Then the road drops down a **steep zigzag**, marking the spot where high ground sloughs off as volcanic forces push out. The steep cliffs offer a good overview of the coast, where steam clouds rise from the spot where molten lava spills into the ocean and instantly vaporizes the water.

At the cliff base, **stop** by Alanui Kahiko pullout. There, one short section of the original road now covered by lava remains exposed, a good reminder that road crews in this park need not fear unemployment. Soon after that, stop at the **trail** for Puu Loa petroglyphs, a 0.75-mi walk each way. Follow *ahu* (cairns) over lava to reach the site. These rock carvings are well worth seeing even for those with only a

Rock carvings create a lively scene on Hawaii's Kona coast.

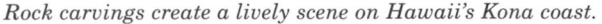

passive interest in archaeology because it doesn't take much searching or imagination to make out the carved figures (humans, animals, circles). While there, look for small pitted holes in this unusually smooth pahoehoe lava; in accordance with native practice, umbilical cords were left in such holes to ensure a baby's long life.

Now paralleling the flatter coastline, watch for Holei Sea Arch near the 19-mi mark and, a short distance later, the trail to the ruins of Laeapuki village. When park rangers open the makeshift Visitor's Center at Kamoamoa Beach, restrooms and drinking water may be available. The area also features a black sand beach, *heiau* ruin, and campground.

Pele permitting, you may be able to extend your foray beyond the end of the road to view molten lava. Even if lava flows are not exposed, you may be able to hike out to Wahaula Heiau, a sacred site spared by lava that obliterated everything else in the area, including a Visitor's Center.

When the time comes to **turn back** and face the **uphill**, you may find that a strong tailwind provides a significant push. Most of the slope is not very steep, and points of interest that you passed by on the outward leg offer a good excuse to rest, breaking the ride up into manageable sections.

Volcano to Hilo: 23 miles

This tour ends with a wonderful 23-mi (26 mi from camping) downhill swoop, after which you can recall the adventures behind and look forward to those ahead. Simply hop on your bike and follow **Belt Road** (Road 11) downhill as mile markers count down the remaining distance to Hilo. Early on, the road's shoulder is wide but bumpy, eventually becoming narrow but more smooth.

Sweep past **Mountain View**, **Kurtistown**, and **Keaau**, where development speeds along orderly subdivisions. Keaau is a commercial center and the turnoff point for a tour of the Puna District (Tour No. 3), a tempting detour of 2 to 3 days.

On the approach to Hilo, the road passes shopping malls and the airport, then comes to a **T** where Road 11 meets 19. Turn **left** on Kamehameha Avenue to pedal to **Hilo** center (1.5 mi). To reach Arnott's Lodge or campsites in public parks, turn right on Kalanianaole Avenue (Road 19) for 1.5 mi (see the Hilo section).

PUNA DISTRICT LOOP
Coastal Attractions

Distance: 33 miles
Riding time: 3 days
Difficulty: Moderate
Terrain: Small rolling coastal hills
Roads: Bumpy pavement
Connecting tour: Tour No. 2

The Puna District, occupying a southeast corner of the Big Island, has the dubious distinction of being Hawaii's most volcanically active zone. On the bright side, it also offers some of Hawaii's cheapest real estate—just don't ask when the next volcanic eruption might be. This tour traces a triangular route through the area, coasting down roads tunneled by overhanging trees. Cyclists witness a sharp contrast between the lush, wet forests of Puna's eastern side and the barren, dry lava that now covers its western half. The entire village of Kalapana and the coastal road to Volcanoes National Park now lie beneath twisted sheets of lava, the victims of a 1990 eruption.

The entire triangle ride demands only a single day's ride, but the tour really requires 3 days—one to pedal in from either Volcanoes National Park or Hilo, one for the triangle tour, and one to ride out again. It is a tour to be covered at a nice, relaxing pace, with plenty of stops and detours.

PRACTICAL INFORMATION. The triangular route begins and ends in Pahoa, a small town located 11 mi from Keaau. Therefore cyclists connecting directly into the tour from Volcanoes via Keaau cover 32 mi to Pahoa, and those arriving from Hilo cover 19 mi. From Keaau, simply follow Road 130 to Pahoa. Unfortunately, this is one of the worst roads for cycling on the island, a busy road with no rideable shoulder. However, this is not at all representative of the roads this tour follows.

Shop ahead in Keaau's large supermarket or at Pahoa before heading down to the coast, where there are no services at all. The ride from Keaau to Pahoa is level or uphill for the most part, with a final 1,000-foot descent to the coast after Pahoa.

This triangle tour is described in three legs for easy reference, with northeast winds favoring a clockwise route. When setting out for a day of exploration, pack a flashlight to light up lava tubes and a snorkel for an underwater angle on Puna.

ACCOMMODATIONS. Accommodations directly along the Puna Coast are limited to a handful of choices. For an indoor stay, try Kalani Honua Cultural Center and Retreat (telephone 800-800-6886 or

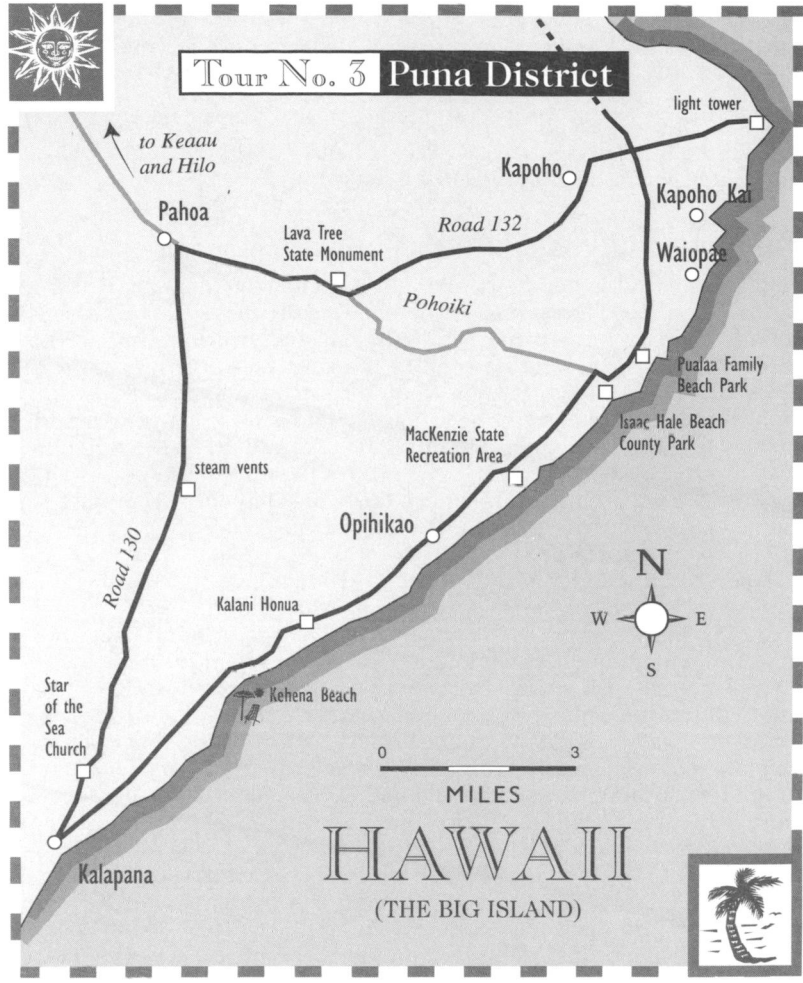

Tour No. 3 Puna District

to Keaau and Hilo

Pahoa

Kapoho

light tower

Kapoho Kai

Road 132

Lava Tree State Monument

Waiopae

Pohoiki

Pualaa Family Beach Park

MacKenzie State Recreation Area

Isaac Hale Beach County Park

steam vents

Opihikao

Kalani Honua

Kehena Beach

Star of the Sea Church

Road 130

Kalapana

N
W — E
S

0   3
MILES

HAWAII
(THE BIG ISLAND)

965-7828; address RR2, Box 4500, Pahoa, HI 96778).

Kalani Honua (meaning Harmony of Heaven and Earth) is a yin-yang sort of meditative retreat, but there is plenty of *aloha* for strays too. Guests who do not practice yoga or eat organic foods are left in peace to . . . well, retreat. A huge lawn, pool, and hammocks make for an extremely peaceful setting. Kalani Honua is located 3 mi southwest of Opihikao on the coastal road, its entrance marked with a large banner.

Indoor accommodations are a visitor's best bet in Puna, a wet region where rain showers pass through periodically. However, determined campers can choose between MacKenzie State Recreation Area and Isaac Hale Beach County Park, both directly on the coast. MacKenzie State Recreation Area is the nicer site, set in a forest over cliffs where spray kicks 30 feet into the air (but no water and no showers). Isaac

Hale is a smaller, more open site with more day use and less privacy. Facilities include unpleasant latrines, outdoor showers, and untreated tap water. Both parks have covered picnic shelters as well, a nice extra in this rainy region.

Pahoa has one small hotel and a few private cottages for rent. Although the town makes a good practical base for this triangle tour, it is not nearly as nice as staying on the coast.

Pahoa to Kapoho: 8 miles

Begin the first leg of the triangle from Pahoa by following **Road 132** toward Kapoho. This is one of the most beautiful roads anywhere in Hawaii thanks to the tunnel effect of massive, overhanging albrizzia trees. Only 2 mi down this road is the first point of interest, **Lava Tree State Monument**. Once upon a time, lava engulfed a stand of ohia trees that stood on this spot. Tree trunks slowed some lava until it cooled and solidified while remaining lava flowed away, leaving pillars cast around trees. In places, lava pillars have toppled, permitting a view of the hollow interiors where trees once stood. Although a sign suggests one hour to hike the loop, 20 minutes is enough time for a quick look around the park.

Those heading directly to Isaac Hale or MacKenzie parks should ride straight for **Pohoiki** after Lava Tree State Monument for another stunning but bumpy ride. Trees arch completely around this narrow lane, and vines dangle down to the road. After a 5-mi cruise down from Lava Tree, the road emerges at a **four-way intersection**. Less than 2 mi straight ahead on a bumpy dirt road is a place of solitude where rough *aa* lava meets the pounding sea. The **lighthouse** that once stood on this spot was spared from destruction when flowing lava parted around it, but unfortunately could not survive man-made forces; eventually the lighthouse was torn down and replaced by the plain, open light tower that marks Hawaii's easternmost point today.

The road to the **left at the four-way intersection** (north) ends less than 1 mi later with a sudden lurch off the pavement. A **dirt road** takes over from there, continuing a few miles farther. This is yet another gorgeous, tunnel-like road through a forgotten corner of Hawaii. Vines hang over the road, birds whistle from thick leafy overgrowth, and spray from puddles tickles your legs. Ride as far as your sense of adventure leads, or even walk a short distance; just be sure to explore the magical atmosphere of this road.

Kapoho to Kalapana: 16 miles

To continue southwest on the next portion of the triangle, turn **right** at the **four-way intersection** for a tailwind-aided ride along the coast. Throughout this coastal stretch, views of surf smashing into sea cliffs pop out in brief snatches beyond a row of trees. The road is bumpy but fun, perfect for an easygoing, face-in-the-sunshine ride. A short distance down the road, you can **turn off** the main road on Kapoho Kai Road (open for public access) and then turn **left** on Waiopai Road to reach an area of interesting tidal pools.

Trees and vines form an enticing tunnel in Puna.

After another 2 mi, keep your eyes open for a **small sign** at Pualaa Family Beach Park. This is a nice (as the name implies) family day-use park where a section of coast has been dammed up, creating a calm, safe pond for swimming. The park is a fun place to visit and watch families barbecuing and kids playing in the water, with pretty scenery to boot.

The next stop is Isaac Hale Beach County Park, just 1 mi past the family park. On weekends, the area attracts many picnickers and surf-ers, and a snack truck pulls in with refreshments. The park is much quieter on weekdays, but even then its compact, open grounds offer little privacy for campers. Park facilities include latrine toilets, un-treated tap water, and picnic shelters. To soak in the natural warm spring just south of the boat ramp, first ask permission for access at a private house neighboring the park.

Near Isaac Hale Park, the road jogs inland. To continue rolling along the coast, **bear left** (do not ride uphill back to Pahoa). The road surface between Isaac Hale and Kehena is terrible, but who can blame county road crews for stalling repairs when it seems that Pele has resurfacing plans of her own?

From Isaac Hale it is 2.5 mi to MacKenzie State Recreation Area where, in addition to surf, cliffs, and pleasant woods, you will be treated to two more points of interest. An information board in the park describes the King's Highway, a portion of which is easy to spot nearby. The "highway" was originally a footpath that was upgraded to a horse trail in the 1800s, still visible as a clear, straight line.

Follow the **King's Highway left** to a sign that forbids vehicles (including bicycles) from proceeding. Right there lies the gaping mouth of a lava tube, which you can follow through to its opposite end on the other side of the road. A middle section of the cavelike tube has collapsed, leaving an open hole called a skylight. To forget about the world for a time, claim a throne on seaside cliffs to watch crashing spray fly high into the air.

Opihikao, a tiny settlement 1.5 mi past MacKenzie State Recreation Area, consists of only a few homes and a white church. From

The mouth of a lava tube gapes near the Puna coast.

there, bounce 3 mi more to **Kalani Honua**, a retreat with a cafe (organic/vegetarian tendency although M&Ms are also available) and harmonizing staff (brace yourself: the manager calls himself Dragon). From Kalani Honua, only 6 mi remain until the next corner of the triangle.

Kalapana Sea View Estates is a fancy name for a small cluster of houses, probably available at bargain prices considering that Kalapana proper now lies under a layer of lava. An assemblage of parked cars and hippies mark the trailhead to **Kehena Beach**, a nude sunbathing strip near the 19-mi mark.

Suddenly the road emerges from scrub lands to barren lava flows and reaches the last corner of the triangle. Sadly, the smoothest part of the road is the short section near the end, the majority of which now lies entombed in lava. Do not turn right for Pahoa before first riding past a NO OUTLET sign to reach the end of the road. There, the smooth asphalt road suddenly disappears under a rough tongue of lava, and that's that. Climb up on the high lava flow overlooking the sea to view a wide expanse of recent lava and imagine what once was. Kaimu, widely considered the most beautiful black sand beach in Hawaii, lies buried beneath this volcanic blanket, a thought both sad and spectacular.

Fortuitously, the diner located here was spared from destruction, being the only place at which to buy an ice cream along this entire coast. Whew! The establishment's owner left offerings of ti leaves and alcohol for Pele at the edge of advancing lava, a pacifying strategy that evidently paid off.

Kalapana to Pahoa: 9 miles

To complete the tour and return to Pahoa, pedal **north** on Road 130 near Kalapana. In less than a mile, pull over to see Kalapana's Star of the Sea Church, moved when it became clear that advancing lava would claim the historic building. While the church awaits a new home, it may not be entered, but you can sneak a look at the stained-glass windows and painted interior from without. Like St. Benedict's Painted Church (Tour No. 1), this building is adorned with three-dimensional, illusionary scenes. One stained-glass window depicts Father Damien, who served the church before moving on to Molokai's Kalaupapa Peninsula.

Road 130 runs **uphill** for the first 6 mi until reaching a peak at 1,000 feet. Steam vents at the roadside show that Pele may still have some tricks up her sleeve in Puna. Finally, **descend** to **Pahoa** to complete the triangular tour. From Pahoa, **retrace** the original route to **Keaau**, a rolling 12-mi ride, and then cruise 8 mi down to **Hilo** or ascend to Hawaii Volcanoes National Park (Tour No. 2 in reverse).

TOUR NO. 4

SADDLE ROAD
Hilo to Waimea

Distance: 64 miles
Riding time: 2 days
Difficulty: Most challenging
Terrain: Climb from sea level to 6,800 feet
Roads: Paved throughout
Connecting tours: Tour Nos. 1, 2

Saddle Road provides a demanding but unique bicycling opportunity, giving cyclists the chance to challenge themselves and gain a new perspective on the Big Island's 14,000-foot volcanoes. Although a paved road smooths the way over the 6,000-foot saddle between Mauna Kea and Mauna Loa, the remote, rarely traveled route remains a challenge that few cyclists accept. This ride is not so much a convenient shortcut between Hilo and Kona as an adventure far off the beaten tourist path.

Although fit cyclists can cross Saddle Road in one long day, that goal is both brutal and unnecessary. The only accommodations along the high road are comfortable housekeeping cabins in Mauna Kea State Recreation Area, which should be reserved in advance. The cabins provide a practical way to divide the tour as well as a treat, since clear evenings atop the saddle permit phenomenal stargazing. After a sound night's sleep, you are ready for the reward, a scenic cruise down to Waimea, the Big Island's ranch town.

Hilo to Mauna Kea State Recreation Area: 38 miles

Bring enough food for the entire ride from Hilo as you will pass no more stores (let alone houses) until Waimea, the end point of the tour. From downtown Hilo, **pedal *mauka*** up Waianuenue Avenue, which has no shoulder to begin with. The road begins to climb immediately, with no breaks until 6,600 feet. Early on, however, **detour** past Rainbow Falls on the outskirts of town (0.5-mi detour). Signs along Waianuenue Avenue lead to the wide falls where spray often breaks rays of light into a full, glimmering spectrum of color. Then **backtrack**, turn **right** on Puuhina Street and **right** again to rejoin Kaumana Drive, the Saddle Road.

Not too far along, another interesting sight distracts bikers from the climb. Kaumana Caves County Park lies directly beside the road, marked by stairs that lead to the underground lava tube. After the cave, few diversions punctuate the remainder of the ascent, permitting cyclists to concentrate on challenging terrain.

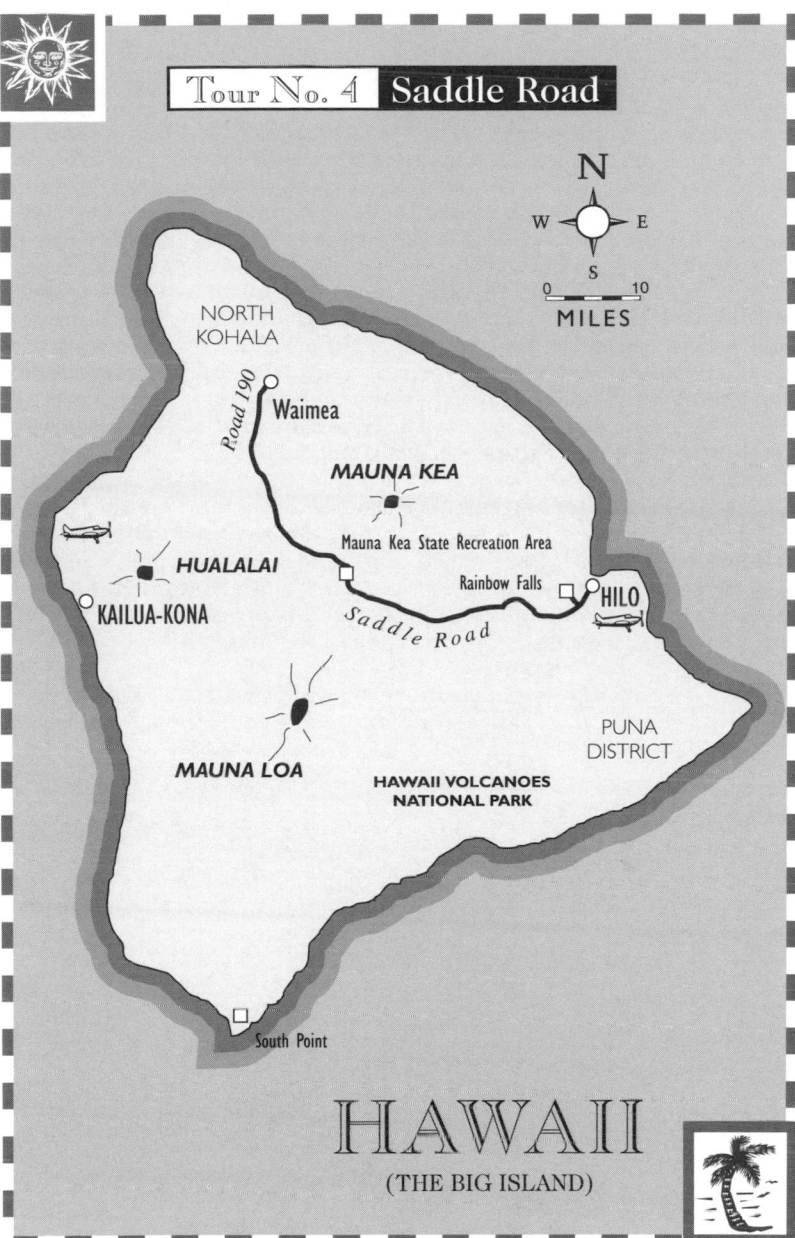

Tour No. 4 Saddle Road

N
W E
S
0 10
MILES

NORTH KOHALA

Road 190

Waimea

MAUNA KEA

Mauna Kea State Recreation Area

Rainbow Falls

HILO

HUALALAI

KAILUA-KONA

Saddle Road

PUNA DISTRICT

MAUNA LOA

HAWAII VOLCANOES NATIONAL PARK

South Point

HAWAII
(THE BIG ISLAND)

Saddle Road is at least decently paved throughout its course over central Hawaii. There is a shoulder until the 19-mi mark, but cyclists will hardly need it as traffic is virtually nonexistent past Kaumana. After the 19-mi mark, the road degenerates to older, **bumpier** pavement for a few miles, making for a less comfortable but reasonable ride. By mile marker 24, the surface is **smoother** again. If it is cloudy (a likely scenario), views will be limited to the surrounding fern-ohia scrub. Ohia is interesting as a successful colonizer on lava due to the plant's shallow root base and its ability to efficiently absorb moisture from mist.

The long climb can be draining, coming in **bursts of short, steep hills** separated by more manageable and gradual inclines. Upon conquering each steep section, immediately pop up a gear to recover for the next assault. Few mile markers and no altitude signs mark Saddle Road; in fact, the road has few distinguishing features at all. Only two side roads branch off the main way (Tree Planting Road and Powerline Road), handy points to use as short-term goals.

At the 25-mi marker, cyclists will be ready to cheer aloud, having reached the **more level**, central section of the saddle. Another plus at this point is the good likelihood of a nice tailwind and a **slight downhill** grade for the last few miles to the cabins. These higher slopes display intriguing scenery when skies clear, with Mauna Kea's steep green slopes pocked by uplifted cinder cones contrasting with the opposite view, where patchwork patterns of lava and scrub mark Mauna Loa's more gradual slope.

Upon entering Mauna Kea State Recreation Area, turn **right** to reach the rental units, called Pohakuloa Cabins. Although the cabins

Cabins in Mauna Kea State Recreation Area offer a snug bed for the night.

are a bit run down, at this point in the day they will represent sheer luxury for weary travelers. All cabins offer hot water, showers, full kitchens, some kitchen utensils, linen, towels, blankets, electric heaters, and small lanais (decks). There is also a pay phone in the park. The roomy cabins sleep up to six occupants, but smaller groups do not have to share. Some cabins also feature woodburning stoves, although wood is not supplied. Reserve a cabin and pick up a key in advance at Hilo's state park office or have it left for you, rather than searching for the caretaker at the end of an exhausting ride.

The state park borders a military reserve, so do not be surprised by the sound of distant (and not distant enough) artillery. Although clouds often shroud the high saddle during the day, an inversion effect ensures dependably clear conditions for wonderfully starry nights. If the sky is not clear by the time you go to bed, rouse yourself in the night to greet an incredible panorama of clear, shining stars. In spring, the Southern Cross and North Star are both visible at the same time, an unusual phenomenon occurring only at this latitude.

Mauna Kea State Recreation Area makes a perfect base for those daring the ride up Mauna Kea or Mauna Loa. A dirt road reaches "only" to the 11,000-foot level of Mauna Loa, while dirt and paved roads lead to Mauna Kea's very summit. Mauna Kea Road climbs to the Visitor's Center at 9,000 feet (paved), followed by a dirt and finally another paved section to the 14,000-foot summit. The 4.5-mi dirt section has a bumpy, scalloped effect, with little relief until the final, smoothly paved 1.5 mi to the top.

Mauna Kea State Recreation Area to Waimea: 26 miles

From your high overnight point at Mauna Kea State Recreation Area, you will reap the benefits of yesterday's challenge with a spectacular descent and unforgettable views. Simply **continue along Saddle Road** toward the Kona coast to begin. The ride is entirely **downhill** with the exception of **one nasty hill** rising at a point 8 mi down the road that jolts dozing muscles back into action. Clear, dry mornings are the norm for this western side of the road, perfect for unobstructed views over the Big Island.

The saddle spreads wide from Mauna Kea to Mauna Loa, and views of Hualalai's impressive cone (over 8,000 feet) open ahead as you progress westward. Sharp eyes may also pick out the solar observatory at Mauna Loa's 9,000-foot level with a fair chance for summit snow to match the white dome. Apparently there is some rivalry between astronomers; Mauna Loa is a solar observatory, a building that earns its own mountaintop location far from the rest on Mauna Kea.

As the road curves north toward Waimea, it passes through deep green ranchlands with spectacular views of Kohala and Maui's Haleakala towering above clouds on the horizon. Cyclists will coast down in a state of awe at one of Hawaii's grandest views. You cannot possibly take it all in while rolling along, so pull over periodically for a good look.

After sweeping along high ground and ranchlands for nearly 20 mi, Saddle Road **joins Road 190** north to Waimea. This nearly level highway has a smooth shoulder, but relentless headwinds drastically reduce progress over the final 6 mi into **Waimea**.

Once in Waimea town, glance back at Mauna Kea for a new view of the summit, the huge mountain mass rearing up from green slopes to a white ridge fully 11,000 feet above Waimea. Opposite Mauna Kea, deep rifts and scooped hillsides mark Kohala's eroded volcanic slope. For more information on the town's offerings, see the Waimea description in Tour No. 1.

From Waimea, cyclists can join Tour No. 1 to Hawi (22 mi) either directly or after an overnight rest. Another alternative is to follow part of that tour in reverse to Honokaa and back to Hilo via the lush windward coast (all downhill to Honokaa except the first 4 mi). Finally, those in a hurry can speed directly down to Kailua-Kona via Road 190 (Mamalahoa Highway), 33 mi away.

TOUR NO. 5

SOUTH POINT EXPLORATION
South Point and Green Sand Beach

Distance: 11 miles
Riding time: Day trip
Difficulty: Challenging
Terrain: 11 miles down/uphill
Roads: Bumpy pavement, then lava/dirt/
sand doubletrack
Connecting tour: Tour No. 2

This ride to the southernmost point in the United States extends off Tour No. 2 from its midpoint, described as a separate tour for easy reference. Road bikes can easily negotiate the paved road down to the Point, although fat tires (or sturdy shoes) are required to continue along the coast to Green Sand Beach. An area of howling winds and stark, elementary scenery, South Point makes a memorable—albeit challenging—detour off the main road.

Ideally, cover the tour as a day trip from a base in Waiohinu or Naalehu. Unfortunately, South Point Road glides a full 11 mi downhill, forcing bikers to tackle the same distance on the uphill return.

To South Point: 11 miles each way

The nearest lodgings from which to base your day is Waiohinu's Shirakawa Motel (telephone 929-7462), the only lodgings in town. The little town also has a small general store (open 8:00 A.M. to 7:00 P.M. daily, Sundays 8:00 A.M. to 6:00 P.M.) but few other amenities. Campers must cruise past Naalehu (supermarket located there) to reach Whittington Beach County Park, near the 61-mi mark of the main road (see Tour No. 2).

South Point Road branches off Belt Road (Road 11) east of the 70-mi mark. Those undertaking the ride from a Waiohinu base need not backtrack west on Road 11 to reach that road, however. Instead, follow **Kamaoa Road** (marked DISCOVERY HARBOR) **west** from the center of Waiohinu, a road lying between the church and gas station. This short-cuts to South Point Road in 4 mi, saving some distance and eliminating an unnecessary climb.

The ride down to South Point follows a **narrow** and **bumpy** but **paved** road for 11 soaring mi. The road quickly narrows to only one lane, but traffic is very light and the surface presents no problem for road bicycles. Of course, this also implies an 11-mi uphill on the return, unless of course you con a ride up from one of the fishermen or tourists down at the point. On the way down, modern windmills churn

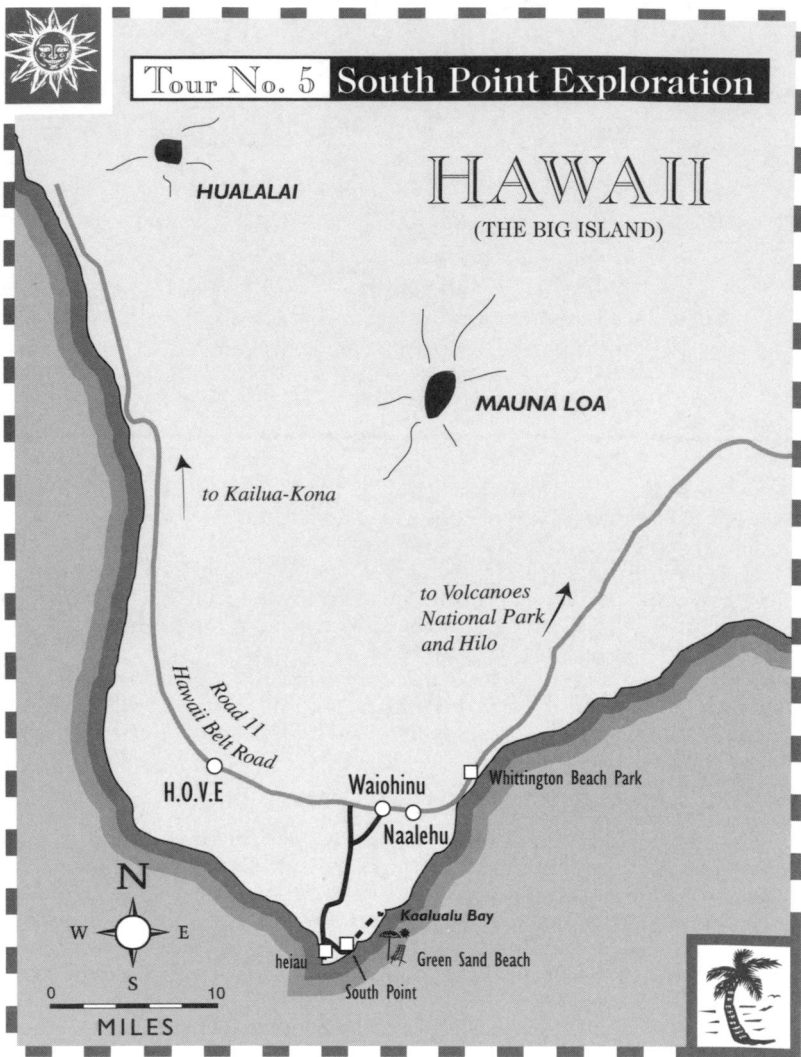

HUALALAI

HAWAII
(THE BIG ISLAND)

MAUNA LOA

to Kailua-Kona

to Volcanoes
National Park
and Hilo

Road 11
Hawaii Belt Road

H.O.V.E   Waiohinu   □ Whittington Beach Park

Naalehu

N
W   E
S
0   10
MILES

Kaalualu Bay

heiau □   🏕 Green Sand Beach
South Point

the air, creating an eerie din on windy days—which means just about every day at South Point. The few wayward trees at South Point all bend low to the ground from the force of easterly winds.

At the bottom of the hill, the road forks. To reach the southernmost point of the United States, **bear right** and pass pullout points for dramatic, cliffy views. South Point proper is marked by a *heiau* and crashing surf. Look for mooring holes in clifftop stones that once tied native fishing canoes to shore. Today, modern fishermen continue the tradition, casting lines from shore or from boats reached by ladders that disappear over the cliff edge. Ceaseless winds may blow dust into your picnic lunch, but it is impossible not to appreciate South Point's raw splendor.

To run away from the few people that visit South Point, pedal **back** to the **fork** and turn **right** to reach Kaulana Bay. Road bicycles can coast as far as the boat ramp at Kaulana Bay, a spot marked only by a few grounded, ghostlike boats and fewer people. The jeep trail to Green Sand Beach begins at Kaulana, an excellent mountain-biking opportunity. Those without fat tires can hike just over 2 mi to Green Sand, where crashing surf and a unique bay create the perfect setting for deep thoughts or a light-hearted dip into the water.

Ride to Green Sand Beach and Beyond

The first mile consists of **rugged** aa lava and loose stones over which you might walk your bike, followed by a **smoother** ride on hard-packed dirt and tough grass suitable for hybrids or road bikes with beefy tires. Only a few short, steep rises mark the otherwise level trail, but a raging headwind may slow your progress noticeably.

Green Sand Beach is easily recognizable as a sharp cut in the coast at the base of a conical hill, its dark green color produced by volcanic and oceanic agents. Lava flow rich in the green mineral olivine cooled in this area, and wave action separated the heavy olivine from other particles, leaving it concentrated on this distinctive beach.

Beyond Green Sand Beach, miles of doubletrack continue paralleling the coast. Mountain bikers can pedal another 4 mi to Kaalualu Bay or meander the intersecting trails that cut overland. Remember to stay on existing trails; there is no need to scar the land with extra sets of tracks when so many established paths already exist.

Mountain bikers and hikers can trek to Green Sand Beach.

MAUI
The Valley Island

Maui is named for the demi-god who pulled the Hawaiian Islands from the sea with his fishing line. Not content with that feat, Maui also went on to lasso the sun to slow its progress across the sky from the island's crowning heights, known as Haleakala, or House of the Sun. Of his time on this special island, Mark Twain wrote, "I never spent so pleasant a month before, or bade any place goodbye so regretfully. I doubt if there is a mean person there. . . . I went to Maui to stay a week and remained five." Bikers may also find themselves stretching out their stay, collecting memories as they roller-coaster over waterfall-laced coasts or sweat up Haleakala's full height.

Maui is an island of mixed images, home to both crowded coastal resorts and the stark, color-strewn moonscape of Haleakala National Park. Its principal town, Kahului, is just another mall-lined commercial center, while Lahaina's historic streets exude a proud character befitting a historic whaling port and Kamehameha's former capital. More than any other island, Maui represents how much Hawaii offers, and how few visitors take advantage of its opportunities. While scores of tourists line Wailea's beaches, few venture a few miles farther to the stark grandeur of La Perouse Bay. Hundreds drive up Haleakala to watch the sunrise, yet only a handful set off on crater hikes. Cyclists are well equipped with the means and initiative to leave the Maui of tourist brochures behind for quiet corners that convince them Maui *no ka oi* (Maui is the best), indeed.

Haleakala's impressive mass makes almost every Maui bicycle tour a challenge. Most seem like obstacle courses of endless rolling hills or interminable climbs. Maui cycling is best suited for those who enjoy challenging themselves with demanding (or demented) tasks like the 10,000-foot ascent of Haleakala or those who can see the reward in a four-day trek around the mountain's considerable bulk. On the other hand, cyclists with more modest goals can also enjoy Maui, taking on shorter rides and working in other activities like snorkeling or whale watching.

Practical Information and Tips for Touring

Although Oahu bears the brunt of Hawaii's tourist trade, Maui is the second most visited island. Massive Haleakala creates most of the island's area, with the eroded remains of an older volcano forming West Maui. The flat isthmus connecting the volcanoes gives Maui its nickname, the Valley Island. Although Lahaina and Wailea are Maui's principal tourist destinations, the island's gateway town is Kahului (with neighboring Wailuku), located in the valley. The area around Kihei is Maui's sunniest, driest region, while the cooler, higher slopes of Haleakala are known as Upcountry, where ranches take the place of coastal resorts.

For tourist information, contact the Maui Visitor's Bureau at (800)

525-MAUI or Box 1738, Kahului, HI 96732. The free *Guide to Maui* magazine available at the airport and in tourist towns includes useful travel tips, maps, as well as coupons for whale watching and snorkeling excursions.

Airports and Ferries

Kahului's airport is Maui's main gateway. The airport is a short but uncomfortable 4-mi ride from Kahului center, with little shoulder space on busy roads in the island's main business center. Follow Kahului signs from the airport to pass Kanaha Pond and ride Road 36 and then Road 32 through the centers of the twin towns.

Small aircraft also service Hana, on Maui's wet east side, and Kaanapali, a resort area on West Maui. The latter (Kapalua West Maui Airport) is located midway between Kaanapali and Napili, 7 mi north of Lahaina.

The Maui Princess ferry line shuttles commuters and visitors between Lahaina and Kaunakakai on Molokai, while Expeditions vessels sail from Lahaina to Manele Bay on Lanai. Both transport bicycles, providing a fun, less expensive alternative to flying. For more information on either service, consult the Molokai and Lanai chapters.

Accommodations

As a popular tourist destination, Maui offers many accommodations options. Only campers may be frustrated by a lack of sites. In some remote areas, cyclists might be limited to a single accommodation choice. For example, camping is the only option in Haleakala National Park (both the summit region and the Kipahulu District on the south coast), while indoor accommodations are the only choice in the Kihei/Wailea area. Therefore, the name of the game on Maui is flexibility and preparation.

ROOMS. Maui's prime resort areas offer many rooms and condos, principally in the Kaanapali area north of Lahaina on West Maui, and Kihei/Wailea on the dry west shore of Haleakala. Main towns like Kahului, Wailuku, and Lahaina also have many hotels, while smaller towns like Hana and Paia offer a few as well. B&Bs dot Upcountry Maui around areas like Makawao and Kula, and many others are scattered throughout the island. There are two independent hostels in Wailuku, both restricted to foreign travelers, which mean they do not officially accept U.S. citizens.

CABINS. State parks maintain housekeeping cabins at Waianapanapa State Park, near Hana (see Tour No. 6). There are also three cabin sites under tremendous demand in Haleakala crater (all hike-in access only). To enter the lottery for reservations, contact Cabin Reservation Request, Haleakala National Park, Box 369, Makawao, HI 96768.

CAMPING. It is impossible to base a tour of Maui entirely on camping in official sites. Maui county sites include Baldwin Beach County Park and Rainbow Park, both near Paia. Neither site is recommendable due to safety concerns: your gear may not be safe at these sites, and women (whether alone or with company) are warned to steer clear of both.

State sites are secure but remote. Poli Poli State Park allows camping high on the slopes of Haleakala (6,000-foot level). Only mountain bikers might consider this remote site (latrines, no showers, tap water must be treated). The second of two state sites is the pleasant, safe, and well-run site at Waianapanapa, a few miles outside Hana. A resident ranger regularly patrols the campground, and cabins are also available. Camping in state parks is free with a permit from the office at the State Office Building (lower level), 54 High Street, Wailuku, HI 96793 (telephone 243-5354). This is the large building at the corner of Roads 30 and 32 in Wailuku.

Haleakala National Park extends from the summit of the volcano to Maui's south shore, an area known as the Kipahulu District. Camping in national park sites does not require a permit or fee but is limited to three nights in each site. Other than backcountry sites within Haleakala crater, there is a campsite in Kipahulu and one at Hosmer Grove, at the 7,000-foot level of Haleakala. Neither site offers showers, and the Kipahulu site has no water at all (but a nearby tap resolves that problem). The last camping option on Maui is a private site in Olowalu, 6 mi south of Lahaina. The grounds and facilities at Camp Pecusa (telephone 661-4304) are no charmers, but the management is pleasant and, most importantly, the site is safe.

Kahului/Wailuku

Maui's gateway town is Kahului, which has overgrown into neighboring Wailuku. These towns comprise Maui's central commercial district with government offices, malls, and the island's main airport. The towns offer convenient stopover points for your first and last day on the island, but little else.

SIGHTS. After taking care of business matters in Kahului, your time is best spent on short rides to nearby points of interest. Halekii and Pihana *heiaus* and the Iao Valley are all only a few miles away from town, rides that leave traffic lights and bustle behind in exchange for peace, solitude, and more appealing scenery (see Additional Suggested Rides). Otherwise buy an ice cream, do your laundry, or rest your muscles in preparation for the challenging rides ahead.

FOOD AND ACCOMMODATIONS. The main street of Kahului (Road 32, Kaahumanu Avenue) and the surrounding area have several large supermarkets. The same street rises gradually toward Iao Valley and Wailuku, halfway up the slope (where there is another supermarket and small convenience store). A number of small bars and restaurants line the side streets of both towns, although Wailuku's offerings tend toward the seedy side.

There are a few hotels and motels along the main road in both towns, none overly appealing. For budget accommodations, try the Northshore Inn or Banana Bungalow, both independent hostels that offer dormitory space as well as private rooms.

The campground nearest Kahului is Baldwin County Beach Park, 5 mi east on Road 36 (Hana Highway) just west of Paia. However, the park may be unsafe for camping, especially for women. The park has a terrible location to boot, directly beside the main coastal road with bright street lights. In short, you are far better off in a hostel or cheap hotel than this site.

Along the Way

HIKING. One of Hawaii's greatest natural treasures, spectacular Haleakala National Park crowns the island of Maui. Tour No. 7 describes the bicycle ride to Haleakala's 10,000-foot summit, but the possibilities do not end there. Even the wonderful summit overlook and the rewarding ride up provide only superficial views of the real attraction—the bizarre moonscape within Haleakala crater. To better experience Haleakala, spend a day exploring the crater on foot.

For practical information on the park, accommodations, and services, see Tour No. 7. To reach the summit without applying phenomenal pedal power, your only options are to hitchhike or pay for a ride up. No buses travel to the summit, but some downhill bicycle tour companies will transport hikers to the top at a reduced rate.

Free, ranger-led hikes with various destinations and themes are offered, so check schedules posted at Park Headquarters. The best day hike is a 12-mi walk on Sliding Sands and Halemanu trails (5-7 hours). That hike descends into the crater's moonscape from the Visitor's Center (9,700 feet), winds around cinder cones and the twisted valley floor (7,000 feet), then climbs back out to join Crater Road at the 8,000-foot elevation level. You can then hitch from there or follow the signed Supply Trail right to Hosmer Grove, an additional 2 mi away.

The magnificent "moonscape" of Haleakala crater

For a short hike (2 mi round trip) follow Halemauu Trail from Crater Road to the crater rim. Halemauu Trail is marked approximately 3 mi up from park headquarters from the main road. With negligible elevation gain or loss, this short hike brings you to a new and different crater overlook point with good views down Kaupo Gap to the coast in clear weather.

Hikers with more grandiose plans should know that Haleakala also offers two campsites and three cabins in the crater (camping requires a permit issued on the spot at headquarters). The ultimate Maui hike is the trek down through Haleakala crater, descending through Kaupo Gap to the sea and the Kipahulu District.

SNORKELING. Molokini is a tiny island between Maui and uninhabited Kahoolawe, the very tip of a submerged crater. Molokini's perfect crescent shape shelters thousands of fish, creating one of Hawaii's most popular snorkel and dive spots. Most charter boats depart Maalaea Harbor, making this day trip easy to manage from a base in Kihei. You can usually find a spot as a last-minute walk-on, but call ahead for reservations during peak tourist weeks and look for trip coupons in tourist brochures. There is also a good chance of spotting whales, turtles, and dolphins during the trip.

Charter boats range from stylish catamarans to motor boats and graceful wooden sloops, most charging about the same price. More importantly, shop around for a boat with limited capacity and a nice crew. Although I was initially disappointed in the chug-chug motor boat I boarded, I was soon counting my luck. The ship's crew was fantastically nice, the boat remained at Molokini later than all the others, and the captain made several detours to get a better look at whales along the way.

WHALE WATCHING. The area between Maui, Kahoolawe, Lanai, and Molokai is an underwater volcanic plateau with depths of hundreds of feet, in contrast to sea levels north and east of Maui that rapidly drop off to over 18,000 feet. These sheltered waters serve as a prime winter breeding and calving area for whales. Although whales are also spotted off other islands, Maui's waters practically teem with the giants in season (mid-February to mid-March, although sightings continue into April). Whale-watching excursions that depart from Maalaea area offer the best chance to gain closer views, although the boats are required to maintain a certain distance from the whales. Shop around for both a bargain price and more importantly, a knowledgeable crew for your trip.

TOUR NO. 6

CIRCLING MAUI AND HALEAKALA
Hana Highway and Maui's South Coast

Distance: 125 miles
Riding time: 4 days
Difficulty: Most challenging
Terrain: Constantly rolling hills, climbs up to 4,000 feet
Roads: Paved except 4 miles of gravel
Connecting tours: Tour Nos. 7, 8

This challenging tour circles the main body of Haleakala, from the waterfall-laced Hana Highway to the remote south coast and Maui's Upcountry. For Hawaii, it is also a lengthy and varied tour, wandering from rainforests to arid volcanic slopes and high green ranches. To conquer unrelenting terrain, cyclists must push themselves constantly over endless roller-coaster hills or miles-long, grinding ascents. However, Maui's prizes befit the toll they exact, coming in the form of rocky cliffs colored by the setting sun or wide, windy views over miles of unpopulated coast.

Although the island attracts many tourists, this tour demonstrates how easy it is to escape to Maui's hidden side where sights and attitudes remain unblemished by development. Although the first few miles of highway pedaling are uncomfortably busy, cyclists will have the road to themselves for most of the route. Thanks to a stretch of gravel on the south shore, this road ringing the mass of Haleakala sees little through traffic. Of course, the gravel also presents a formidable obstacle to bicycles. Mountain bikes or hybrids can negotiate the 4-mi gravel section more easily than regular road bikes, which might rattle unhappily along or even force riders to get off and push.

If it were easy to manage, the ride would not be as unique an adventure. Despite the logistical drawbacks, this remains one of the most memorable rides in all Hawaii. Tourists using road bikes might compromise by riding only as far as Hana or Kipahulu, investigating the possibility of a flight from Hana's small airport.

Kahului to Hana: 56 miles

For accommodations and other practical information on Kahului and neighboring Wialuku, refer to Maui's introductory section. Day one presents an early trial on this difficult tour, covering a long distance over constantly rolling terrain. However, this stretch may be divided into two shorter days by stopping at the YMCA Camp in Keanae or one

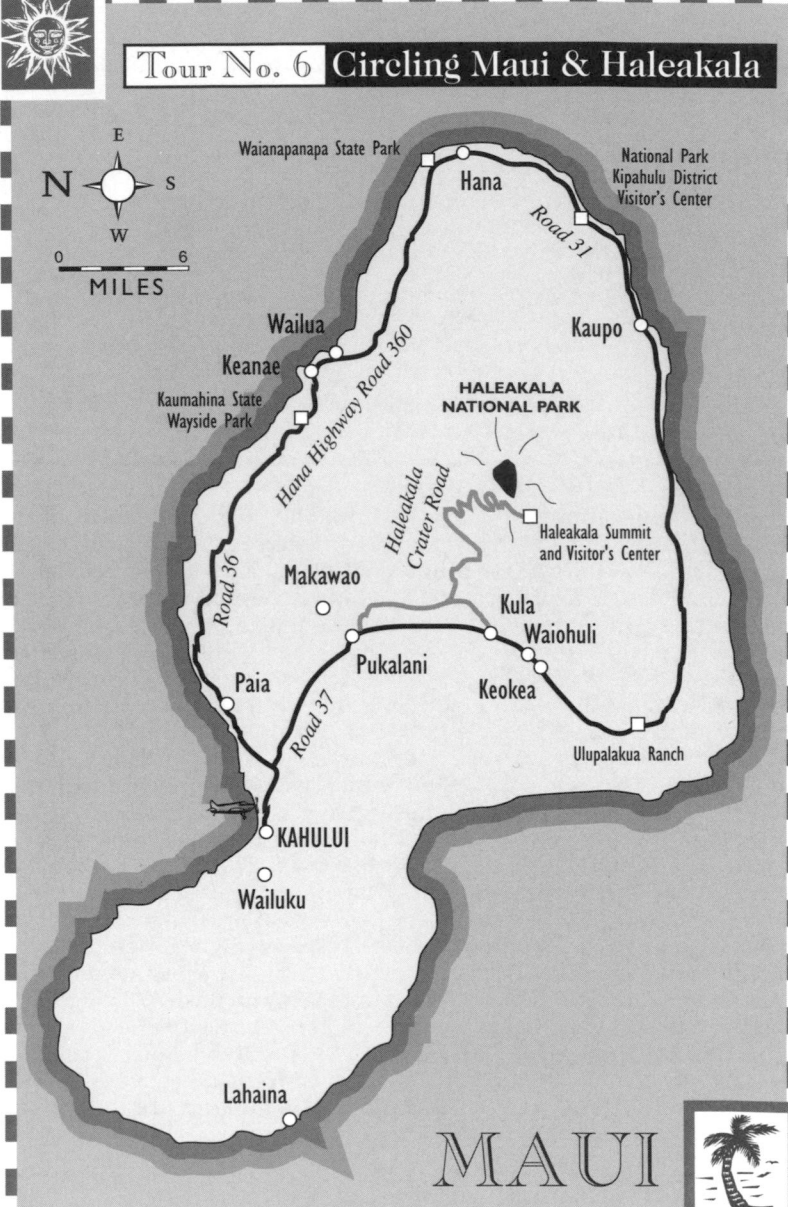

Tour No. 6 Circling Maui & Haleakala

MAUI

of the few B&Bs scattered along the route. There are no stores along the route except fruit stands and a snack wagon at Halfway to Hana Point, so come fully prepared with lunch and snacks for the day. From an athlete's point of view, the roller-coaster ride provides intense interval training for Maui's greatest challenge, the ascent of Haleakala.

In winter, keep an eye out for the occasional offshore spout of a whale throughout this coast-hugging ride. The ride follows shoulderless Road 36 from Kahului to its eastern endpoint.

From the center of Kahului, follow signs to the **airport** (Road 32) and keep **right** on Haleakala Highway (Road 396). This road curves several times around the airport/heliport area but avoids traffic and the long meander of Road 36. At a traffic light and major intersection, turn **left** on Road 36 (Hana Highway).

The Hana Highway offers little to no shoulder space, but traffic is usually bearable and greatly decreases as you progress eastward. One look at the crowded beaches near Paia should make you feel glad for the road as you watch wind and board surfers narrowly avoid chilling collisions.

At some point along this shore, pull over for a last look westward to West Maui's misty mountains with distant Molokai poking out on the horizon behind. After **Paia** the ride takes on the character it retains throughout the rest of the day, with **steady rises and falls** in landscape. On the east coast of Maui, endless sharp clefts in the coastline consign cyclists to constantly pedaling up, only to zoom down the next slope. Long, steady inclines gradually give way to long, steeper inclines. After 18 mi, Road 36 becomes 360, a narrow, winding road still called the Hana Highway.

Punishing terrain aside, the ride is pure joy as each valley curve reveals yet another lush waterfall or rocky cove. The Hana Highway is also famous for its endless string of one-lane bridges, a place to exercise caution. Small side streams drip across the road in places, creating slippery areas. Enjoy the views, but pay attention to the road.

When Road 360 begins, **mile markers restart at zero**. After the 6-mi mark, save one gear and use caution on a steep ascent; one hairpin turn there can be incredibly steep if you are forced to take it at a tight angle. Generally traffic is light and patient, although the occasional nervous driver may refuse to pass you and jam four or five pickup trucks behind, all blaring their horns. If a driver is too timid to pass, it is best to pull over completely and let the backup through. However, just as many drivers will cheer encouragement and admiring comments along the way, adding a little pep to your pumping legs.

Many waterfalls are visible directly from the road. Clever cyclists will keep a bathing suit handy for a cool, rejuvenating dip in the pool beneath a waterfall. For roadside relief, let yourself get sprinkled by one of the miniature waterfalls that cascades to the roadside. The most Eden-like waterfall is **Puohokamoa Falls** (at the 11-mi mark), a picture-perfect waterfall with a clear, round pool at its base.

A good place for a break past the halfway point of the day is **Kaumahina State Wayside Park** (past the 12-mi mark). The park offers picnic tables, toilets, and nice views of the craggy Keanae peninsula ahead (no drinking water). Those with the patience and interest

Wailua's picture-perfect Coral Miracle Church

should hold out a little longer for a break at **Keanae Arboretum**, where short trails meander through lush patches of both native and introduced vegetation.

A short distance farther down the road, **Keanae** itself is signed to the left. The round-trip ride down to the tip of the small peninsula is only 1.5 mi and the return climb back to the main road is not too bad, so give it a go. An 1860 **mission church** stands on the lower peninsula (only one word can describe these little guys: quaint). Waves crash into twisted lava formations on the coast, putting on a mesmerizing show. **Back on the main road**, stop once again to take in a high view of the peninsula's patchwork of flooded fields.

To reach Keanae's YMCA (telephone 242-9007), turn off the road halfway between mile markers 16 and 17. If you stop at the Keanae YMCA you cut this day's distance to only 46 mi, leaving 10 mi to Hana. A small snack bar stands a short distance farther at **Halfway to Hana Point**. The faucet outside the stand is your best hope for refilling water bottles on the way, so drink up and refill before moving on.

For another short **detour** past the 18-mi mark, turn **left** at a triangular intersection (an unmarked dead end to Wailua). Only a short distance down the big hill stands the **Coral Miracle Church** (the second church on the left). When the church was under construction, a violent storm washed coral blocks ashore to conveniently provide building materials and washed away the excess after the church's completion. Like many other Hawaiian churches, this building contrasts the primary colors of its structure and its backdrop, a photogenic sight.

Back on the road, brace yourself for a **long climb**. The road rises for nearly 3 mi of serious, sweaty climbing, then another mile of very gradual **up and down** slopes before a **final descent**. Encouraging signs on the order of FALLING ROCK and ROAD NARROWS line the road, but so do grand views like the one back to Wailua's Coral Miracle Church with its thin tower pointing clearly out of the lush tropical scene. Tempting Tarzan vines dangle along the upper road, creating a thick rainforest atmosphere.

After the long climb, the road runs mostly **downhill** to Hana. Honesty-system fruit and flower stands stocked with pineapples, papayas, passionfruit, and bananas dot the roadside. Who can resist those "sexy pink" flowers? Another multilevel waterfall comes into view from a bridge, before another **long climb** puts you back to work again.

Finally you will **descend** a long hill and pass Hana Gardenland Nursery. Note the first left after that; Ulaino Road runs down to the coast there, leading to the largest *heiau* on Maui, a potential **side trip** for the next morning. Past the 32-mi mark, a sign points out **Waianapanapa State Park** to the left. Park facilities include outdoor showers, toilets, drinking water, picnic tables, and rental cabins. The nice campsite is full of travelers and well patrolled by the resident warden, a very safe and quiet area. In the area you will find a nice black sand beach, a seaside rock arch, and a small *heiau*. For a diverting walk, follow the ancient "paved" coastal trail for up to 3 mi to Hana. Beware, however, that "paved" is literally a rough term. As a thrilling, somewhat spooky antidote for the hot ride, take a dunk in a cold pool in one of the nearby caves.

Hana lies only 3 mi away from the park. As you near town, keep **right** at the police station to avoid a long down and uphill to Hana Bay. There are also a few inns and hotels in town for those seeking indoor accommodations. Ride straight to the south end of town to reach the Ranch Store and landmark Hasagawa General Store, both just beyond the church (open daily until 6:30 P.M., including Sundays). Hana's services are the last food and gas supply points along this tour until Ulupalakua Ranch, two days away.

After this big day, cyclists are probably satisfied just to breathe a sigh of relief and unwind in a quiet seaside spot. Those with excess energy may be tempted to hike the historic trail between Waianapanapa and Hana. The largest *heiau* on the island, Piilanihale Heiau, stands on the property of Hana Gardenland Nursery at the end of Ulaino Road, which you passed on the way into Hana. The grounds are open for limited hours, so it is best to stop by the main nursery building on the main road to ask first.

Hana to Kipahulu: 11 miles

The short ride from Hana to Kipahulu provides a good break between two taxing days on this tour and also serves to shorten the following day's route through a remote area. The short hop allows for a slow departure from your lodgings, or time for a cool soak at Kipahulu.

Before leaving Hana, load up on groceries for two day, as the next store is located at distant Ulupalakua Ranch. The last gas station on the road out of Hana distributes photocopies of a handy national park (Kipahulu District) information sheet.

Hana Highway (Road 360) becomes **Piilani Highway (Road 31)** beyond town, beginning with the 51-mi marker. This road is well **paved** up to Kipahulu but the terrain continues in the same **rolling** spirit of the previous leg, with slightly more gradual slopes. Overly optimistic maps indicate several interesting sights, such as a *heiau* and petroglyphs along the road, but most are extremely difficult to find.

The road **curves** sharply past more waterfalls and houses both modest and grand. In no time, cyclists will **enter** Haleakala National Park's Kipahulu District. This section of the national park was a late addition dedicated with the help of Charles Lindbergh and the Nature Conservancy, among others.

Perhaps as an attempt to discourage tourism, the Kipahulu District has no running water. Toilets consist of fancy latrines, and there are no sinks or running water. You can wash yourself with a cooling soak in a nearby stream, but otherwise there are no facilities of any kind. Not to panic, however! Cyclists can obtain water 1 mi west at the little pink-roofed Kipahulu Church. Walk behind the church on the right side and look for a slightly overgrown faucet at the church wall. To be sure, treat or boil the water, filling up as many containers as you can for the afternoon and your campsite. While there, detour by the nearby grave of Charles Lindbergh at the Congregational Church. In this starkly beautiful area, it is easy to understand his memorable comment, "I'd rather live a day in Hawaii than a month in New York."

The only accommodations at Kipahulu is camping in the national park, one of the best campground locations in Hawaii. To reach the campground, go behind the upper toilet block and follow a gravel road with small signs to the campground. Instead of settling for the drab field at the end of the road, grab a seaside spot in the shade of a tree. From there you will have a front-seat view of the best show in town, starring rolling surf and rocky cliffs, with guest appearances by whales and sea birds. Later, you can tune in to a sunset and watch constellations rotate slowly around the night sky while a Kohala lighthouse sweeps the Big Island's distant shores with its piercing beam of white.

As for other area opportunities, visitors can hike along Oheo Gulch and find a pool to claim for their own. Although some maps refer to Seven Sacred Pools, there is really no such thing. The term was invented as a tourist-attracting gimmick, a bastardization of traditional terms that native and local groups take exception to. Therefore do not bother counting pools, just set out and find one that suits your taste.

Better yet, hike up to Waimoku Falls (2 mi; about 1 hour) or simply find a pool along the way if you are not up to a long trek. The cold stream provides refreshing relief on a dry, sunny day and after a hot, albeit short, ride. An afternoon's relaxation in this beautiful area will soothe both muscles and mind, preparing you for the difficult ride ahead.

Kipahulu to Kula: 38 miles

This challenging day is marked by a handful of historic churches and constant uphill slopes, along with the "three Vs" of Hawaii: views, views, views. Fill at least three water bottles as there are no reliable

The pools of Oheo Gulch invite cyclists to take a plunge.

resupply points until Ulupalakua Ranch. Dire warnings about road conditions ring more or less true. Although most of the ride covers adequately paved roads, cyclists must battle 5 mi of terrible gravel at one point. Only mountain bikes or beefy hybrids should be ridden here, but determined road bikers can probably push their wheels over this section.

The first 4 mi from Kipahulu are a **well-paved, twisting roller coaster**, some hills so steep they are not even worth pedaling up. At the 38-mi marker, pavement gives way to **gravel** mixed with short **dirt** sections. However, a gorgeous coastline compensates in part, one highlight being little white **Huialoha Church** (1859) on a picture-perfect headland on the way to Kaupo. About 0.5 mi past the 35-mi mark, the surface improves slightly to **bumpy pavement**, leading into **Kaupo** (7.5 mi from Kipahulu). Although there is a small general store and snack truck in "town," don't count on either being open.

Beyond Kaupo, the road degenerates again to not-so-terrible **gravel**, which becomes decent **pavement** 9 mi from the day's starting point. The road to Ulupalakua consists of **patchy pavement**, but even that is a wonderful treat after the gravel section. As you pedal along, you will revel in views of the rocky shore, ochre-colored volcanic slopes sweeping down to the sea's deep blues. A few miles along, a **rock arch** stands out among other twisted rock formations along the coast.

As you tackle hill after hill on this ever-rising road, it is important to supply your body with energy in the form of snacks and drinks. Use gears intelligently and make the most of short downhill sections to recover and regain momentum. Try to keep a positive attitude by focusing on the scenery and not the challenging inclines. Winds are usually helpful here, at times whipping bicycles along at a steady clip. Happily, there are no cars to speak of on this road, an extra complication cyclists can do without.

As you round Haleakala's southwest corner, high views of neighboring islands open up, beginning with scarred Kahoolawe and little Molokini, then Lanai and Molokai. As you rise higher and higher from the coast, the sound of wind sweeping through brush replaces the crash of ocean surf, creating a feeling of Big Sky country combined with the azure Pacific.

Inland, the domes of Science City atop Haleakala become visible as you round the volcano's southwest side. You will finally reach **Ulupalakua Ranch** (28 mi from your starting point; no accommodations), which is more ranch than town. One tiny portion of the ranch is **Tedeschi Winery**, an excellent place for a break with shade and picnic tables. A general store just down the road offers all the basics and essential snacks. A free, 20-minute tour of the winery begins every hour to half hour (between 9:30 A.M. and 2:30 P.M.) and includes free samples of vintages such as a unique pineapple wine.

The tiny, 23-acre vineyard lies to the left of the road as you pedal **north** from the ranch, its grapes specially developed for Ulupalakua's climate and soil. The state "highway" that begins here is a dream come true, a vast difference from the bumpy county road behind. Locals joke that county road crews are extremely efficient—they finish work at 4:30 and are home by 3:15.

Straight down to the left spreads the highly developed Kihei area. A **jeep road** leads from Ulupalakua to Makena on the coast, but may not always be passable. Far below, little crescent-shaped Molokini can be easily distinguished by the armada of charter boats that surround it— and for good reason, as the islet is an excellent snorkeling destination.

Beyond Ulupalakua, only a few gradual **uphill** miles remain until you reach the day's end point. The road continues its steady bend northward, opening panoramic views across the central valley to West Maui and the curve of Maalaea Bay. Shops, restaurants, and cafes line the little towns of **Keokea** and **Waiohuli**.

Regular customers greet newcomers at Ulupalakua's general store.

Kula, a last 3 mi down the road, has a few B&Bs and two grocery stores (located 2 mi north of the junction of Roads 37 and 377 on an intermediate road between the two). Those insane enough to consider hauling up to Poli Poli State Park at this point in the day (Kula is at 3,000 feet elevation, Poli Poli at 6,600) can bear right on 377 and turn right up Waipoli Road. Otherwise, there are no camping opportunities anywhere in the area. Kula makes an ideal base from which to begin an ascent of Haleakala (Tour No. 7). Cyclists not ready for that challenge, on the other hand, will have an easy, quick downhill cruise to Kahului, where more budget accommodation options are available.

Kula to Kahului: 20 miles

From Kula, the **road divides** into two **parallel branches,** Road 37 (Kula Highway) and Road 377 (Haleakala Highway). Cyclists planning to pedal up Haleakala should follow the latter for 3 mi to reach the marked right turn for Haleakala Crater Road. Before beginning the long climb up, however, stock up on supplies in Kula. Otherwise, cruise down the lower road (37), which eventually joins the busiest section of Haleakala Highway through **Pukalani** and down to Kahului. Although the road widens to two lanes of speedy traffic, an extremely wide shoulder allows cyclists to keep out of harm's way.

On this 20-mi downhill ride, cyclists descend from over 3,000 feet to sea level, an effortless and quick ride. Before you know it, you will be back in **Kahului**, ready to collect yourself again and head out for Tour No. 8 around West Maui.

UP AND DOWN HALEAKALA
An Ascent of Maui's Highest Peak

Distance: 41 miles
Riding time: 1 to 2 days (not including hiking time)
Difficulty: Most challenging
Terrain: Climb to 10,023 feet (3,055 meters)
Roads: Well paved throughout
Connecting tour: Tour No. 6

Maui's Haleakala, the House of the Sun, towers 10,000 feet (3,000 meters) above sea level, its summit a 41-mi ride from Kahului. With a smoothly paved road all the way to the top, Haleakala is one of the premier bicycle ascents in the world. This ride is unique as the only place in the world where one can pedal from sea level to 10,000 feet in 40 mi. Those who climb Haleakala join an exclusive club. The day I pedaled up, only five cyclists ascended, while over 100 descended. The reason for this multiplication? Cruising down Haleakala is one of the most popular outdoor excursions on Maui, and visitors can fork over about $100 for bicycle rental and shuttle service to the top. In spite of all the sweat, there is a lot to be said for the experience of ascending, making your visit much more significant when you finally reach the summit and then descend. On the other hand, the ascent of Haleakala is not for everyone. Challenge yourself, but remember to recognize your limits.

Surprisingly, Haleakala is also extremely underused in spite of its easy access. Hundreds of visitors drive to watch the sunrise from atop Haleakala, only to leave minutes later. Few invest any time in hiking the park's trails or wandering through the informative Visitor's Center. Although this is a shame, the low numbers are also a boon to determined outdoors people, who will find their chosen paths uncrowded and unspoiled.

LOGISTICS. Although this route is described from a starting point in Kahului, cyclists can link directly into the ride from Kula, a stop along Tour No. 6. Due to the challenging and remote nature of this tour, it is important to plan several aspects of the trip before setting out, including accommodations, general information, and services atop the volcano.

While the Haleakala ascent is a serious climb, several factors make the challenge more manageable than it may at first seem. First, Haleakala Crater Road is evenly graded throughout, allowing conditioned cyclists to ride with one gear in reserve at most times. The steepest sections lie between mile markers 5 and 6 near the base. The

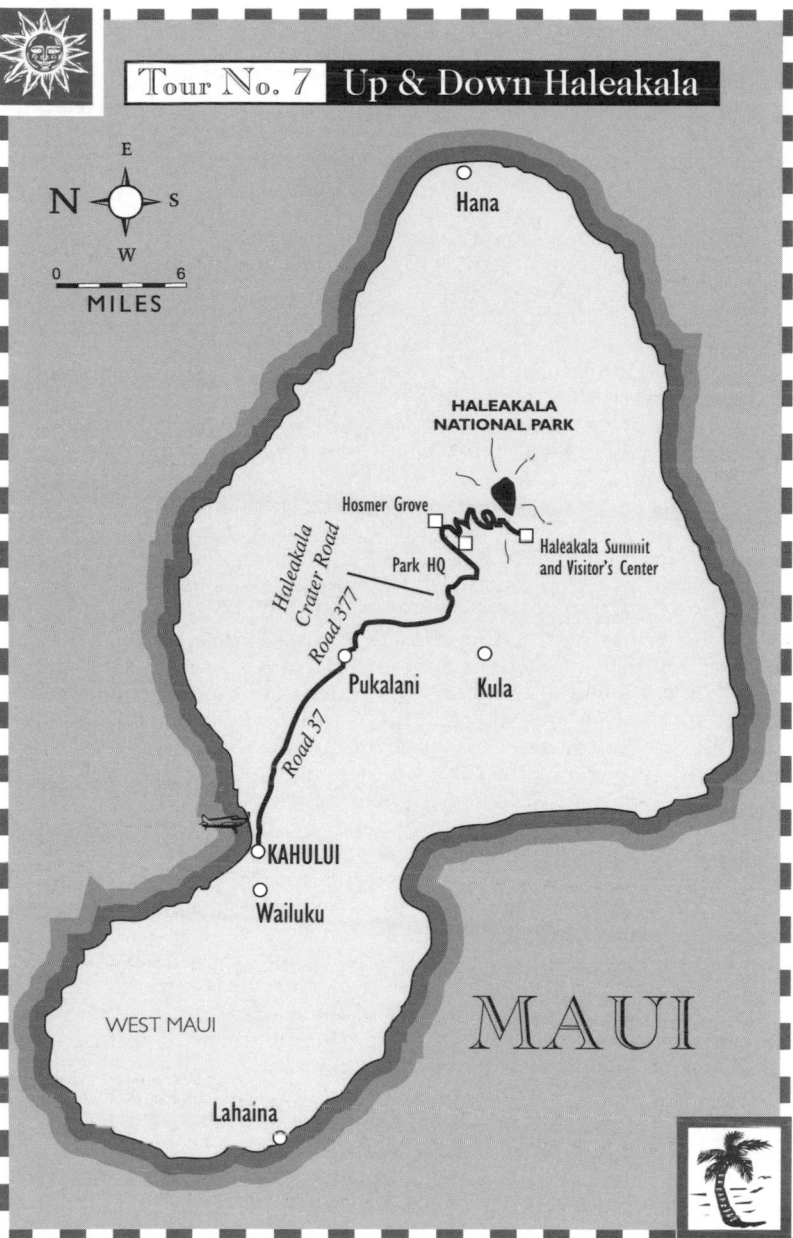

Tour No. 7 — Up & Down Haleakala

top half of the road (a second series of switchbacks after Hosmer Grove) actually has a slightly easier grade than the bottom.

Furthermore, the ride breaks up well into manageable sections. Unless you climb Haleakala as a day trip based from Kula or (heaven forbid) from Kahului, your best bet is to camp at the free Hosmer Grove site. Hosmer Grove lies just above the halfway mark of Crater Road, neatly dividing the climb. First, you will ascend 10.5 mi from the base of Crater Road to Hosmer Grove with full gear, where you can stop to set camp, eat lunch, and rest. Afterward, continue the last 11 mi to the summit with the dual advantages of an unloaded bicycle and slightly easier switchbacks. No problem!

SUPPLIES. Bring all food and supplies for your entire Haleakala stay from Kula or Kahului, because there is no food sold in the park, not even a vending machine. Unfortunately, the crazy consequence is that you must pedal spaghetti up a volcano, but so it goes in the life of a committed cyclist (or one who should be committed). Hosmer Grove facilities include grills and drinking-water taps, but no shower. During the low season, only a handful of visitors camp at Hosmer, most of them late arrivals eager for a head start for the next morning's sunrise. In peak season, the site can become quite crowded, but as a relatively early arrival, you should not have a problem squeezing in. Hosmer Grove is the only campground on Haleakala accessible by bicycle.

PARK INFORMATION. The National Park Service operates two outlets for visitor information. Park Headquarters near Hosmer Grove at the 7,000-foot level offers general information and displays (open until 4:00 P.M.), and a Visitor's Center at the summit distributes more hiking information and has good interpretive displays (closing at 3:00 P.M.). At the Visitor's Center, colorful murals depict the story of the demi-god Maui who lassoed the sun, leaving the dangling ropes as reminders that are still visible as rays at dawn and dusk.

The park's sole pay phone is located at headquarters, where a number of silverswords grow. The friendly staff will go out of their way to help visitors who demonstrate a genuine interest and thoughtful approach. Devote some time to informative exhibits there and learn more about the area's unique flora and fauna, as well as elements that threaten them. For example, you will learn that some native birds burrow into the volcanic slopes and that silverswords have shallow root systems and are therefore sensitive to the weight of footsteps. Details like these will help you protect the park and make the difference between seeing and experiencing Haleakala.

ACCOMMODATIONS. The only accommodations in the national park itself are the Hosmer Grove campsite, located at 7,000 feet near park headquarters (see above). All other park accommodations are hike-in sites. Cyclists depending on indoor accommodations must complete the ascent as a day trip based from distant Kahului (a daunting thought) or, better yet, a B&B in Kula.

Ideally, calculate three days for Haleakala: one for the ascent, one for a day hike in the crater, and one to descend and perhaps connect into the next tour, such as the one to Lahaina (Tour No. 8).

WEATHER. Weather atop Haleakala is often clear even when lower slopes are cloudy. Likewise, the volcano's crater is usually clear when lands below are clouded, creating the mesmerizing effect of clouds lapping at the crater's low edge like waves on a beach. For the same reasons, Mauna Kea and Mauna Loa on the Big Island can often be seen from the summit, both volcanoes poking their often snow-capped peaks above the clouds. Of course, in perfect conditions your view will seem to reach to the very end of paradise. Current park weather reports can be heard by dialing 572-7749.

During the day, even the high, breezy summit can be comfortably warm. By night, however, temperatures drop dramatically, so campers should pack a few extra layers. Dependable, bright raingear is a must on Haleakala, to be used for both weatherproofing and safety on a potentially misty descent.

DOWNHILL TOURS. Several different tour operators advertise downhill tours of Haleakala, charging $100 or more for a van trip up, breakfast, and a descent by bike. Those persevering through the ascent, on the other hand, will pay with sweat but will come away with a far more rewarding experience. Some downhillers shout encouraging cheers to cyclists heading up, while others can only produce enlightening comments like "It's easier this way." Ignore those and the people

One of Haleakala's unique features: a silversword

who shout "You're going the wrong way"—little do they know which way is right. In any case, you will be everyone's hero on your long gritty trek up, amassing a fan club of dozens by the time you reach the summit.

Kahului to Crater Road: 20 miles

Ideally, begin the Haleakala ride by connecting in from Tour No. 6 via **Kula** at the 3,000-foot level. Those beginning in central **Kahului** must tackle the full 41-mi, 10,000-foot climb at once. If you choose the latter route, simply follow the **Haleakala Highway** (Road 37) up—and up and up! The easiest way to reach that road from downtown is to pedal **Road 396** past the **airport** until it intersects with the **Hana Highway** (Road 36) just **east** of Kahului. From that point, begin climbing steadily toward the island's central point on **Road 37**.

Haleakala Highway is the main thoroughfare for most Upcountry-bound traffic, but wide shoulders grant cyclists plenty of breathing room. The road climbs steadily past **Pukalani**, then splits into two arms, with Haleakala Highway bearing off to the **left** (now **Road 377**). Within 6 mi, you will reach the base of the main climb itself on **Road 378, Crater Road**.

Crater Road to Summit: 21 miles

Calculate 5 to 6 hours for the **21-mi ascent** from the base of Crater Road at 3,000 feet. I was passed by three lean Swiss racer-types who summitted in closer to 4 hours, each giving me an encouraging cry of *"Hopp Schweiz!"* as he went by. No matter what your pace, be sure to bring high-energy snacks and drinks for the challenging ascent.

You will pass a number of **protea farms** and small roadside stands that sell the large flowers as you immediately begin tackling a **series of switchbacks**. Until the park entrance near Hosmer Grove, the road has good **shoulders** and signs that warn motorists of bicycles. The second part of the ride to the summit has **no shoulder**, but traffic is extremely scattered by that point, with far less circulation by afternoon.

Road 378 begins at the 0-mi mark and 3,000 feet, reaching 5,000 feet and a steeper section at the 5-mi mark. Once past the 7-mi mark, the road begins a long **northeast** jog with a slope gradual enough to allow a short breather. Finally, 10 mi up, you will reach the official **park entrance** and pay to enter. Rangers at the booth show respect but no mercy for visitors hardy enough to pedal up, so expect to pay up. Get your money's worth by picking up trail information and a Hosmer Grove trail guide there.

The **turnoff** to **Hosmer Grove** is marked shortly past the fee station, with the **campsite** located just 0.25 mi down a **side road** at 6,800-foot elevation. Hooray for you! There, you can take a long break to set camp and eat lunch before tackling the second half of the ride. Even if the first half has you beat, take heart: the less steep top portion will feel like a breeze with an unloaded bicycle, although you must remain patient for another two hours of pedaling.

Not long after you set off again, take a short break at **Park Headquarters** (at 7,000 feet, 13-mi mark). Look through informative displays there and ask all your questions about hiking, ecology, and so on. Then, on the quiet ride up, listen for nene, not just your labored breathing and slowly rotating chain. The nene is Hawaii's state bird, an endangered relative of the Canada goose. Together with the unique silversword plant and other species, the nene represents Hawaii's threatened native flora and fauna that remain in only a few protected areas throughout the islands.

The 15-mi mark comes at an elevation of **8,000 feet.** As you climb higher above the clouds, there is a removed feeling of leaving earth, an atmosphere enhanced by the bizarre lava-strewn landscape and sea of white below. Haleakala provides a photo opportunity like no other, where you can snap a "bicycle on top of the world" picture as proof of your achievement.

Once past the 18-mi mark, keep **right** for the summit **or bear left** to Lelewii Overlook for a crater view and a break. The last 2 mi of the road are more exposed to wicked winds, but nothing can stop you now. You will reach the **Visitor's Center** on the crater rim at the 20-mi mark. First, however, keep **right** and grit your teeth for a last 1 mi to Haleakala's very **summit** to top 10,000 feet. You will be dog tired but proud as can be to reach the official summit marker, another good place to take a jubilant photo for the brag album.

In addition to a huge sense of accomplishment, cyclists will be rewarded with incredible views from what will seem like the most beautiful place on earth. Haleakala's red-hued crater spreads like a huge bowl below, marked by cinder cones and streaks of gray ash. The southern horizon is guarded by the majestic volcanic peaks of Mauna Kea and Mauna Loa on the Big Island of Hawaii. The names help identify each peak: Mauna Kea means "white mountain," the bumpier, often snow-capped point on the left, while Mauna Loa means "long mountain," the massive, smoother slope on the right. White domes of nearby Science City observatories (closed to the public) round out the impressive scene.

After relishing your hard-earned time at the summit, you can **descend** to the Visitor's Center to look through displays and get a closer view from the very edge of the crater. From this point, you can also gather inspiration for a hike into the crater the next day and watch the sun slowly stretch shadows across the land, obedient to Maui's wishes that daylight not rush away too soon.

The Reward: Cruising Down Haleakala

Pat yourself on the back, zip up your jacket, and get set for the glorious descent back to Hosmer Grove, but **be careful!** After a tiring day, it is more difficult to focus and reflexes are slower to act, so take it easy and enjoy a safe, steady glide.

When descending from Hosmer Grove with all your gear, **take special care** as well. Drivers may not be attentive, so **keep your speed down** and watch those **tight turns**. You may descend through a

foggy level of limited visibility, another point of concern. Finally, watch out for **cattle grids** on the road after leaving the national park. Above all, keep your attention on the road and remain in full control at all times, and you will enjoy a safe, fun descent from the mountain.

Sunrise at Haleakala

Ideally, make your experience of Haleakala complete by waking early to watch the sun rise after a night in Hosmer Grove. There are almost always other campers there who drive up to catch the spectacle and would be happy to give you a lift.

Check at headquarters the day before for the exact time of the sunrise. The best colors begin to light the horizon about 40 minutes before the actual sunrise. Sunrise atop Haleakala is all it is cracked up to be, from the vast nighttime panorama to the melting colors of the approaching sun.

It is a shame that so many come so far to see the sun rise, only to speed away again at daybreak. Haleakala offers far more than a rewarding ascent and pretty viewpoint. Colors in the sky that fade away with daylight remain within the multihued crater throughout the day, one of the most accessible and spectacular hiking destinations in Hawaii.

Of course, any mere mortal (and even a bicycling demi-god) will certainly be tired after the ascent and a strenuous hike, but you only live once. Hikes of various lengths and degrees of difficulty are described in free brochures, and rangers are happy to help visitors choose a suitable route. The most comprehensive, 1-day hike in Haleakala follows Sliding Sands Trail into the crater and climbs back out via Halemauu Trail, with a chance to get close-up views of cinder cones and silversword plants along the way.

TOUR NO. 8

WEST MAUI
Wailuku, Lahaina, and Beyond

Distance: 63 miles
Riding time: 2 days
Difficulty: Challenging
Terrain: Easy valley cycling, challenging coastal rolls
Roads: Paved throughout
Connecting tour: Tour No. 6

While Haleakala makes up the mass of Maui, an older formation, the West Maui Mountains, provides a rugged counterpoint to the main volcano's smooth slopes. This short ride touches on a little of everything Maui is known for, both popular attractions and little-known hideaways. From the island's commercial center in Kahului, the tour cruises down Maui's central valley to Maalaea Bay, home port to the island's whale-watching fleet. From there, the route curves north, overlooking neighbor islands like Kahoolawe and Lanai as it traces the coast of West Maui to Lahaina.

Lahaina simply exudes character and is one of the most popular tourist destinations on Maui. The whaling port and early missionary outpost first served as Kamehameha the Great's capital. Where royalty and rowdy sailors once walked, Lahaina's streets are now touristy but quaint, cluttered with shops, traditional hanging signs, and a palatable feeling of history despite the modern scene. From there, the route continues circling West Maui, with views extending to Molokai on the horizon. Few visitors venture out around the entire range because the narrow, winding road is not open to through traffic. However, its smooth surface is just fine for road bikes, leading the way around the beautiful, barely populated north shore. This is an exciting ride of constant interest as one of few tours during which you will enjoy close views of other islands. Local bikers even circle West Maui as a long day trip, another fun but rushed possibility.

Wailuku to Lahaina: 24 miles

For accommodations and sightseeing information on Kahului/Wailuku, see the Maui introduction. This ride originates from Wailuku, Kahului's neighboring town, to follow a quieter road south across Maui's central valley. Set off by pedaling **Road 30 south** (Honoapiilani Highway), which begins beside the state building at the corner of Main and High streets in Wailuku. Even cyclists starting from Kahului or the airport should follow this road rather than more

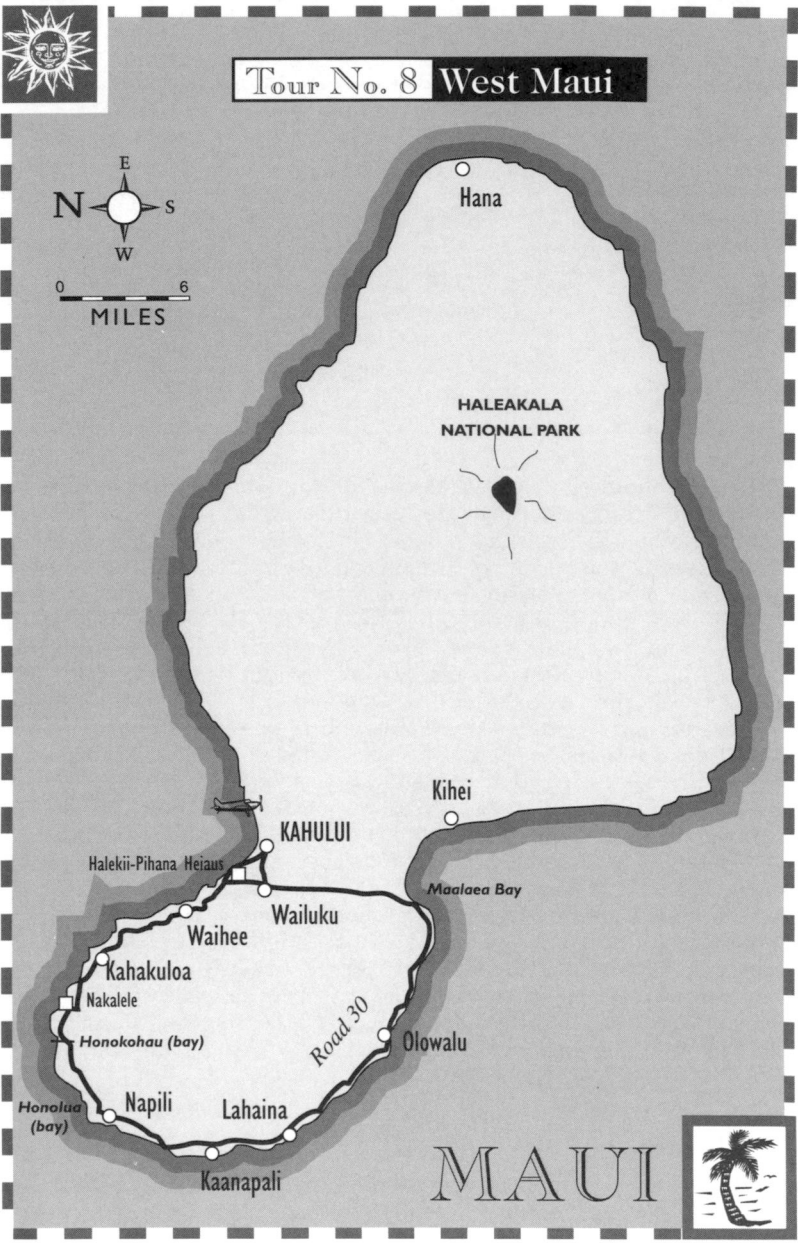

Tour No. 8 West Maui

direct Road 380, a thoroughfare plagued by heavy cross-valley traffic. Quiet Road 30 handles only light traffic, with at least a narrow shoulder throughout.

Prevailing winds should zip you along this southward leg at an effortless clip, reaching **Maalaea Bay** in no time. The bay harbors most of Maui's charter boats that offer daily whale watching, snorkeling, and diving trips. Many stop at little Molokini for snorkeling and diving at this perfectly crescent-shaped islet that lies between Maui and Kahoolawe. Passing Maalaea, continue along Road 30 all the way to Lahaina, a potentially gusty coastal ride. Traffic will increase once 380 and other roads merge, but a good wide shoulder runs consistently alongside.

Superb views make the short ride speed by even more quickly, with scarred Kahoolawe and then little Lanai coming into view as you round the coastal bend toward Lahaina. Take advantage of the scenic lookout point beyond Maalaea for excellent photo opportunities of Haleakala and the neighbor islands.

Then, 3 mi beyond Maalaea harbor, you will reach a **short tunnel**. Wait for a lull in traffic to dash through or walk along the narrow tunnel shoulder. When seas are calm, the area between the tunnel and Olowalu is an outstanding whale-watching spot as relatively shallow waters favor safe calving. In winter, dozens of cars pull over to watch unforgettable displays of whales breeching.

Campers can pull over at **Camp Pecusa**, located before the 15-mi mark and Olowalu General Store. Watch carefully for a small mailbox bearing the camp's name by a tsunami siren (an orange siren atop a tall post), 4 mi past the tunnel. The campground is no charmer, but it provides safe, cheap lodgings 6 mi from Lahaina (telephone 661-4304).

Only 0.5 mi farther, you will reach **Olowalu** and face a dilemma— to trespass or not to trespass? A small but interesting collection of **petroglyphs** lines a cliff face 0.5 mi behind the store, a tempting detour. Rock-art hunters can find the site by turning **right** (inland) immediately past the store, then taking the first **left**, and then the first **right** at a white water tower. Ride toward a small lump of a hill on the right side of the road and look for remains of a **metal railing** on the cliff face. Petroglyphs dot that rock wall, including human figures and abstract patterns. Having said that, trespassing is by no means encouraged.

Several appealing white beaches stretch between Olowalu and Lahaina, including Launiupoko and Puamana beach parks. Cyclists passing early in the day might be tempted to stop there, but curiosity to see Lahaina may drag you onward. Of the several exits from Road 30 into the historic town, take **Shaw Street** to emerge on the waterfront just south of the town center.

Lahaina first played an important role as capital of the newly unified islands under King Kamehameha. Later, the town boomed as a center for the lucrative whaling industry, a period most evident in the town's style and atmosphere. Raised sidewalks, painted wooden shop signs, and a square-rigged ship in the harbor all remind visitors of the town's past. Of course, frozen yogurt parlors and tourist boutiques also dot the town and tourists crowd the streets, but Lahaina's charm is undeniable.

Boats in Lahaina's small harbor offer cruises, excursions, and ferry service to Lanai and Molokai. Ideally, visit either or both of those small, sparsely developed islands using this service. For example, you can aim for an early arrival in Lahaina, look around town all afternoon, and catch an early evening ferry to one of the neighbor islands.

Cyclists planning to stay over in town and soak in the nighttime flavor can choose from several hotels and B&Bs in town (most fairly pricey). Ask for directions to a nearby supermarket or take your pick from among Lahaina's many quaint restaurants.

Lahaina is small but densely packed with both historic sights and sunburned tourists. Stroll through the huge main square in town—the one that hides under the shade of the world's largest banyan tree. Of the fort that once stood on this square, only a few coral blocks remain (see the two seaward corners). A dog wearing a lei and sunglasses guards the entrance booth for the *Carthaginian* (admission fee), a replica square-rigged ship. The shady green square beside the ship makes a nice spot to picnic or soak in the scene, although you make easy prey for eager-to-talk hippies who seem to see any biker as a spiritual sibling. In that square, you can also see the remaining foundation of Kamehameha's Brick Palace, the first Western-style building in Hawaii.

From that area, head north to window-shop more stores, or turn sharply inland to wander quiet side streets where sloping roofs and

The Carthaginian *recalls Lahaina's whaling days.*

rambling lanais give a better sense of Lahaina in sleepier days between whaling calls. A small stone building served as a reading room where sea captains spent shore time. Their crews, on the other hand, devoted their shore leave to other pursuits, creating a trying situation for the town missionaries. The main street behind the Pioneer Inn is lined by a long, lava wall neatly delineating Lahaina's original missionary house. Today the building is an interesting museum, although the admission fee raises an age-old dilemma: museum admission or ice cream?

Farther north on Main Street, stop in the Crazy Shirts store (*makai* side) to see the mini whaling museum inside, complete with photos, scrimshaw, and the figurehead of the original *Carthaginian*, which sank outside Lahaina in 1972. Across the street, take note of the Wo Hing Temple, a reminder of one of Hawaii's most prominent immigrant groups (now a museum).

Lahaina to Wailuku: 39 miles

The second leg of this tour completes the circle around West Maui, a sparsely developed area of spectacular views. The sight of Molokai accompanies cyclists along much of the ride, and each bend in the narrow road brings a new cliff or jutting peninsula of West Maui into sight. Although your map may show a long unpaved stretch around the north end of Maui, be assured that the road is paved the entire way.

Begin the challenging ride by heading **north** on Road 30 from Lahaina. At 5 mi, **choose** between branching off to the **left for a coastal road** that passes hotels and narrower streets with views or **staying on the more direct main road**. On Road 30 cyclists will have the advantage of a wide safe shoulder, but views are limited to glimpses over condominium rooftops. Kaanapali is one of Maui's biggest resort areas, but the development quickly gives way to untamed slopes.

Traffic eases by the time you reach **Kaanapali** and is practically nonexistent by **Napili**, leaving you in peace for the remainder of the day. At Napili, you will reach the last large **supermarket** and the first of the day's many **hills** as well as (potentially) the first headwind. When winds are up in this exposed area, they can really howl, so try to pick a calm day for the ride. The north end of Maui sees virtually no traffic, only the occasional surfer or adventurous tourist.

By the 32-mi marker, you will begin rolling over rugged north-shore terrain in earnest. There, the road becomes extremely windy, twisting around every small curve and climbing every sudden, steep rise. Mile markers along Road 30 count up to 36, until the road becomes **Kahekili Highway (340)** and counts down 21 mi to Wailuku. In **Honolua** (*bay*), far below your roadside view, scores of surfers dodge each other as they ride the waves of this popular surf break.

To finish off your ride along Road 30, **descend** into **Honokohau** (*bay*), reaching the 36-mi marker. From there, cyclists confront two incredibly steep **uphills** in succession, a test of your will (or your aversion to pushing a loaded bicycle). The hills can be surmounted without dismounting, although you may crawl along at a painful 3 miles per

A cyclist's only companions on the remote West Maui ride

hour to do so. Continuing past ranch and scrublands, pounding sea to your left and lush mountains to the right, you will reach a **sharp curve** with spectacular views of two bays and the twisting road ahead (0.75 mi past the 21-mi marker). After passing Nakalele light station, keep an eye *makai* for a **blowhole** that sprays with every powerful wave.

Thrilling **descents and more climbs** draw Kahakuloa Head steadily nearer, its vertical mass acting like a beacon. As more of the headland comes into view, you will reach a short downhill section of **poor pavement** for 100 yards, then pedal uphill on good pavement. On the right at the top of that hill is the **Bellstone** (before the 16-mi mark). Supposedly the stone emits a bell-like ring, but it's hard to get more than a weak clunk out of it, and you only bruise your knuckles in the process. Still another **long climb** to the 9-mi mark rewards your efforts with views of a high waterfall cascading down the opposite side of the gulch. Keep an eye out for carved *kii* (statues) behind a gate to the right before crossing the valley. Then pass over the **waterfall** at the 9-mi mark and begin a well-earned **descent** to Kahakuloa.

Near Kahakuloa, signs say ONE LANE ROAD—and they mean it. The newly paved road narrows to one car's width for several miles, so watch those tight turns. **Kahakuloa** is as far away from it all as a Maui village can be, a scattering of houses through a deeply cut valley, all dominated by the obelisk-like bulk of Kahakuloa Head. Cyclists who have already spent time touring the islands should feel fulfilled upon reaching this point, since they were able to see it from so many distant points, including the Hana Highway and distant Molokai. The road winds past a picture-perfect missionary church with Kahakuloa Head and rushing ocean waters as its backdrop.

From Kahakuloa, it is a long 2 mi **uphill** on the same narrow lane. The minute you climb away from Kahakuloa Bay, you will be rewarded with panoramic views of Haleakala's north slopes and the Paia area, a view that widens steadily as you approach Wailuku. After the initial climb, you will cruise **down** into a few sharply cut valleys only to slog out of them again, the landscape gradually **leveling** as you near Maui's central valley.

Distract yourself along the last challenging section by keeping an eye seeward to spot a rock arch (after the 6-mi mark). Finally, you will ease downhill to **Waihee** and the outskirts of **Wailuku**. Those heading to Wailuku should keep **right** on Road 330 to pedal another 2 mi to Main Street. Cyclists heading to **Kahului** can avoid an unnecessary climb by turning **left** on Road 340 instead, keeping along the curve of the bay for a final 2 mi. For those with a bit of energy to spare, this is a perfect time to work in a short **detour** to Halekii and Pihana *heiaus*.

Back in Wailuku or Kahului, you can recuperate from the ride and prepare for your next venture, be it another Maui tour or a flight to the next point on your itinerary. Before moving on, however, be sure to look back for the distinctive shape of Kahakuloa Head, satisfied with your ride around West Maui's unspoiled shores.

ADDITIONAL SUGGESTED RIDES

Iao Valley

Iao Needle, an obelisk-like shaft that reaches 2,250 feet in the center of a lush valley, is one of Maui's most recognizable landmarks. The Needle is only 4 mi from Wailuku, an uphill ride that makes a good half-day excursion.

To begin the ride from Kahului, pedal up Road 32 (signed for Lahaina) to Wailuku. At the top of Main Street, most traffic turns south on Road 30; instead, continue straight up (and up) on Road 320 for Iao Valley. Almost every ride on Maui, it seems, provides good uphill training for the Haleakala ascent.

Although many tourists come to Iao, few leave the parking lot and fewer still venture off the single trail to the overlook. Ideally, make the most of the beautiful scene by finding your own private pool in the gurgling, clear waters of Iao Stream.

Halekii and Pihana *Heiaus*

Halekii and Pihana *heiaus* comprise a small state monument site near Kahului and Wailuku, another good side trip to fit in with tours or to fill extra time before or after a flight. These *heiaus* represent the religious center of Maui's central valley where early island chiefs resided. A short-and-sweet interpretive display marks the well-preserved temples, making this one of the few temple complexes in Hawaii that is both readily accessible and easily appreciated. In addition to historic buildings, the park offers wide views of the island's central valley and slopes of Haleakala, as well as West Maui's misty slopes.

The state monument lies 3 mi northwest of Kahului near Waiehu. From the intersection of Roads 330 and 340 near Waiehu, follow 340 for 0.75 mi. Then turn inland at Kuhio Place and take the first left (on Hea Place) to pedal up a short hill to the historic site. Information boards address both the geology and human history of Maui, and the ruins remain quite clear (although Pompeii it is not). Halekii and Pihana *heiaus* do not require much time to tour quickly, and therefore make a good brief detour from the West Maui tour (No. 8).

Makawao

Makawao (pronounced mack-a-wow) is one of Maui's most typical Upcountry towns that exudes the area's *paniolo* (Hawaiian cowboy) flavor. The area makes an ideal getaway from lower Maui's tourist scene, with many local B&Bs offering cozy accommodations for those with time to spare. As a sleepy two-road town, Makawao is a place for visitors who wish to explore Maui's less traveled dead-end roads, not those who seek the resort or nightlife scene.

To reach Makawao, pedal up Baldwin Avenue from Paia on the coast, an ascent of 1,600 feet. Although the town is also accessible via Haleakala Highway (Road 37) more directly from Kahului, Baldwin

Iao Needle, Maui's distinctive landmark

Avenue offers a more scenic and quiet ride. On the way up, you will pass Rainbow Park of Jimi Hendrix Rainbow Bridge fame. Although the county park officially permits camping, Makawao B&Bs make the best accommodations in this area.

Makawao town is a small, old-fashioned place with an eclectic mix of old Maui families (missionary descendants like the Baldwins), traditional *paniolo* elements, and recent arrivals who sport dreadlocks and tie-dye shirts. The town maintains a good sense of humor about it all: for example, a banner on the local Mexican restaurant calls "Come in and eat—or we'll both starve!" Pickups line up outside Makawao Hardware Store to buy horse feed and supplies; inside, fluffy little chicks for sale are marked with blue or pink "male" and "female" stickers.

An annual summertime rodeo is held at Makawao's arena (home of the local roping club). All in all, Makawao makes a terrific side destination to partake of Maui's Upcountry flavor.

Kihei/Wailea

Finally, the only area of note on Maui not yet described is Haleakala's sunny southwest side, near Kihei and Wailea. Cyclists heading from Wailuku toward Maalaea on the way to Lahaina can easily detour to this popular coastal strip. Road 350 south and then Kihei Road lead cyclists south past white beaches and promising tidal pools, taking in views of West Maui, Molokini, Kahoolawe, and Lanai all the way. The last part of the ride crosses Maui's most recent lava flow to reach La Perouse Bay, an undeveloped and starkly beautiful corner of Maui, perfect for further exploration on foot or by mountain bike.

MOLOKAI
The Friendly Isle

Molokai is compact in every sense. Only 40 mi in length, it is possible to watch the sun rise from the east end of the island and pedal across in time to watch the sun set on the opposite shore. Molokai also remains in a past long gone on highly developed islands like Oahu and Maui. Not a single stoplight marks the island, and building codes prohibit any structure taller than a palm tree. Mega-resort development plans for the west end of Molokai have been successfully thwarted by concerned islanders, while bicycling, on the other hand, is neither discouraged nor strictly limited.

People stop to chat on Molokai, truly the Friendly Isle. Its 6,700 inhabitants make it the most Hawaiian of the principal islands, with the highest percentage of native ancestry. Remains of the original native culture, such as fishponds, line the island's southeast shores, while *heiaus* still stand atop quiet hills. Traditional missionary churches, macadamia nut farms, and dramatic views such as that over Kalaupapa Peninsula keep cyclists busy traversing Molokai in search of the next scenic highlight.

However, Molokai does not offer something for everyone. This island attracts cyclists who enjoy long, uninterrupted views and who do not depend on stopping for cool drinks at roadside stands. Molokai's peace and quiet make it ideal for those who find entertainment in waves and passing clouds, not bars or town streets.

Practical Information

Molokai lies in view of Oahu, Lanai, and Maui and is officially part of Maui County. Kalaupapa Peninsula is separately governed as Kalawao County. The island receives very few tourists and would like to keep it that way. There are few accommodations options and traveler services on the island, in fact few services of any type. That is not to say that you will feel unwelcome there; especially as a cyclist, you will find that residents take a special interest in you. Visitors to Molokai must remember to plan ahead because the island has no bicycle shops and grocery stores are few and far between.

Use the University of Hawaii Press's *Reference Maps* or a similar map for touring Molokai. Do not use a map that adds Molokai and Lanai to a map of Maui, as the two smaller islands will not be treated in equal detail. A map with only Molokai and Lanai, on the other hand, will be fine.

The friendly people at Molokai Visitor's Association will do everything they can to help visitors enjoy their stay. The associations's office is located at the corner where Roads 460 and 450 meet (hours Monday to Friday 9:00 A.M. to 5:00 P.M.). Telephone (800) 800-6367 from the United States and Canada, or write to Box 960, Kaunakakai, HI 96748.

Tips for Touring

Molokai is a very windy island, perhaps because its long sloping shape makes a good target for winds whipping over open ocean. Pity the cyclist heading north or east when tradewinds roar over Molokai. If time permits, try to organize your days around weather conditions. Take a beach day when northeasterlies pick up, and get an early start when all is calm.

While Molokai's mountains are not particularly high, the constantly rolling terrain poses a considerable challenge on some rides. The island's easiest tour covers the east side to Halawa (Tour No. 9), but a ride to the stunning Palaau Lookout requires a long climb from coastal Kaunakakai straight over the island's central ridge. Similarly, reaching the island's remote west shore also requires a long haul over hills that seem to roll higher with every mile.

The island poses some logistical challenges to cyclists as well. Although all roads emanate from a single point (Kaunakakai) in a spokelike arrangement, distances are often too long to allow comfortable day rides. Cyclists must either push marathon there-and-back rides in one day or confront accommodations problems. With either approach, bikers cannot avoid backtracking over long stretches. The best approach is to move from one extreme of the island to another. For example, base first in Kaunakakai and cover the Halawa Valley tour in a day trip. Then pack up and pedal to the west end and stay there overnight before eventually returning to the island's central airport or the ferry dock.

Airport

Molokai has one small airport located on the island's central plateau (Hoolehua Airport), with little more than a large waiting area, car-rental desks, and a parking lot. The island is serviced by Hawaiian Airlines, Aloha Island Air, and Air Molokai. Cyclists heading to Kaunakakai and points east should turn right out of the airport parking lot, then right again to reach Road 460 (Maunaloa Highway), signed to town. If you are heading directly to the island's west end, turn left and left again to reach 460 West. Other than a pricey convenience store at the Papohaku resort area, there is one grocery store in Mauna Loa and another north of the airport in Hoolehua.

A small airfield on Kalaupapa Peninsula is serviced by Aloha Island Air and Air Molokai. Visitors are permitted on the peninsula by permit only; for more information see Along the Way.

Ferry

Like Lanai, Molokai is very easily combined with tours on Maui, thanks to a ferry service that connects the islands. Ferries are an appealing alternative to air travel as there are no bicycle shops on Molokai. Bicycles are less likely to be damaged on a ferry, whereas they are routinely smushed on interisland flights.

The *Maui Princess* ferry service offers two departures each way daily between Lahaina on Maui and Kaunakakai on Molokai. The ferry departs Lahaina at 7:00 A.M. and 5:00 P.M. and Kaunakakai at 5:45 A.M. and 3:55 P.M. (telephone 800-833-5800, on Maui 661-8397, on Molokai 553-5736). Bicycles travel free and may remain loaded. However, you should at least remove items such as frame-fit pumps that might easily fall off. Although travel time is officially 75 minutes, count on at least 90 minutes due to baggage transfer. Apparently the draft of the *Maui Princess* is too deep for Lahaina harbor, and therefore a smaller ferry shuttles passengers and baggage to deeper waters, where everything is transferred to the larger ship. You may find it difficult to watch as your bike is handed out over open water, however (perhaps it is a good idea to unload your panniers, after all).

Don't grimace if a group of schoolchildren boards the ferry—they may provide a nice surprise. Soon ukuleles and guitars may emerge and the whole company will be singing along as the ferry bounces over rough channel waters. Locals are amazed if you plan to spend even a week on the island, offering a clue as to Molokai's tourism level.

Accommodations

Molokai, a small island with a small population and few visitors, offers limited accommodations. The few campsites, hotels, and B&Bs tend to cluster in a few compact areas. However, all parts of the island can be reached from some type of lodgings at least in a day trip. Due to the irregular distribution of accommodations, it may be best to cover a few tours as day trips from one home base before moving on.

ROOMS. Indoor accommodations concentrate around Kaunakakai or Papohaku on the west end. Kaunakakai has a handful of hotels, but the town offers little besides a conveniently central location. Visitors who arrive by ferry can cover the Halawa Valley (Tour No. 9) or Palaau Lookout (Tour No. 10) rides as day trips from a base in Kaunakakai. A few hotels string out for a few miles east of Kaunakakai, as do the island's few B&Bs. The central part of Molokai has no lodgings at all. Molokai's only other rooms are at the Papohaku condominium/resort area. Prices are high, but the west-end location is beautiful.

The few B&Bs on Molokai are all scattered eastward from Kaunakakai. Most Molokai B&Bs seem to hold fast to the 3-day minimum, although they may make an exception for needy cyclists. On the other hand, 3 days is a practical stay for those using a home-base approach or simply relaxing.

CAMPING. Despite the fact that Molokai is part of Maui County, camping permits for Molokai sites are issued only on Molokai (perhaps another bureaucratic tangle designed to discourage campers). To camp in one of Molokai's two county sites (One Alii or Papohaku beach parks), you must acquire a permit and pay a small fee. Contact the County Department of Parks and Recreation, Box 1055, Kaunakakai, HI 96748 (telephone 553-3204 or 553-5141). The office is located in the Mitchell Pauole Center on Kaunakakai's east edge (ride to the end of Ala Malama Street; open weekdays 8:00 A.M. to 4:00 P.M.).

The two state parks that allow camping (free with a permit) are

Palaau and Waikolu lookouts. Send for permits or wait for a ranger to find you at these sites. For Palaau State Park, contact the Division of Parks, P.O. Box 153, Kaunakakai, HI 96748 (telephone 567-6083). Waikolu's campsite falls under the direction of the Division of Forestry

Molokai's "highways" present few hazards.

and Wildlife (on Maui), Box 1015, Wailuku, HI 96793 (telephone 244-4352). Rather than chasing around rangers on Molokai, it may be easiest to pick up a permit at a state office on Maui or another island.

Most of Molokai is undeveloped, and locals seem to have no objections to discreet free campers at sites like Halawa or Moomomi beaches. However, water supply is a problem in these remote areas.

Kaunakakai

Kaunakakai is Molokai's main (and practically only) town, the gateway for visitors who arrive by ferry. With a bit of imagination, one can see a touch of the Old West in this one-road town with its false-front buildings—just transform the pickup trucks into horses. The town has every practical necessity and little else: a gas station, two supermarkets, one bakery, a natural-foods store, and a library. Kaunakakai has little to offer visitors aside from a convenient point from which to base their explorations of Molokai.

Surprisingly, supermarket prices are roughly equivalent to those on larger islands. However, prices are higher at all other points on Molokai. The two main supermarkets are open from 9:30 A.M. to 8:00 P.M. daily, Sundays until 2:00 P.M. In addition, fresh supplies are available at the Saturday farmer's market in town.

The few visitors who come to Molokai usually head to Papohaku condos. Kaunakakai has a few hotels and nearby B&Bs for indoor accommodations. The nearest park that permits camping is One Alii Beach County Park, 3 mi east of town off the "Kam" Highway (a highway only on the Molokai scale). It is a nice, grassy site directly on the water, although disadvantages include high winds and the legitimate hazard of falling coconuts. The park has water, indoor showers, and picnic tables.

Along the Way

KALAUPAPA. Kalaupapa Peninsula is both a sad and splendid place, an isolated spit of land that served as a leper colony since 1865. The most famous figure of Kalaupapa is Father Damien, a Belgian priest who worked in the colony, eventually falling victim to the disease himself. By the 1940s, leprosy (officially known as Hansen's disease) could be medically controlled, although the colony remained in isolation for another two decades.

Today the peninsula is still inhabited by former patients who have been granted the right to remain in their village. Visitation remains strictly controlled to protect their privacy, as the area is now designated a National Historic Park. Those interested in visiting the peninsula must join a guided tour by making arrangements with the tour guide, Richard Mark of Damien Tours. Inquiries regarding his walking and van tour of Kalaupapa should be addressed to P.O. Box 1, Kalaupapa, HI 96742 (telephone 567-6171).

TOUR NO. 9

HALAWA VALLEY RIDE
Kaunakakai to Halawa

Distance: 30 miles
Estimated time: 1 to 2 days
Difficulty: Moderate
Terrain: Flat coastal road, except hilly final miles to Halawa
Roads: Paved and untrafficked
Connecting tours: All Molokai rides

The Halawa Valley tour is simply the best ride on Molokai. All along the route, the high ridges of interior Molokai rise in rich greens, while the blues of Pailolo Channel and the open ocean color the opposing view. This is also the only level ride on Molokai, an easy breeze back and forth along the coast that passes ancient fishponds, traditional missionary churches, and offshore islets. The highlight of the ride is Molokai's Halawa Valley, a tight, deep cleft in the island's east shore, its lush scenery crowned by a picture-perfect Hawaiian waterfall. Cyclists can undertake the ride as a long day trip or a 2-day event, with the opportunity to hike right up to the falls in Halawa.

LOGISTICS. The ride from Kaunakakai to Halawa Valley is 30 mi each way, or a 60-mi round trip. For a day trip, that distance is long, but 21 mi of easy terrain and a brisk tailwind on the return make the ride more manageable than it may initially seem, especially on an unloaded bicycle. On the other hand, some may be tempted to forego the worthwhile hike to Moaula Falls when faced with a long return trip on the same day.

In all cases, shop in Kaunakakai, because only a small general store (at Wavecrest Resort, 13-mi mark) and a few fruit stands dot the road to Halawa. Halawa itself is a small settlement with no shops of any kind.

ACCOMMODATIONS. Although Kaunakakai accommodations force you to undertake this tour as a long day trip, they provide the most practical lodgings. The trip might be shortened by staying in one of the easternmost B&Bs along this coast (such as Pukoo). Most B&Bs require a 3-night minimum stay, but some will fill vacancies with shorter-term guests.

To make the tour into an overnight venture, campers may consider remaining at Halawa. Unofficially, locals report that camping is common and tolerated on the beach at Halawa, land owned by Puu O Hoku Ranch. The only public facilities in the area, however, are picnic tables, toilets, and untreated tap water at Halawa Beach County Park (a grassy lot above the beach).

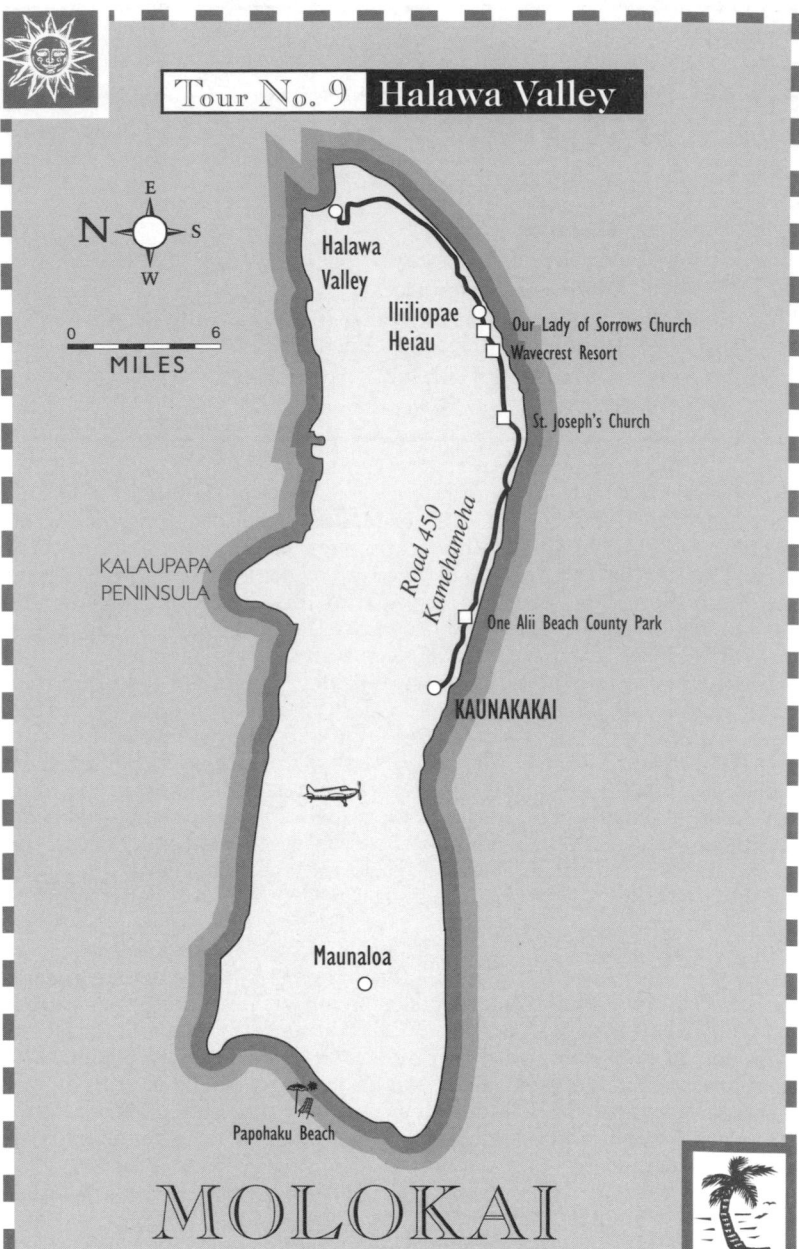

Tour No. 9 | Halawa Valley

N E S W

0 — 6
MILES

Halawa
Valley

Iliiliopae
Heiau

Our Lady of Sorrows Church

Wavecrest Resort

St. Joseph's Church

Road 450 Kamehameha

KALAUPAPA
PENINSULA

One Alii Beach County Park

KAUNAKAKAI

Maunaloa

Papohaku Beach

MOLOKAI

Kaunakakai to Halawa: 30 miles each way

Kamehameha Highway (450), the road running **east** from Kaunakakai to Halawa, is a quiet two-lane byway, contrary to its impressive name. Not only is "Kam Highway" perfectly paved, it also runs dead flat along the coastline until the 21-mi mark. After that, cyclists must tackle a few miles of rolling terrain before finally descending into Halawa Valley. Wind poses the greatest potential obstacle during this ride, with a good possibility of a headwind on the outbound leg, then an easy cruise home on the return. At times, ocean breezes rush through Pailolo Channel between Molokai and Maui with incredible ferocity, hitting this exposed coastline directly. With luck, a hearty wind will clip you home at speeds over 20 miles per hour.

Molokai's shores become rockier and windier as you progress eastward, with Maui joining Lanai on the horizon and finally craggy little Moku Hooniki comes into view. This turtle-shaped island was once used for bombing practice, another example of how Hawaii's unique lands have been (and some continue to be) thoughtlessly abused.

A number of interesting sights pleasantly delay eastward progress from the outset, each demanding only a few minutes interruption (just as easily stretched into, say, a chocolate break). You will pass **One Alii Park** and then **Kawela Place of Refuge** and **Pakuhiwa Battlesite** early on, but the latter is difficult or impossible to see. Kawela Beach County Park is easy enough to find, but its *puuhonua* (place of refuge) perches far out of reasonable reach (just imagine the plight of refuge seekers attempting to enter).

The first viewable point of interest is crisp, white **St. Joseph's Church** with its tall, thin tower (at the 11-mi mark). The building is one of four churches built by Father Damien outside Kalaupapa, of which only two remain (St. Joseph's and Our Lady of Sorrows). By the time you leave Molokai, you may be tired of hearing the story of Father Damien, but then again his work deserves the acclaim. Just skim through the visitor's book of the church to see how vivid his legacy remains.

Just 0.25 mi beyond the church, look right for an overgrown **sign** that marks the site of the 1927 Smith-Bronte landing. The men earned their place in aviation history by completing the first mainland-to-Hawaii flight, although they fell short of their original target, Oahu. **Wavecrest Resort** at mile marker 13 operates a small general store beside the road, your last chance to purchase food or snacks. A short distance down the road on the left stands a true blast from the past—an old-fashioned general store (closed), complete with antique gas pump and rusty Coca-Cola sign that still swings in the breeze.

Next comes **Our Lady of Sorrows Church,** originally another of Father Damien's works. The structure you see is a reconstruction of the first church, which caught fire in the 1960s. Apparently everyone pitched into reconstruction efforts; even doggie footprints mark the cement step on the east side of the church. Before setting off again, take a moment to examine the coastline opposite the church for clearly visible remains of an ancient **fishpond.** Native islanders constructed walled inlets into which fish could swim but not swim out of, keeping a fattened stock readily on hand. Although invasive mangrove wreaks havoc on these structures, many fishponds can still be seen along Hawaii's shores, appearing as light lines arching along the coastline.

After the 15-mi mark, a **wagon crossing sign** reminds cyclists how rural this "highway" remains—even playing children and dogs outnumber cars along this road. About 0.5 mi past the 15-mi mark, Kam Highway crosses a small **bridge**. The first dirt road on the **left** after that leads via private property to **Iliiliopae Heiau,** Molokai's largest. If the road is corded off and signed against trespassers, look for the owner's phone number printed on the cord; those interested can ask a local resident or call from along the road for permission to visit on the return trip from Halawa. The impressive platform structure dates back to the fifteenth century and is located less than 0.5 mi from the road.

After that point, few other specific sights mark the ride, freeing cyclists to progress more quickly and enjoy the superlative scenery. Beyond the road's 21-mi mark, cyclists encounter more challenging conditions. Put your muscles to work over 1 mi of **gradual uphill**, 2 mi of **serious climbing**, 1 mi of **ups and downs**, and finally a steep 2-mi **downhill** swoop into Halawa Valley. Since bicycles that go down must come up, this means a 2-mi uphill grind on the return trip over the dead-end road, but that's for later.

From the curving road that descends into the valley, cyclists command tremendous views of **Moaula Falls** (250 feet), the lush green valley, and the twisted cove carved into the coast. Once down in the valley itself, you will see small houses and a tiny green church that make up **Halawa**. The road **dead ends** at the beach, passing the sheltered picnic area of Halawa Beach County Park first. Littered with gnarled branches of driftwood, the windswept beach makes an inspiring setting for a well-deserved picnic lunch.

Those not too tired by the ride can set out for Moaula Falls **on foot**. Calculate about 1 hour to reach the wide, cold pool at the base of the falls. The **trail** begins as a dirt road that runs west in front of the little green community church and narrows soon after. Watch carefully for orange markers or white piping that follows along the correct track.

Despite the initial climb out of Halawa Valley, the return trip is a breeze—literally. A stiff afternoon wind should help you backtrack over familiar ground in satisfying time. On the way back to their lodgings, cyclists can pull over at one of the sights missed earlier in the ride, or simply plop down under a seaside palm for a short break.

PALAAU LOOKOUT AND CENTRAL MOLOKAI
Kaunakakai to Moomomi Beach

Distance: 40-mile circle
Riding time: Day ride(s)
Difficulty: Challenging
Terrain: Challenging climbs across windy Molokai
Roads: Paved and peaceful
Connecting tours: All Molokai rides

This varied ride tours several different sights around high, central Molokai. The trip can be undertaken as an independent venture or covered in sections as detours from other island rides. Climbing steadily from Kaunakakai, the ride first heads north to Palaau Lookout, pausing to visit a restored sugar mill on the way. At Palaau, visitors marvel at both the beauty of the Kalaupapa Peninsula as well as at its terrible history as a former leper colony.

From Palaau, cyclists can detour slightly west before returning to Kaunakakai to visit a working macadamia nut farm that lives up to Molokai's friendly reputation. Finally, cyclists can also swing down to the coast at Moomomi Beach for a remote, windswept panorama over Molokai's north shore. Like Tour No. 9, limited accommodations force most cyclists to plan this ride as a somewhat awkward day trip based from Kaunakakai.

Kaunakakai to Palaau: 10 miles

The first leg of this eclectic tour rides north across Molokai to reach the island's most photographed vista, the Palaau Lookout over Kalaupapa Peninsula. Begin by pedaling from **Kaunakakai** toward Mauna Loa and the **airport** on **Maunaloa Highway** (460). The shoulder is always suitably wide for bicycles although it is a bit gravelly in areas. Never mind, this is Molokai, where traffic is practically nonexistent to begin with, and it is rare to see two cars pass in opposite directions at one time.

First this road heads 2 mi **along the shore**, then bends **north** to begin a long **uphill** that extends all the way to Palaau Lookout. At a signed junction 2 mi later, bear **right** for Kualapuu. In **Kualapuu** (another 2 mi ahead), pedal **straight** on for another 2 mi to **Kalae**. This can be a difficult, sweaty uphill, particularly if Molokai's typical howling winds kick in. On the other hand, the challenging terrain is compensated for by wide views to west Molokai, the island's drier side, as well as close-up views of coffee plantations. You will also pass fields where fowl roost comfortably in little rooster chalets, arranged in neat rows. Cockfighting (a Southeast Asian import), although illegal, is popular among some circles in Hawaii.

For a break at the ride's 8-mi point, stop by Kalae's **Meyer Sugar Mill**, signed left off the road. The entrance fee to the restored mill includes a personally guided tour by one of the sweet volunteers who run the museum (mostly retired folks). The mill was built in 1878, taking advantage of a new treaty that opened trade of Hawaiian sugar with the United States. The mill only operated for a decade or so, but recent renovations ensure its future under a new role. Restoration efforts seem to be an unqualified success; now that the mill is restored, a cultural center and museum focusing on Molokai is already under construction.

The final 2 mi from the sugar mill to Palaau Lookout are mostly **uphill**. It is only a short ride from the state park entrance sign to the viewpoint. On the way, note a covered picnic area to the left and a small dirt road that leads to the state campsite. The **campground** is nicely set back from the road, but facilities are minimal (picnic tables, unpotable tap water, no showers). The narrow **trail** down to Kalaupapa begins on the **right** immediately before the sign for Palaau State Park. Visitors are not even permitted to walk part of the way down the trail without a permit or arranged tour. (See Along the Way.)

Two short, clearly marked **trails** begin from the parking area at the very top of the hill. A 1-minute walk brings you first to **Palaau Lookout**, where a series of informative tablets relate aspects of the peninsula's history. Kalaupapa was for years a place of death where lepers were isolated under terrible conditions. Not until the 1930s could Hansen's disease, as it is officially known, be effectively treated. Today some former patients remain by choice, and the area is highly restricted to visitors as part of a national historic park.

The sight is stunning, literally for the fascinating and awful history of the peninsula, and visually for its raw physical grandeur. Sheer cliffs drop vertically onto the flat peninsula, the product of a late lava flow. The juxtaposition of these immense land masses at right angles to each other forms an unforgettable sight, some of the highest *pali* (cliffs) in Hawaii.

Back at the parking area, follow the second trail marked **Phallic Rock**. The 5-minute walk leads through a cluster of boulders and finally to Phallic Rock itself. No question about it, this is indeed quite a rock; you can't miss it. It is one of many phallic formations around the islands, but certainly the most famous (and well-endowed).

From Palaau it is **10 mi back** to Kaunakakai. If the climb up had you licked, you will enjoy the cruise back down with excellent views of Lanai and Kalohi Channel. To extend your Molokai explorations, on the other hand, follow other, nearby routes to visit more sights or head directly to the island's west end.

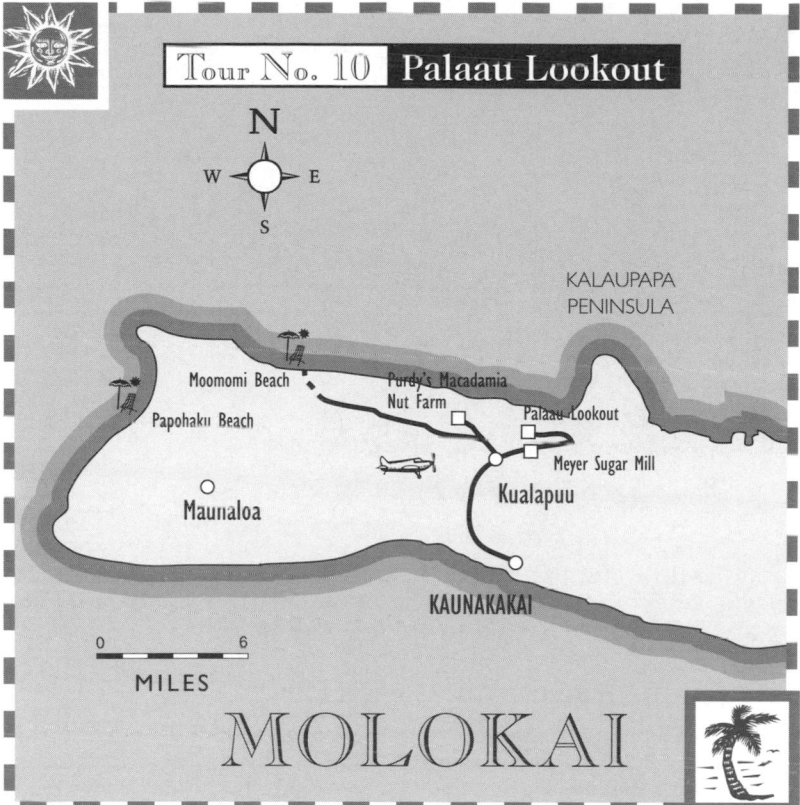

Detour to the Nut Farm: 6 miles

Before zooming straight back to town, it is worth a detour west to Purdy's Macadamia Nut Farm, 6 mi from Palaau via Kualapuu. From **Palaau**, **backtrack** until the **right** turn on **Road 480** to **Kualapuu**. For 2 mi, you will pass more coffee fields and Molokai's only high school, then turn **right** on Lihi Pali Avenue, where a small sign indicates **Purdy's Farm** in ⅙ MILE. Actually, the distance is twice that but who's counting? The farm is marked on the right side of the road (open daily until 3:00 P.M.).

Upon entering the seventy-year-old grove (free admission), visitors will be warmly greeted by Tuddie Purdy or his mother, who will obligingly demonstrate all steps in "mac" nut production, from picking to drying and shelling. All in all, the detour is worthwhile for both the nuts and the charming folks who show you a little of what the Friendly Isle is all about.

Purdy's Macadamia Nut Farm displays its harvest.

For a quick return to Kaunakakai, **backtrack** to **Kualapuu** and enjoy huge views along the 8-mi downhill run. If it is still early and you are eager for more, continue on to Moomomi Beach.

Moomomi Beach: 6 miles each way

Although a bit out of the way, this ride reaches one of the most starkly beautiful, isolated destinations on Molokai. It may be covered as an extension of the Palaau ride or separately as a half- to full-day ride. Locals sometimes camp overnight at Moomomi, a tempting prospect. On the con side, however, a lack of practical amenities such as drinking water at Moomomi argue for more comfortable lodgings elsewhere.

Farrington Highway is a long, desolate road that few cars travel, running **west** along north central Molokai. From **Purdy's Macadamia Nut Farm**, pedal 4 mi to the end of Farrington where the **dirt road** begins. The outbound ride along Farrington Highway runs **mostly downhill** past scattered homesteads, although a few long slopes lead into uphills. When pavement ends, a red **clay and dirt trail** continues straight ahead to Molokai's north coast.

If the weather has been dry, road bikes should have no problem descending this 2.5-mi-long dirt road as it is quite smooth. The road's side tracks are plenty wide and smooth for just about any bike—just beware of renegade kiawe thorns. You do not want your bicycle to share the fate of abandoned cars on the roadside.

Soon you will emerge on a rocky, windswept **coast** where the full, humbling force of nature can be felt in crashing surf and howling wind. The Moomomi area is also unique as one of the last relatively untouched dune systems in Hawaii, home to many endemic species and nesting site of green turtles.

Adventurous cyclists can continue bouncing **eastward** along a seashore track, or walk 15 to 20 minutes west to reach sandy **Kawaaloa Bay** and other beaches. However, do not be tempted to swim anywhere along the pounding, rocky coastline even if conditions seem calm, as even strong swimmers have drowned here.

Simply **retrace** your route back toward Purdy's, turning **right** for **Maunaloa Highway** at the **intersection** with Puupeelua Avenue. A direct ride back to **Kaunakakai** is 13 mi. Alternatively, cyclists may wish to ride directly to the airport or Molokai's west coast via Maunaloa Highway (Road 460).

Windswept shores of untamed Moomomi Beach

TOUR NO. 11

WEST MOLOKAI
Kaunakakai to Papohaku

Distance: 23 miles one way
Riding time: 1 day
Difficulty: Challenging
Terrain: Long rolling hills
Roads: Quiet roads, good pavement
Connecting tours: All Molokai rides

To catch sunset views from Molokai's west end, follow this challenging ride across the island's rugged central mountains. Although cyclists must work hard to reach their goal, both Maunaloa and Papohaku reward efforts generously. Maunaloa is a small, sleepy town, most interesting for its atmosphere of times long past in other parts of Hawaii. Kids fly kites and old-timers sell pop from dusty bottles in the small general store. Even visiting cyclists can slip into the tranquil scene by settling comfortably into the shade of a banyan tree and watching time go by.

From Maunaloa, the tour cruises down to Papohaku, known as Hawaii's longest white sand beach. West-end resorts are literally hideaways that blend into the landscape without interrupting scenic views. At Papohaku cyclists can comb the beach for shells, bounce over mountain-bike trails, and gaze across the ocean to Oahu. On a clear day, you can even make out Diamond Head, the chaotic modern world of Honolulu seeming like a distant place in space, time, and memory.

Kaunakakai to Maunaloa: 17 miles

Although the ride is described from Kaunakakai, arriving cyclists can shorten the distance significantly by connecting directly into the ride from the airport. In terms of accommodations, there are no lodgings between Kaunakakai and the west end, where cyclists can choose between a county park campsite and pricey hotels.

Cyclists must work constantly over undulating terrain, gaining elevation steadily to Maunaloa and the turnoff to Kaluakoi. From there it is all downhill to Papohaku Beach, meaning a big climb out followed by downhills back to the airport and Kaunakakai. The distance from Kaunakakai to Maunaloa is 17 mi; a start from the airport saves 7 mi.

Beginning from **Kaunakakai**, head up **Road 460 west** (Maunaloa Highway), climbing up to the island's central plateau. Near the airport, enjoy a bit of a breather on more level terrain before tackling the higher slopes of west Molokai. Traffic is always light or nonexistent on Molokai, and the shoulder is good all along the state "highway" to Maunaloa.

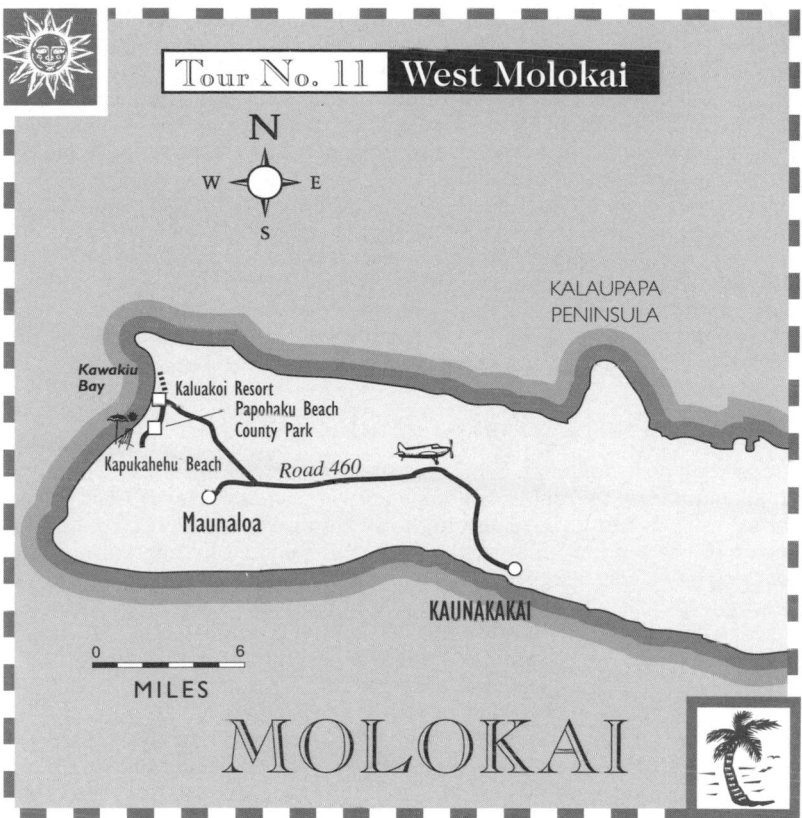

Not long after the airport, cyclists reach a 2.5-mi **uphill**, followed by a combination of **long up- and downhills** rolling steadily **westward**. This arid half of the island is characterized by sparse, scrubby cover reminiscent of African plains. In fact, Molokai Ranch operates a wildlife park complete with zebras and giraffes, and the island has been used as an African set for movie productions.

At the 15-mi mark, take note of the **right** turn signed for Kaluakoi Resort, the only road down to Papohaku Beach. Unless you are in a hurry to zoom straight down, however, pedal **straight** ahead a last 2 mi along the **main road** to **Maunaloa,** a typical plantation town.

Neatly laid out on Molokai's upper slopes, Maunaloa was the Dole company town until recently when the company pulled out of the island. Latin American suppliers undercut the higher costs of production in Hawaii, bringing a virtual halt to the state's pineapple industry. Today Maunaloa is still a sleepy little place and headquarters of Molokai Ranch, which controls most of the island's western lands.

Maunaloa has a general store, a post office, one restaurant, and a few shops. You can't miss Big Wind Kite Factory for its impressive banyan tree and all the banners waving madly outside. The friendly staff there will show you around their workshop, giving visitors a new appreciation for finished products like a clever, hula-girl windsock. When business dies down and the wind kicks up, the shop owners will run out and lend their kites to local kids, making the whole field below town explode in color, activity, and laughter. It's a nice scene typical of Molokai's down-home atmosphere.

The crafts shop attached to Big Wind Kite Factory is also worth a look, offering one of the most extensive Hawaii/Molokai book selections on the island, from star guides to natural history and Kalaupapa biographies. Maunaloa's general store is open from 9:00 A.M. to 7:00 P.M. daily, Sundays 2:00 to 10:00 P.M. There are no accommodations in town unless you can free camp nearby, but Papohaku's good camping and indoor lodgings are only a short downhill ride from here.

Maunaloa to Papohaku: 6 miles

Stock up on supplies in Kaunakakai or Maunaloa since there is only a small, overpriced market at Kaluakoi and an even more overpriced restaurant. From **Maunaloa**, **return** to the **15-mi mark** and enjoy the 4-mi **descent** to the resort. This west-end area is marked by golf courses and luxury homes, just the place to shop around if you happen to be in the market for vacation property in the high six-figure range. Generally, **Kaluakoi** is a low-key resort, as tasteful as development might be called. Disappointed purists can escape the condos by heading for Papohaku Beach County Park and quiet beaches to the south.

West-end hotels and condominiums are pricey but would make a fabulous splurge, and vacancies are often easy to come by. Budget cyclists can pedal 1 mi farther south to Papohaku Beach County Park, Molokai's nicest campsite. The clean, grassy spot is set back from a broad white sand beach, with indoor (cold) showers, drinking water, and picnic tables. Be sure to pick up a permit for the site from Kaunakakai first, however.

Surfboards line the park in Maunaloa.

Wide, uncrowded sands characterize Papohaku Beach.

Kaluakoi Road continues **south** from the resort for nearly 4 mi, marked by occasional public beach access paths. Long, white sand beaches are tempting, but swimming is not safe except at Dixie Maru (Kapukahehu) Beach, the southernmost point.

Back at Kaluakoi resort, the Fun Hogs shack offers bicycle rental, kayaks, surfboards, and possible help for emergency repairs. Those with sturdy bikes can follow trails 1.5 mi north to Kawakiu Bay to explore off the beaten track. If you need a break from strenuous activity, take a leisurely walk south to Kaiaka Rock, the impressive cliff south of the hotels, where land meets sea in spectacular crashes of surf. Although cyclists face a hefty 7-mi climb away from the west end upon departure, for now just enjoy the area's quiet splendor. After the initial ascent, the ride will be **practically all downhill** or flat to the **airport** (13 mi) and **Kaunakakai** (20 mi).

LANAI
The Pineapple Isle

Little Lanai makes a unique bicycling destination off the standard tourist track thanks to the island's sleepy, compact character. Each of the island's tours offers something extraordinary, like historic ruins at Kaunolu Village, powerful scenery at Shipwreck Beach and Garden of the Gods, and ecologically significant zones like Kanepuu Preserve. Native rock carvings and Manele Bay's pretty beach promise to pack your time on Lanai with activity.

As a small island with few roads and fewer accommodations options, Lanai lends itself to unconventional touring approaches. All island tours are designed as day trips from Lanai City or Manele Bay. Cyclists can establish a comfortable base at one point and move in for days or even a week, setting off on a new ride every morning. Although distances are quite short, terrain provides a constant challenge. The island is shaped like a pyramid with its high point in the center, all roads emanating like spokes of a wheel with its hub at Lanai City. Few roads interconnect, requiring frequent backtracking, and the lack of a coastal ring road consigns cyclists to cruising down to every coastal point, only to turn around and climb back up.

Finally, Lanai's last challenge is that of road surface, with only 23 mi of pavement. Lanai's best scenery is accessible via a network of dirt roads that roam over the island, not one of them marked with annoying NO TRESPASSING signs. Most of these smooth clay or dirt tracks can be pedaled with road bikes, but mountain bikes are recommended for unrestricted access to Lanai's wonders.

In spite of these challenges, cycling is actually one of the best ways to widely travel the island. Rental cars are prohibitively expensive, and their range is strictly limited by rental companies. Cyclists are therefore among the most independent and unrestricted travelers on all Lanai. When you return to your campsite or hotel at the end of the day, other visitors will envy your unfettered travels over the little island that keeps its prizes hidden out of the way.

Practical Information

Lanai is very small. How small? Well, there is no postal delivery on Lanai; everyone has a post office box. The island's only town, Lanai City, boasts a total of two public phones. It is so small that residents even begin to recognize and greet cyclists who stay more than 1 or 2 days on the little island.

Due to Lanai's size and situation, prices are higher than those on other islands. If Maui's prices are 5 percent higher than Oahu's, Lanai's are 5 percent higher still, so calculate a little extra into your budget. There are no bicycle shops on Lanai, so plan on being self-sufficient with repairs. Those in need of technical help might try asking at a gas station or the Lodge at Koele, which rents bicycles.

View of little Lanai from West Maui

Pick up a free Lanai map on a plane or at an island hotel. You will still need a good road map for navigation, but the free map's pictorial representation will also prove useful. Most road maps cover Molokai and Lanai on a single sheet, but avoid those that combine both islands on one sheet with Maui as the smaller islands inevitably receive secondary treatment. In any case, route finding on Lanai is very easy because there are simply few roads to follow.

For years Lanai was a sleepy one-company, one-crop island, but things are changing. The pineapple business is dead, and new owners hope to promote Lanai as an exclusive resort with two fancy hotels that charge a few hundred dollars a night. The new business director formerly headed the Curry Company, the concessionaire that operated businesses in Yosemite National Park (potentially bad news; in Yosemite, development and economic gain ranked far above environmental and cultural awareness. On the other hand, the company makes an effort to support the local school, so it can't be all bad). Although changes will not come overnight, Lanai is sure to undergo readjustment to whatever the future holds.

All distances indicated on Lanai tours assume a base in Manele Bay. Those staying in Lanai City can usually subtract a few miles from the total (noted within each description).

Lanai does not have its own tourist office, although a basic brochure and free map are distributed by businesses on the island. For local lore, look for *True Stories of the Island of Lanai* by Lawrence Kainoahou Gay, available at hotel shops and around town.

Tips for Touring

A mountain bike is best for all Lanai tours, although a sturdy touring or cross bike will do for many of the routes. Road bikers can combine limited biking with hiking to extend their range, but be prepared to undertake considerable walks to some remote sights.

Lanai cycling is a charm, but not a breeze. Northeast tradewinds complicate matters on some legs of the tours, and hilly terrain ensures daily climbs no matter where you head. Happily, however, access is not an issue on Lanai. Although one company owns the entire island, all lands and roads are left open for public access. All roads on Lanai are open to visitors and residents alike, and free camping is widely tolerated.

The Lanai tours may be covered as short day trips, but be careful not to let your usual precautions slack. Carry first aid, extra water, and food on all rides. Do not assume that you will return to your base for lunch, for example; pack enough for a delay of several hours, just in case. Even if kiawe thorns don't get you, you might be tempted to tarry at a scenic point.

Touring Approaches

Lanai is the perfect place for a home-base tour, which is a good thing since there are few alternatives. Cyclists can fly or take a ferry to Lanai, settle into the campground or a hotel, and cover all the day trips from that base. This approach makes a nice alternative to the standard pack-and-go routine and is perfectly suited to Lanai's small size. The two places that offer lodgings are Manele Bay, with a campground and expensive hotel, and Lanai City, with a few B&Bs and hotels (see Accommodations for specifics).

Camping at Hulopoe Beach near Manele Bay is a good option both in terms of budget and convenience. The campsite is located just 0.3 mi from the ferry landing on one of cliffy Lanai's few beaches (9 downhill mi from the airport). The disadvantage of making a base here is that every ride will begin with a 3-mi uphill, climbing from the coast to the high plateau above. On the other hand, every ride will end with a 3-mi downhill run with great views of the ocean and Kahoolawe. The other possibility in this area is the Manele Bay Hotel, but at a few hundred dollars a night the hotel is an unlikely option.

Otherwise, establish your base in Lanai City. This is a more central location that subtracts a few miles off every tour and begins almost every ride with a downhill. However, the area is more cool and damp than Manele Bay, and of course there is no beach. In poor weather, it may barely drizzle at Manele Bay, while clouds lock up views and rain pours on Lanai City.

Airport

Lanai's airport consists of a shed and a runway serviced by Hawaiian Airlines, Aloha Island Air, and Air Molokai. The airfield is 4 mi west of Lanai City on Road 440/Kaumalapau Highway (a name almost longer than the road itself). To pedal into town, simply turn right and head toward the island's central rise. Continue straight ahead at the only intersection for Lanai City, or turn right on Manele Road to reach Manele Bay with its hotel and campground.

Ferry

The ferry provides an ideal way to combine a trip to Lanai with tours on Maui. The Expeditions line runs a ferry from Lahaina on Maui to Manele Bay on Lanai (telephone 661-3756). Boats depart Lahaina at 6:45 A.M., 9:15 A.M., 3:15 P.M., 5:45 P.M., and Friday at 12:45 P.M. Manele Bay departure times are 8:00 A.M., 10:30 A.M., 4:30 P.M., 6:45 P.M., and Friday at 2:00 P.M. You can roll your bicycle directly onto the small ferry yourself, and the friendly crew may even waive the bicycle fee.

On a calm winter day, the ferry ride doubles as a whale-watch while crossing the relatively shallow channel between Lanai and Maui. On a clear day, passengers can see Lanai, Molokai, and Oahu far down the channel.

Accommodations

Visitors can count Lanai's accommodations options on their fingers. Cyclists of all budgets will find a suitable situation on Lanai, although their options may add up to exactly that—one. The island's two newest hotels are the Lodge at Koele (in Lanai City) and the Manele Bay Hotel, where rates begin at a few hundred dollars a night. There is one other hotel in town, the Hotel Lanai. Two homes in Lanai City offer B&B stays, the Lanai Bed and Breakfast, Box 956, Lanai City, HI 96763 (telephone 565-6378) and Pineapple Isle Lodging (telephone 565-7065).

There is one campground on Lanai, located directly on Hulopoe Beach below the Manele Bay Hotel. Make reservations with the Lanai Company at least a few weeks in advance to secure a campsite (Box L, Lanai City, HI 96763; telephone 565-8232).

Lanai City

All 2,500 residents of Lanai live in Lanai City, the company town established by Dole. You can judge the term "city" the same way you judge all those "highways" in Hawaii; the entire place measures a dozen square blocks, the absolute picture of a planned company town. Most houses are of the same style, streets are laid out in a perfect grid pattern, and a large central park lies at the center of it all. Yes, you guessed it, this green is called Dole Park. In fact, the only surprise is that the town is not named Doleville or Dole City. However, that is not to say that Lanai City lacks individuality. Neat rows of company-built homes in town are tended with obvious pride, with gardens and flowers lining the yards.

In town, the main supply depot is Richard's Grocery/General Store, which carries all necessities. Store hours are 8:30 A.M. to 5:30 P.M. daily, closed 12:00 to 1:30 P.M. and all day Sunday. There are also a few smaller shops, restaurants, two pay phones, a library, and a post office in town.

Manele Bay

Manele Bay is 8 mi from Lanai City on the south side of the island. Manele Bay is exactly that—a bay; there is no town, no shops, and no businesses on this side of the island (or any side, for that matter; only in Lanai City). Manele Bay is simply a boat-landing point, one of the few on this cliffy island. Otherwise the Manele Bay Hotel provides all the action on this part of the island, but its restaurants and poolside grill are pricey.

In another sense, there is plenty of action at Manele Bay and Hulopoe Beach: the action of the waves, dolphins that play early in the morning, and sunrises and sunsets that cast colors over Lanai and Kahoolawe on the horizon. It is a beautiful, serene spot in a sheltered location.

Those arriving by ferry should pedal up the paved road to reach the hotel or campground. Take the first left to Hulopoe Beach (0.3 mile) instead of pedaling uphill on Manele Road (440). The official camping area is tucked away at the upper far end of the beach (right upon entering the parking area). The lower east end of Hulopoe Beach Park fills with unofficial campers on weekends, which local policemen say is quite all right. Lanai, you see, is a very relaxed place. It is best to camp officially, but if you are stuck you can squeeze by unofficially. Overall, Hulopoe Beach Park is a place for family barbecues where ukuleles and guitars come out at sunset and people laugh for hours while the stars smile back.

A permit to camp in the official area is rarely checked, and few people camp in their assigned spots anyway. The campground and beach have grills, picnic tables, toilet facilities, and cold-water, semi-private showers on the beach.

TOUR NO. 12

SHIPWRECK BEACH
Road and Mountain Biking

Distance: 17 miles from Manele on pavement,
up to 13 miles more on dirt roads
Riding time: Day trip
Difficulty: Challenging
Terrain: 8-mile descent/ascent
Roads: Well paved, dirt roads along coast
Connecting tours: All Lanai rides

This ride coasts out to Lanai's northeast shore, a fun outing that breezes by one of the best panoramas of the island. From either Manele Bay or Lanai City, cyclists cruise down a smoothly paved road to one end of a 6-mi strip known as Shipwreck Beach. The downhill ride takes in views of West Maui, Auau Channel, and Molokai, drawing steadily nearer the sight of a rusted wreck that still stands grounded off shore. Pavement ends at the beach, where dirt roads take over to lead mountain bikers north to rock carvings or south along the pebbly coast. However, kiawe thorns seem to bristle everywhere along the trail, threatening to blow the air out of your plans to explore. Although swimming is not recommended on Shipwreck Beach, you can keep busy beachcombing and soaking in views. The only real drawback of this ride is the long uphill that cyclists must tackle to return to town, a problem that plagues most Lanai tours.

Shipwreck Beach

To begin this ride from **Manele Bay**, ride up **Manele Road (440)** to **Lanai City**. At the corner where 440 bends sharply west, turn **right** for several blocks, then **left** on Lanai Avenue to pedal through the center of town. Cyclists staying in Lanai City can pick up the ride there, leaving the town center behind.

It is 1 mi from the center of Lanai City to the Lodge at Koele. You can't miss the Lodge, decorated with a huge mural that extols the glory of pineapples, artwork unpleasantly reminiscent of propagandistic socialist style. Continue 1 mi **uphill** as the well-paved road narrows and bends around the north end of a mountain ridge. Look right 1 mi beyond the Lodge to note the paved road that leads to the beginning of Munro Trail, another excellent day trip on Lanai (Tour No. 14).

After the road **curves northeast**, you will whoosh **downhill** for 7 thrilling mi to the **coast** and Shipwreck Beach. Along the way, a huge panorama opens up to encompass endless ocean waters, West Maui, Molokai, the beach below with hulk of a wreck clearly visible,

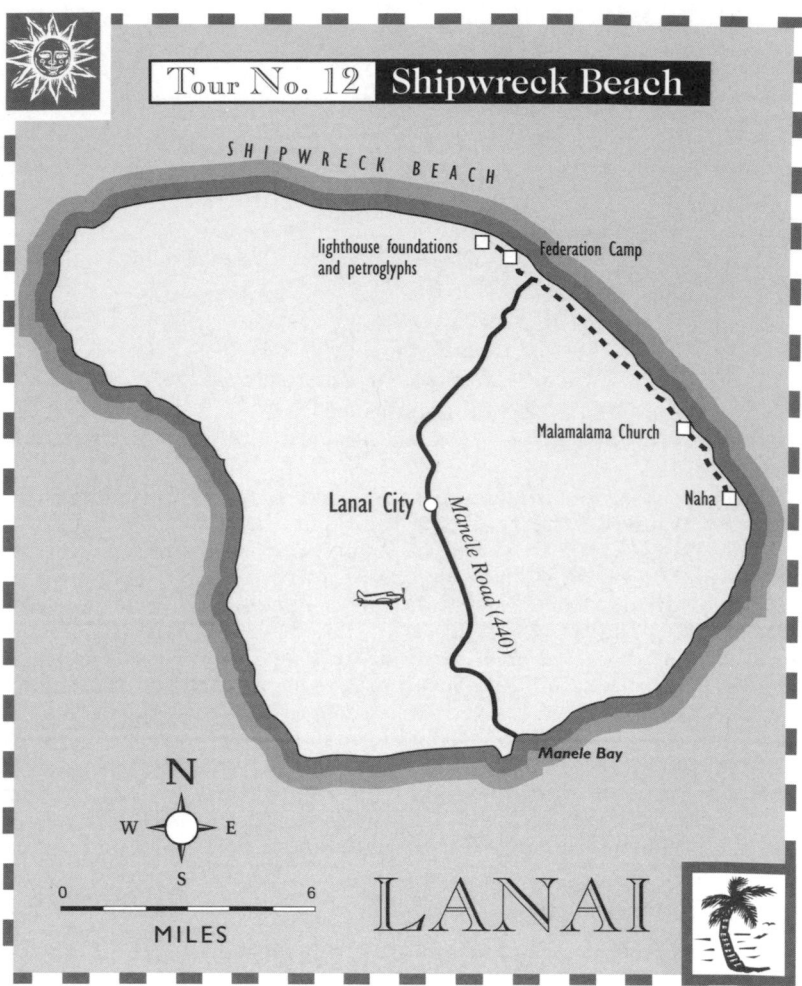

and **endless curves** of twisting road unfolding below. When you reach the **end of the pavement** at the bottom of the hill (17 mi from Manele, 9 mi from Lanai City), two dirt roads **branch** out in either direction. Those with thin tires may think twice about pedaling onward at this point, although hybrids and mountain bikes can push ahead.

The **left road extends west** less than 2 mi before ending at the foundations of an old lighthouse near the shipwreck (obviously not the most effective lighthouse). Short hikes from there lead to native rock carvings or the shipwreck. The **coastal road** that **runs south (right at the T)** offers more possibilities—but beware on either branch! I made it less than 200 yards before an unmistakable hissing sound interrupted my progress—kiawe thorns had struck again. Four punctures later, after extracting two half-inch thorns from one tire alone, I gave up. Therefore, if this view and a short walk aren't enough for you, proceed only with extreme caution, a spare tube, and plenty of patches.

Cyclists heading **west** toward the shipwreck will pass **Federation Camp**, a hodgepodge of beach shacks. White markings from the inauspicious lighthouse foundations lead to a few, simple petroglyphs. The carvings are located a few minutes' **hike** inland, to the right of the path.

Cyclists unintimidated by kiawes can head **south** along the other road. The **dirt road** runs **just inland** of the beach, with some open patches that are blissfully clear of kiawe. Locals prefer to drive directly along the beach, a viable option for cyclists along the hard-packed stretches. Faint **fishponds** still line the shore, as do more modern additions, like rusting metal containers and other debris. Of the original settlement at **Keomuku**, 6 mi south, only **Malamalama Church** remains (1903). Aside from a few more fishponds, the coast farther south is largely uninterrupted by specific sights. The road's **endpoint** at **Naha** totals 13 mi (and countless punctures) from the end of the pavement.

An island pony lives the good life on Lanai.

TOUR NO. 13

GARDEN OF THE GODS
Road and Mountain Biking

Distance: 15 miles to Garden of the Gods,
5 miles more to Polihua Beach
Riding time: Day ride
Difficulty: Challenging
Terrain: Gradual to the Garden, steep drop to the coast
Roads: Smooth dirt road then rough track
Connecting tours: All Lanai rides

Only a short distance from Lanai City is Garden of the Gods, an area of eerie rock formations and red-hued landscape. Road bikes should have no problem on the smooth dirt road running out to Garden of the Gods, but only mountain bikers can continue beyond to Polihua Beach, an isolated stretch of sand below. All cyclists heading out in this direction will pass through Kanepuu Preserve, one of the last stands of native dryland forest in Hawaii. While the ride to the Garden of the Gods covers gentle terrain, the coastal extension descends sharply, meaning a challenging uphill return trip.

Manele Bay to Garden of the Gods: 15 miles

The dirt road from Lanai City to Garden of the Gods (7 mi) consists of hard-packed, smooth red soil with only a slight uphill gradient. Cyclists based in **Manele Bay** should begin by pedaling **up the hill** on the usual route to **Lanai City**. Turn **right** at the **bend** in Road 440 as if toward the center of town, but then take the **first left** on unmarked Fraser Avenue (a Buddhist temple stands on this corner). Fraser runs past Dole Park, coming to an abrupt end at the north end of town.

From there, continue **straight** ahead on a dirt road. After passing **under powerlines**, make a **sharp left** turn. At an **intersection** 0.4 mi later, turn **right** to follow a **fenceline north**. In another 0.4 mi **bend slightly left** with the road (do not take the right fork). This wide, open area offers good chances of spotting Axis deer, and consequently good chances to spot hunters, who are generally friendly. Nevertheless, this may not be the day to show off your Bambi suit; opt for bright safety colors instead.

Measuring 4 mi from the end of the pavement in Lanai City, you will come to and pedal straight through a **clump of trees**. A fence and grating shortly thereafter mark the boundary of **Kanepuu Preserve**, managed by the Nature Conservancy. This 400-acre area was originally fenced by George Munro, who recognized the need to protect na-

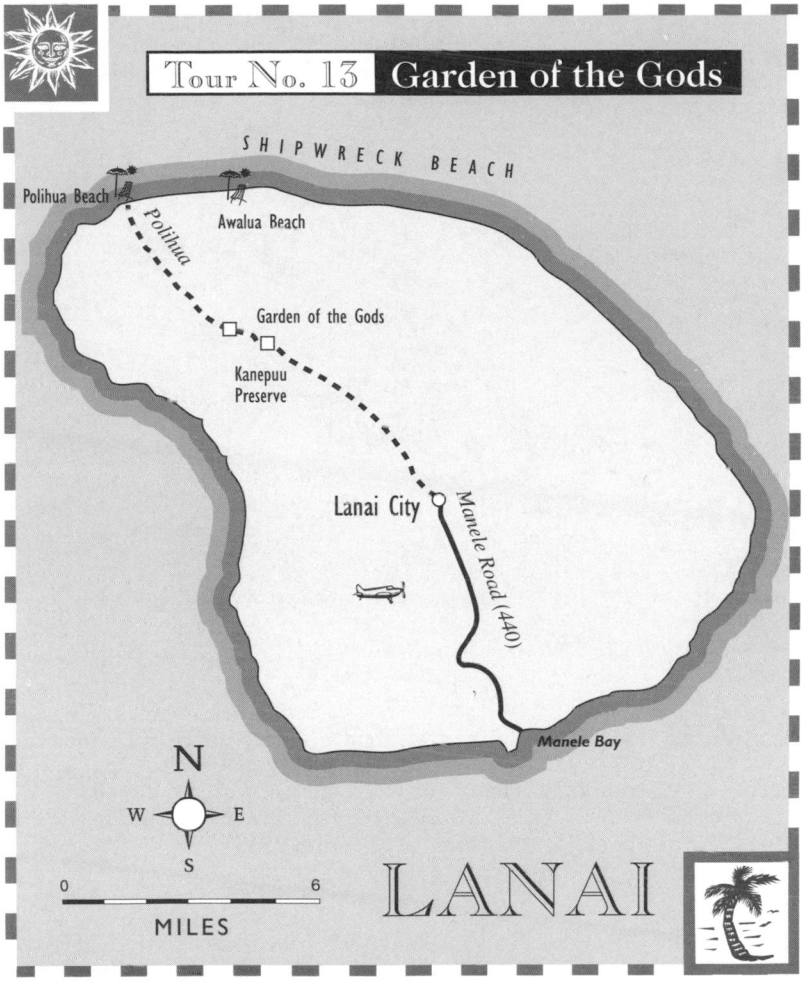

Tour No. 13 Garden of the Gods

SHIPWRECK BEACH

Polihua Beach

Polihua

Awalua Beach

Garden of the Gods

Kanepuu
Preserve

Lanai City

Manele Road (440)

Manele Bay

N
W   E
S

0   6
MILES

LANAI

tive forest from cattle that were grazing the landscape bare. The area represents one of the last stands of native dryland left in all Hawaii and on Lanai in particular, including endangered Lanaian sandalwood.

Follow the main road **straight** through the small preserve, ignoring a side branch marked LAPAIKI on the right. Upon crossing **another grate** and leaving the preserve, you will emerge in **Garden of the Gods**. In the "garden," rocks lie strewn around a reddish landscape overlooking the ocean and Molokai, the eerie effect enhanced by human hands that have stacked rocks in precarious towers.

The few visitors who venture out this far rarely explore beyond, leaving adventurous cyclists with a quiet, solitary ride to **Polihua**

Rock towers perch precariously in Garden of the Gods.

Beach via the dirt road straight ahead (**Polihua Road**). Also note **Awalua Road**, which drops off to the right as you exit Kanepuu Preserve, another challenging mountain-bike route (5 mi downhill). The rough track leads to **Awalua Beach**, the northwest end of **Shipwreck Beach**. Sure enough, Awalua also sports its own beached wreck, another victim of the ocean's brute force.

Polihua Beach: 5 miles

From **Garden of the Gods** it is less than 5 mi down to Polihua Beach. Ride **straight down Polihua Road** and bear **right** at the first unmarked fork. Just over 1 mi from Garden of the Gods, you will reach a **marked split** with Polihua signed to the **right** (Kaena to the left). From that point the road degenerates, making a mountain bike your best bet. Be prepared, however, for the prospect of walking your wheels back up due to the dual obstacles of uphill and headwind on the return trip. Meanwhile, watch for treacherous patches of deep sand and kiawes on the way down.

Polihua is a perfect ribbon of white sand with a huge panorama of Molokai's entire south coast, inspiring a flow of memories for those who visited that island, or a flow of imagination for cyclists planning future explorations. High winds make the beach a showcase of nature's raw beauty rather than a place to catch some rays and relax. Swimming in these powerful channel waters is also not recommended.

Polihua gets its name from the endangered green turtles that nest here (*hua* means eggs). Unfortunately, their fate is still insecure, especially since locals persist in driving trucks across the beach. A dirt road continues for a short distance to the **east** if you are not content with the first beach. Polihua would be an unparalleled private camping site, but with no water source the prospect is impractical. On the other hand, that may be for the better, helping Polihua Beach remain relatively undisturbed.

Remote Polihua Beach draws few visitors.

THE MUNRO TRAIL
Mountain Biking

Distance: 28-mile circle
Riding time: Day ride
Difficulty: Challenging
Terrain: Steady climb to 3,370 feet
Trail: Good dirt track but slippery when wet
Connecting tours: All Lanai rides

The Munro Trail traces Lanai's highest ridgeline to Lanaihale, the island's 3,370-foot peak. The trail is named for George Munro, a visionary New Zealander who planted the trees along the ridgeline and set aside protected tracts of Lanai's native forest. The trail (actually the width and quality of a jeep road) does not simply run straight along, it twists and turns, always keeping you eager to see what comes next. Its smooth surface permits hybrids or even road bikes equipped with knobby tires to pass, although the clay can become treacherously slick in wet conditions. On a good day, all the Hawaiian Islands except Kauai are visible from Lanaihale, although on a bad day you might be lucky to see as far as West Maui.

This high ridgeline is the last point on the island to shake itself free of clouds, so choose your day carefully if you have several to spend on Lanai. From Manele Bay, a full loop around the Munro Trail measures 28 mi (18 mi from Lanai City), 13 of them on the dirt track. No matter when you set out to conquer the trail, you are likely to have the entire length to yourself, feeling far, far away from "civilization."

The Munro Trail

From the center of Lanai City, follow **Lanai Avenue** toward and past the Lodge at Koele. Just 1 mi beyond the lodge, turn **right** onto a paved side road with a stop sign. The pavement ends at a Japanese **cemetery** 0.3 mi later. From the three dirt roads that branch out from there, follow the **left branch** marked MUNRO TRAIL TEMPORARY ACCESS. The original trail began along the middle track, but visitors are now forced into a slight detour since the Koele Golf Course now stands in the way.

Therefore follow the left fork, bearing **left** 0.3 mi later (not right through a white gate to the golf course). Initially, the trail bends far east and runs downhill before turning back on course along a ridgeline. The first half of the trail is a steady succession of uphills interspersed with short, level sections for a breather.

The road surface is good enough for bikers to free their eyes from their usual fixed position a few feet in front of their tires. For the most part, the trail is nicely carpeted with scattered pine boughs (fortunately George Munro did not devote his efforts to planting kiawes), with only a few patches of gravel.

For the first 6 mi the trail steadily gains elevation until peaking at **Lanaihale**, the island's highest point (3,370 feet). From the top, 360-degree views will have you spinning in circles, looking over central or southwest Lanai, then Maui and Auau Channel. In perfect conditions, even Oahu and the Big Island can be seen from Lanaihale, with only Kauai too distant to see. There is no better place to picnic, rest, and soak in the scenery on a nice day. However, you might be in danger of

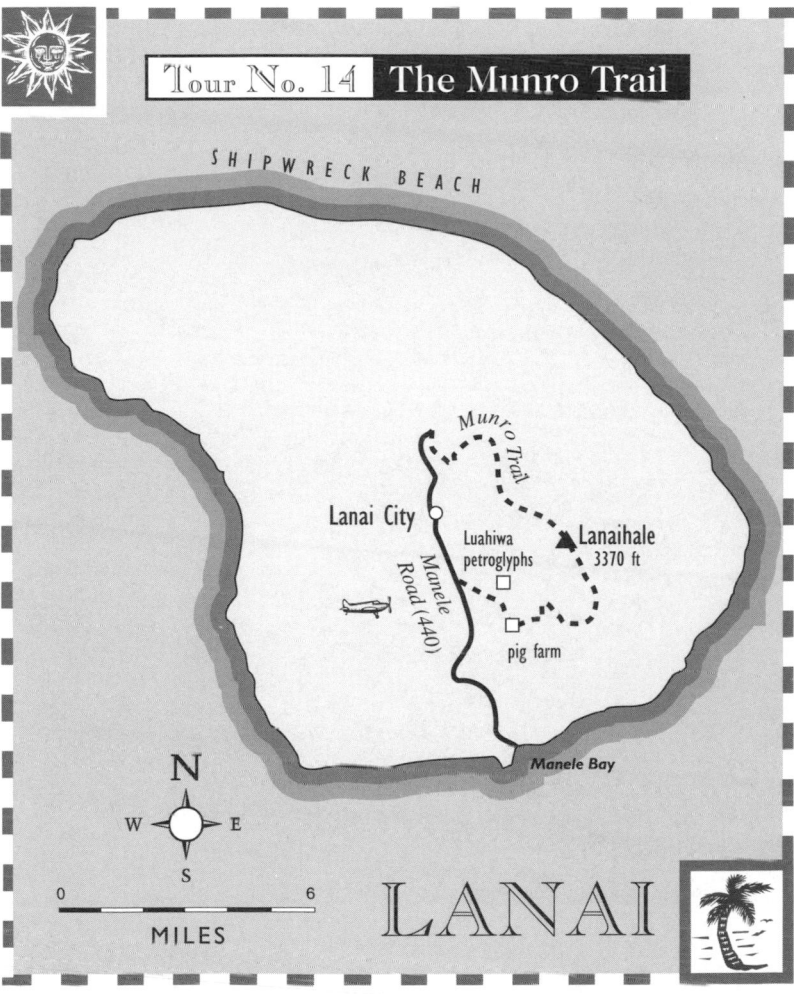

soaking in another way, since the high ridge is often shrouded in rain clouds.

From Lanaihale, Munro Trail descends in fairly **steep** jumps, so proceed cautiously. After an overlook point marked **Kapoho**, the trail bends **right** and comes to a sign for Puumanu. Turn **right** on the bottom of this hill and then ride **straight** toward the crater's center point and the flat metal roof of the pig farm. At the next intersection, turn **left** to bend around an ancient cinder cone and continue riding **downhill** toward the pig farm.

Pedal **straight** past the farm to reach paved **Manele Road (440)** and return to your base in Lanai City or Manele Bay. Unless you are impatient to move on, however, this is a perfect time to add the Luahiwa Petroglyphs to your itinerary as they are located only 1 mi past the pig farm. To do so, take the first right after passing the driveway of the farm, then take the next right, which puts you on the zag part of the petroglyph directions (see Additional Suggested Rides).

View from the Munro Trail

KAUNOLU VILLAGE RUINS
Manele Bay to Kaunolu and Lanai City

Distance: 30-mile circle
Riding time: Day ride
Difficulty: Challenging
Terrain: Long slopes to and from coast, level sections between
Roads: Smooth dirt roads, short gravel sections
Connecting tours: All Lanai rides

This circular tour spins around southwestern Lanai in a full loop that cyclists can hook into from either Lanai City or Manele Bay. First, cyclists head out on dirt tracks to the seaside ruins of Kaunolu Village, one of the best preserved archaeological sites in Hawaii. From there, the ride extends to Lanai's equally cliffy east coast before curving inland and crossing the central basin to Lanai City and Manele Bay. Although the excursion again requires a long descent to the coast and therefore another climb on the return, the overall distance is short and punctuated by several good rest stops. The entire ride can be covered in a half day or be stretched into a full day.

Manele Bay to Kaunolu

From Manele Bay, pedal **uphill** toward Lanai City. Although the 3-mi climb is a difficult way to start your day, the road's steady gradient helps to a degree. Finally, you will **crest the hill** and emerge on open Palawai Basin, the expanse lined with rows of untended pineapples, now a defunct industry.

At the top of the 3-mi hill is a **stop sign** where the road takes a sharp right. Turn **west (left)** on a dirt road there. Cyclists beginning the ride from Lanai City should simply go straight at that stop sign instead of left for Manele Bay. This is a bouncy gravel road through endless pineapple fields that gradually changes to a smoother clay surface (road bikes with knobby tires will do). **After crossing beneath** electrical wires, turn on the **fourth turnoff to the left** marked with a small wooden sign for Kaunolu (2.7 mi from the end of the pavement).

Follow these small signs **downhill** for 2.5 mi. Unfortunately, down is a word cyclists come to dread on Lanai because most finish in dead ends, creating nasty reverse consequences. At one point, the dirt track turns back east but straightens again shortly afterward. Watch for treacherous patches of loose gravel on the way down to the coast.

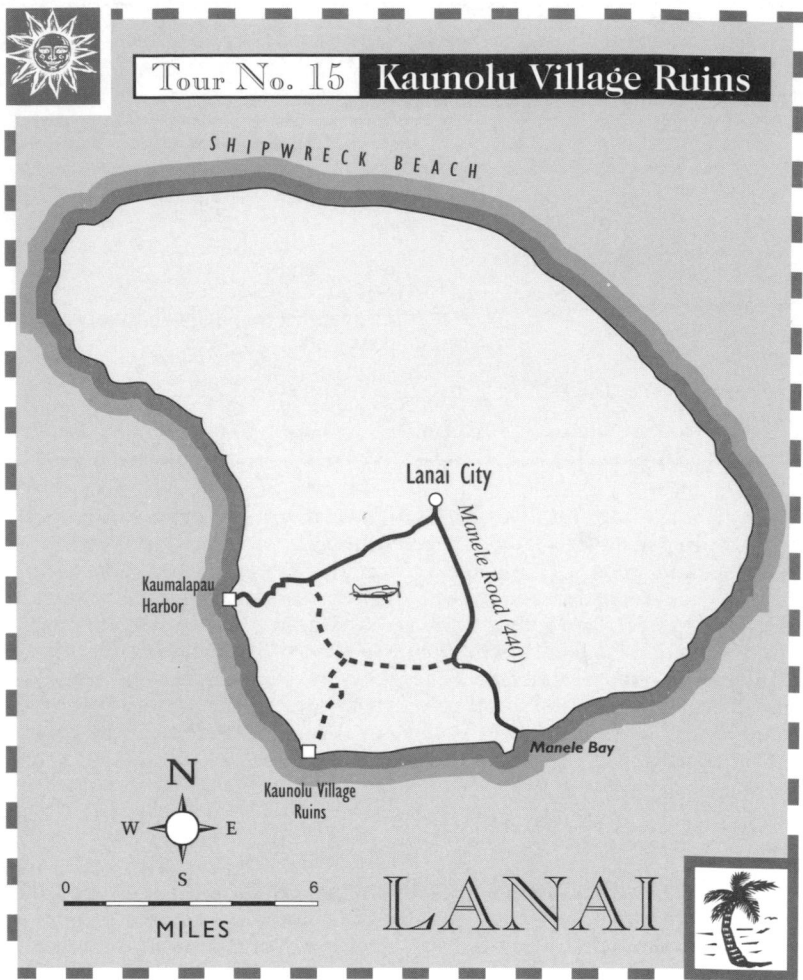

Tour No. 15 Kaunolu Village Ruins

SHIPWRECK BEACH

Lanai City

Manele Road (440)

Kaumalapau
Harbor

Manele Bay

Kaunolu Village
Ruins

N
W · E
S

0   6
MILES

LANAI

Soon you will reach a **parking area** and the beginning of an **interpretive trail**. You can lock your bicycle near the trailhead and follow the one-hour interpretive walk from there. Kaunolu Village are the best preserved ruins on Lanai, and one of only a few sites in Hawaii with good interpretive markers.

As you wander through the village ruins, plaques describe the structures you see: house platforms, a watchtower, canoe sheds, and fishing shrines. One large building was Kamehameha's house, as Kaunolu was a favored fishing getaway of the king. Kaunolu combines great natural beauty with historic interest, a place where seabirds soar against a backdrop of sheer cliffs and clear, turquoise waters.

Even if you are not interested in hiking the entire trail, at least visit

Extensive ruins draw intrepid cyclists to Kaunolu.

the last four sites, starting with Kamehameha's house, then crossing the gulch to the *heiau*, a nearby seastack, and Kahekili's Leap, a 65-foot drop into 12 feet of water.

Kaunolu to Kaumalapau Harbor and Lanai City

Back at the upper dirt road, **continue circling west** around the corner of the island, Molokai coming into view as you round the point. Simply follow a **fenceline** along the main dirt road here. When it branches into three arms, follow the **middle section** that curves **right** then continues straight to intersect **Road 440**.

Eventually, you will reach a stop sign and pavement on the west end of Road 440 (now Kaumalapau Highway). From this point it is—yes, you guessed it—3 mi **down** to Kaumalapau Harbor. Unless you are the type of biker who likes to fill in all possible lines on a map of your voyage, there is not much point in going more than partway down to the little harbor, now marked only by silent machinery. Instead, **descend** just 0.25 mi past the 2-mi mark for excellent views of Lanai's cliffy coast and Molokai in the distance. Turning around at that point will subtract almost 4 mi from this tour's total.

Prevailing winds are likely to fight eastward progress to Lanai City on Road 440, but the distance is only 4 mi once you pass the airport.

Once outside Lanai City, make a sharp **right** turn with Road 440 to return to **Manele Bay**, crossing **Palawai Basin** and gliding down to the bay.

ADDITIONAL SUGGESTED RIDES

Luahiwa Petroglyphs

This ride can fit in with any of the Lanai tours or as a short excursion of its own. Lanai's largest concentration of petroglyphs (rock carvings) clusters on the east edge of Palawai Basin, just 2 mi off Road 440. After the ride in, finding the rock carvings involves a short hike along a rough trail.

To reach the petroglyphs, take Hoike Road off Manele Road (440). This road is marked on most maps but not with a sign from the main road. From Manele Bay, it is 6 mi to the turnoff on the right. You can recognize the turn by the yield sign there and a few short pine trees, the only ones along this road. For those coming from Lanai City, the turnoff is on the left, 1.5 mi south of the sharp bend in Road 440.

Take a moment at the turnoff to get your bearings. Straight ahead rises the east edge of Palawai Basin, delineated by a long mountain ridge along which the Munro Trail runs. At the top edge of the basin stands a white water tower, with a similar gray tank below and to its right. Another 0.25 mi to the right is a scrubby slope with a few trees. Those with keen eyes can make out boulders scattered among the lowest slopes; the petroglyphs are etched into thirty-four boulders in that area.

With those bearings in mind, set off along Hoike Road, which zigs southeast toward a pig farm. After 1 mi, you will pass a corral area and then ride 100 yards up a slight incline. Then take a sharp left to zag back northwest along the edge of the basin. The petroglyph area is only 1 mi farther.

Look for a break in the pipeline to your right along this northwest zag. This is the only access point to the upper road (above the pipeline and powerlines), which leads to the base of the boulder area. Ride that upper road for 0.5 mi, then pull over and walk up to the boulders. A series of small paths runs up to and between the boulders along the slope, but be careful to watch your footing, not just the rocks.

Carvings scattered across these boulders depict human and animal figures as well as other shapes. Some carvings are quite obvious, while others are extremely weathered. Many boulders may seem "blank" at first glimpse, but careful examination will reveal faint figures hiding in rocky shadows.

OAHU
The Gathering Place

Fittingly, Oahu means "the gathering place." Oahu is Hawaii's most populous and most visited island due to its accessibility and its status as a major Pacific crossroad. Don't be fooled, though, into believing that Oahu is completely spoiled by tourism and development. Some of the best bicycle tours in the Hawaiian Islands circle Oahu, taking advantage of level, coastal roads. Oahu's scenery rivals the best of Kauai or the Big Island without the high, unavoidable climbs found elsewhere. On the dramatically eroded Windward Coast, cyclists pedal a narrow line between sheer inland cliffs and offshore islets, while vast tracts of the interior remain untouched by development.

As Hawaii's gateway island where 800,000 of the state's 1 million residents live (one-third of them in Honolulu), Oahu can be quite busy. Therefore cyclists planning an Oahu tour should be comfortable cycling busy roads—or learn to adapt quickly. However, all these statistics overexaggerate the situation. Outside Honolulu, many roads are quiet and only small towns crop up between long stretches of rugged scenery and agricultural lands.

Apart from the chaos of Honolulu, Oahu makes a fun, interesting destination for cyclists of many types. Moderate terrain attracts those who plan a vacation of easy cycling, and compact geography permits thorough coverage of the island within a short timeframe. On the other hand, cyclists who enjoy pitting themselves against obstacles and getting away from it all can also find a niche on Oahu by heading off on more rugged tours such as the little-traveled route around Kaena Point (Tour No. 17) or trails high above the bustle of Honolulu.

Practical Information

Oahu is the most popular tourist destination in Hawaii thanks to the convenience of Honolulu's International Airport. The Hawaiian Visitor's Bureau covers Oahu in great detail (see Part I: Planning), and various tourist information magazines like *The Guide to Oahu* are distributed at hotels and shops. Oahu is also the only island with good public transportation in the form of The Bus. Although you may not put your bicycle on The Bus, you can take advantage of the service to visit sights around Honolulu or to reach a distant area if time does not permit pedaling there.

Waikiki is one compact part of Honolulu where amusement consists exclusively of the beach and nightlife. To visit museums, historic sights, and other points of interest, you must catch a bus or pedal a few miles from Waikiki. Just remember that buses to top attractions like Hanauma *(bay)* and Pearl Harbor fill quickly and early, so wait at a strategic stop and come prepared with exact change.

For the most part, the road tours suggested for Oahu are extremely straightforward and easy to follow. It is easy to find suitable maps for touring Oahu, with several series offering a range of scales. One good place to search is the Pacific Map Center at 250 Ward Avenue, above the Bike Way store.

Tips for Touring

Oahu is one of the older Hawaiian islands, and therefore its volcanic slopes are severely eroded into spectacular cliffs and formations. Two volcanic ridges parallel each other on Oahu's windward and leeward sides, with a smooth valley between. In contrast to the high population density of Honolulu, much of Oahu remains undeveloped and unsettled, especially the forested interior.

In spite of its high population and Honolulu traffic, Oahu is one of the easiest islands to tour because its coastal roads remain relatively level. Both sides of the island may be toured in a few days, during which cyclists encounter only a few hills. The greatest obstacle on either coastal tour (Tour Nos. 16 and 17) is the 1,000-foot-high saddle between the Koolau (windward) and Waianae (leeward) mountain ranges. Yet even that climb is extremely gradual and straightforward, putting up little resistance to determined cyclists.

Once outside Honolulu, Oahu shows its small-town character. Still, the towns are not so widely spaced that the next bicycle shop or grocery store is ever far away. Roads are well maintained and marked, and traffic is rarely a problem outside the city sprawl. Consequently, few other islands in the chain can rival Oahu as a practical, scenic destination with tours of only moderate difficulty.

The Hawaii Bicycling League (see Part I: Information Sources) distributes a free newsletter through Oahu bicycle shops that lists free group rides. These are a good way to meet local bikers and hear about their favorite spots on Oahu.

Airport

Honolulu International Airport is the main gateway for the Hawaiian Islands and an important hub for the entire Pacific region. Both long-distance and interisland flights depart from Honolulu International; just pick the airline of your choice.

Arriving visitors heading for Waikiki can choose several ways to reach their destination. If you had a tiring trip or it is late, it is easiest to pay for a cab ride to your hotel. You can also try your luck with one of the Waikiki shuttle services that depart the airport constantly, but many use microbuses that will not accept bicycles. As long as it is daylight, do not hesitate to simply bicycle to Waikiki, the natural starting point for any Oahu tour. About half of the 9-mi ride follows bicycle lanes, the other half being directly on high volume but reasonably slow-paced roads. With the directions below, you should have a simple ride into Waikiki.

Honolulu International Airport to Waikiki: 9 miles

Estimate about an hour for the easy ride into Honolulu and Waikiki. Before leaving the airport ask how to access **Nimitz Highway** to avoid ending up on H1, a real highway. Often airline magazines include a detailed map of the airport, which would facilitate your departure. Nimitz is directly underneath H1, part of a two-tier road arrangement. A separate bicycle lane runs along the opposite side of Nimitz (westbound side), so **cross over** and turn **right** (east to go toward Waikiki) when you exit the airport. The lane itself is in good shape, but massive pillars block the view at crossing points, so proceed with caution. After a time the lane ends, depositing cyclists on **Dillingham Boulevard**. Rising ahead like a beacon is the obvious landmark of Diamond Head, highrises of Waikiki spreading before the mountain. How quickly things change—photos from forty years ago show that the view to Diamond Head was lined only by palm trees.

After 1 mi turn **right**, following signs **back to Nimitz Highway**. There, turn **left** on Nimitz to head for Waikiki. (Those heading for the campground on Sand Island should go right on Nimitz, doubling back to the west. Signs will lead you to the Sand Island Access Road, a distance of 5 mi from the airport.)

A designated **bicycle lane** eases your way along Nimitz Highway until it ends 2 mi later at **Fort Street** in downtown Honolulu. When the bicycle lane ends, simply continue straight. On the right you will see the masts of ships at the Maritime Museum. Nimitz becomes **Ala Moana Boulevard**, which passes green Ala Moana Park and crosses a bridge into Waikiki. Pause for a moment at the east entrance to Ala Moana Park to view a whale mural on a building in Waikiki, a creation of the artist Wyland. His "Whaling Walls" showcase Hawaii's undersea world on similar sites across the islands.

Ala Moana Boulevard curves up and **splits** into Kuhio and Kalakaua avenues at Waikiki Gateway Park with its statue of King Kalakaua. From there consult a local map (available in the airport or at hotel desks) to reach your final destination. Most streets in Waikiki are one-way only; Kalakaua Avenue is the main eastbound street through the resort area.

To ride **back to the airport**, simply **reverse** this route. Only the trailhead of the bicycle lane for the last stretch to the airport is tricky to find. Begin by riding **west on Ala Moana**, which becomes Nimitz. From downtown Honolulu, ride the **bicycle lane** for nearly 2 mi. When it ends, turn **right up Waiakamilo Avenue** and turn **left onto Dillingham Boulevard at the second light**. Ride **straight** 1 mi ahead as if to ascend the ramp to H1; the bicycle lane begins at the **base of the ramp to the right**. Pedal the now-familiar bicycle lane until the **left** turn to the airport on Rodgers Boulevard.

Accommodations

Oahu offers accommodations aplenty for all budget levels. Budget accommodations can even be found in Waikiki, where nothing is too far from the beach. Read tour descriptions for suggestions and consult the listings of a good guidebook to judge all available options.

ROOMS. Hotels and B&Bs dot all Oahu, although the vast majority are concentrated around Honolulu. A number of official and independent hostels are located directly in Waikiki, although cleanliness and order are characteristics shared only by a few. Outside Honolulu, Oahu's only hostel is Backpackers in Waimea (see Tour No. 16).

CAMPING. In spite of its development and tourist crowds, Oahu offers many camping areas where cyclists can escape to a quieter world. It is possible to completely circle Oahu using only campgrounds, making Hawaiian travel laughably cheap. However, security is a major issue for campers on Oahu; put safety before budget when choosing a site (see below).

All state and county campsites on Oahu are closed on Wednesday and Thursday nights, so plan for a private campground or indoor accommodations then. Both state and county sites are free with a permit. Except for popular holiday times and long weekends, it is easy to secure permits on short notice. The county allows camping at twelve parks, the state at five. For a complete list and permits, contact the County Department of Parks and Recreation, 650 S. King Street, Honolulu, HI 96813 (telephone 523-4525), or State Division of Parks, 1151 Punchbowl Avenue, Room 310, Honolulu, HI 96813 (telephone 587-0300). The two offices are in neighboring buildings separated by a wide lawn. While at the State building, stop by the Division of Wildlife office in Room 325 for free topographic maps of trails open to hiking and/or mountain biking.

Many public campsites are uncomfortable and/or insecure due to threats of theft and the predominance of homeless encampments. Few sites are overseen by resident rangers or even regular patrols. Women traveling alone should not camp at any Oahu parks except the safest sites listed below. Even men or women traveling with a companion might not be comfortable or safe at some sites. Before planning to use a site, ask about security there and read descriptions in tour outlines. For example, even the county office discourages camping anywhere on the Waianae (Leeward) Coast. Having issued these dire warnings, however, I must admit that I camped with a companion in several Oahu sites (including Waianae parks) and encountered no serious problems.

A few sites are reliably safe for all campers, even single women. Inland sites are traditionally quiet and secure because few troublemakers venture out to them. Those include Keaiwa Heiau State Park in Aiea Heights and Hoomaluhia County Botanic Garden above Kaneohe. The latter is a beautiful park with a resident warden and gates that close each night for extra security (write to Box 1116, Kaneohe, HI 96744, or telephone 233-7323). You may feel a bit lonely in these sites but definitely secure.

Another reliable option is Malaekahana State Recreation Area, north of Laie on the Windward Coast. The park offers cabins and free tent sites in a public use area as well as camping in a secure, gated area (telephone 293-1736 for information). Kualoa County Regional Park, near Chinaman's Hat on the Windward Coast, offers free camping in an area that is gated at night and staffed by a caretaker. Finally, YMCA Camp Erdman is another good choice. The camp is located in Mokuleia, near Kaena Point (telephone 637-4615).

Honolulu and Waikiki

In the words of Paul Theroux, Honolulu "is not really a city but a highly complex small town." For some, Honolulu is an exciting resort with interesting people from all over the world, but to others the city is a sad monument to the destructive powers of development. For cyclists, the city proffers both bad and good factors. The traffic and confusing road network are enough to drive any cyclist mad, but city resources include bicycle shops and friendly allies in the state's most populous bicycling community. All characterizations aside, it is difficult to avoid Honolulu in any case. Nor should one shun the city outright; Honolulu has plenty to offer people of all purposes and pursuits.

Waikiki is one section of the city of Honolulu, a compact beach area chock full of highrise hotels and neon lights. Waikiki sprawls under the shadow of Diamond Head, one of the most recognizable landmarks in the world. You may shake your head at honeymooners, pensioners, and lei-bedecked foreigners in Waikiki, but then you might just enjoy yourself. Waikiki Beach also serves as a surprising escape at night when streets pulse with bar music. On the beach those sounds are distant, and the twinkling stars feel much closer.

For all its development and congestion, Honolulu still retains some seas of calm like Tantalus, a towering peak right above the city. A ride or hike there, only a few miles from downtown, transports you to a jungle world that seems much farther away. Historic buildings in Old Honolulu also offer calm respite from glaring highrises only blocks away.

Whenever cycling in Honolulu, avoid rush hours. Choose quieter side streets or narrow roads on which cars are forced to proceed slowly, or use The Bus for local sightseeing. Put all your cycling strategies to work on the city streets: signal all turns, claim a safe space for yourself on the side of the road, wear bright clothing, and follow bicycle lanes when possible.

FOOD. Waikiki is dotted with countless convenience stores that charge prices considered outrageous even in Hawaii. The only fairly priced supermarkets within bicycle range are a Foodland in the rear of Ala Moana Shopping Center and three large supermarkets in a row stretching west from the point where Kalakaua Avenue meets Beretania Avenue (just outside Waikiki to the northwest). There are plenty of restaurants and fast-food places about, some serving meals at good value, others offering poor fare. As if in league with restaurateurs, few hostels and hotels in the area offer self-catering kitchen facilities.

ACCOMMODATIONS. Waikiki options alone are far too numerous to detail here. Rest assured that accommodations of all types and budget ranges are available, although quality and location vary in direct proportion to rates. A number of official and independent hostels offer bunks in Waikiki, but two or more people can do just as well in a basic hotel room. B&Bs do exist in the city and surrounding areas, but it may not be worthwhile to seek out small side streets for a site far from the center. Hostels are rarely full, but for hotels a few weeks' advance booking is recommended.

The nearest camping is Sand Island State Recreation Area, located 9 mi from Waikiki and 5 mi from the airport. Reach the park via the Sand Island Access Road off Nimitz Highway. Facilities include cold showers, picnic tables, grills, and toilets. The park offers partial views of Waikiki, full views of the harbor, and lies in full noise range of the airport. A few homeless camps are scattered around the area, although most are low profile and the park is large enough to give everyone their own space. However, it is still not a comfortable place to camp, especially for women.

SIGHTS. The Bishop Museum, widely considered one of the best Pacific collections in the world, is a good place to begin a trip to Hawaii. Extensive exhibits cover every aspect of Hawaii, from geology and ecology to native arts, culture, and recent history. Pedal to the museum on 1525 Bernice Street (northwest from Waikiki), or hop on Bus 2 (School/Middle Street). Admission is steep, a blow somewhat lessened if you coincide your visit with the timing of a hula show or living exhibits in which traditional handicraft making are demonstrated (usually weekdays; call 847-3511 for schedule). The exhaustive collections include countless artifacts and crafts from all Pacific islands, featuring such curios as a carved meat platter "large enough to hold a pig or small dog." Most memorable among delicate artworks are stunning feather capes used by royalty. Many little tweeters gave their all for these masterpieces, but others got away only a few tailfeathers the poorer.

Entrance to the highly acclaimed planetarium is also included in museum admission. Check the theme of each program before waiting in line, however, as several different shows are offered daily and some are more interesting than others.

Historic Honolulu is chock full of interesting sights from the era of monarchy and missionary influence. The downtown ride described below tours many of those sights. Other destinations of merit are Chinatown and the Hawaii Maritime Center, both near the downtown

The Falls of Clyde *graces Honolulu's harbor.*

area. *Hokulea* and the *Falls of Clyde* are both moored at the Maritime Center, which also contains exhibits on whaling and other maritime periods. For more day trips from a Honolulu base, consider a trip to the U.S.S. *Arizona* Memorial in Pearl Harbor, or head up to Diamond Head or Tantalus (see Additional Suggested Rides).

Downtown/Punchbowl Area

Almost all the principal historic sights in Honolulu can be toured in one effort, being highly concentrated in one area. Either pedal or bus to the downtown area to begin. If biking, plan your route around one-way streets. You can reach Honolulu's historic downtown by following Ala Moana Boulevard west, then turning up Richards Street or Alakea Street. The historic center lies between King Street, Richards Street to the west, and Punchbowl Street on the east, with Chinatown just west.

Downtown Honolulu dates from the missionary and late monarchy period; for a taste of native Hawaii, you will have to visit the Bishop Museum or wait to get out to the countryside.

Visually and geographically, Iolani Palace stands at the center of historic downtown. The building is the only royal residence in the United States, although it housed only three monarchs before Hawaii became a republic. The most tragic of them was Queen Liliuokalani, Hawaii's last monarch, who was deposed and imprisoned in the palace, an insult to the Hawaiian people who were systematically deprived of their lands and leaders. A kukui tree planted by President Roosevelt (FDR) still shades the palace grounds.

Across the street stands the lei-draped statue of Kamehameha the Great before Aliiolani Hali, an impressive colonial-style building. Kamehameha was the first to unite all the Hawaiian islands with both brutal force and astute leadership. This statue is actually a recast of the original, which was lost at sea en route to Honolulu. Many maintain that this is no chance, as the statue should rightfully belong at the king's birthplace in North Kohala on the Big Island. Indeed, after the second casting was erected in Honolulu, the first was recovered and placed in Kohala.

Pedal or walk one block east to Kawaiahao Church, an early church made of coral blocks. Walk a stone-paved path around the building and past a fountain to reach the most interesting part of the church, a small cemetery. Tombstones there read like a Who's Who roster of missionaries and big business families—Cooke, Castle, Bishop, and Alexander. Hawaii's first missionaries struggled in their new home, but their descendants came to control virtually all Hawaii. The same list would closely match the membership of Hawaiian country clubs today, showing how little things have really changed.

One block farther west is the Mission Houses Museum, a cluster of some of Hawaii's oldest buildings (admission charged but grounds free). These modest buildings demonstrate how the new arrivals tried to impose New England standards on Hawaii's tropical climate, paralleling their attempts to do the same with attitudes and values. On Saturdays, special programs by staff dressed in period attire demonstrate craftwork and early printing.

Iolani Palace marks the center of historic Honolulu.

Back at Iolani Palace, you can look for the statue of Liliuokalani between the palace and the modern state building behind it. Behind the state building stands Washington Palace, currently Hawaii's governor's mansion. A plaque in front of the mansion is engraved with Queen Liliuokalani's "Aloha Oe" hymn, Hawaii's unofficial anthem. A few other points of interest dot the area, including the Church of Our Lady of Sorrows and the Territorial Building. Spacious green lawns heighten the sense of grandeur of these historic buildings, contrasting with the cluttered, choking atmosphere of nearby highrises. For clutter of a more interesting type, explore untouristy Chinatown, just a few blocks away.

To extend your explorations from the downtown area, head up to Punchbowl Crater for a good city overview. Yes, cyclists, it is uphill, but only to 500 feet. Just think of the ride as good training for the tours ahead. To ride there, pedal up Queen Emma Street and follow green signs to Punchbowl National Cemetery (not up Punchbowl Street, which is one way in the wrong direction). When Puowaine turns into Tantalus Drive, make a sharp right turn to Punchbowl Crater, a road lined with flags. As a military cemetery, Punchbowl is a solemn place and not a recreational park, so you are not permitted to pedal within the crater. However, you can walk your bike (10 minutes) up to the overlook for broad views over all Honolulu, Diamond Head at one extreme and the Pearl Harbor area on the other.

While you are already there, 500 feet on the way to Tantalus, why not continue directly into that ride? Well, the 2,000-foot climb may dissuade you, but look on the bright side—from Punchbowl, only 1,500 feet remain. The long climb is absolutely worth undertaking at some point for its tremendous views and, better still, its sense of peace and natural order. The Tantalus section of Oahu's Additional Suggested Rides describes the circular route (9-mi loop from Waikiki).

Pearl Harbor/U.S.S. *Arizona* Memorial

The state of Hawaii hosts over 100,000 visitors per day on average, and approximately 99,999 of them seem to visit the U.S.S. *Arizona* Memorial at Pearl Harbor at the same time each day. Indeed, the memorial is Hawaii's most visited attraction, now run by the National Park Service with a staff largely augmented by veteran volunteers.

The memorial is a very interesting place for reasons beyond historic value. Park programs and rangers do a good job of conveying various dimensions of the surprise attack that led to the United States's entry into World War II, at the world, national, and personal level. The free

U.S.S. Arizona *Memorial at Pearl Harbor*

75-minute tour includes film footage of the bombing and a boat trip out to the *Arizona* Memorial, a structure that spans the hull of the sunken ship. Visitors can be as interesting as the site itself. Many represent living history as veterans who survived the attack or who passed through Honolulu on their way to other Pacific theatres. Visitors also include a significant number of Japanese tourists, creating an interesting dichotomy at the site. Those who consider Japanese visitation inappropriate, however, should think twice and consider the number of U.S. citizens who visit the memorial at Hiroshima.

Early arrival at the *Arizona* Memorial is optimal; by mid-morning, the wait for a mandatory (but free) tour can stretch into hours. Either work in a visit with one of the long Oahu circle tours (Tour Nos. 16 or 17) or day trip from Honolulu. From Waikiki hop on Bus #20—but get an early start, or you'll do no hopping. Buses to popular tourist attractions like Pearl Harbor and Hanauma (*bay*) become so full by 9:00 A.M. that they often drive straight past designated stops.

Along the Way

Two prime hiking and mountain biking areas near Honolulu are Tantalus (see Additional Suggested Rides) and Keaiwa Heiau State Park, high above Aiea and Pearl Harbor. Keaiwa Heiau State Park permits free camping (with permit from the Honolulu office), although the high damp area makes a better day destination than overnight rest stop. Aiea Loop Trail is a circular route that takes 2 hours to cover on foot, or 1 hour of technically demanding biking. The loop trail passes fine vistas over Pearl Harbor and undeveloped interior valleys, and visitors may also stop by the park's historic *heiau*.

Tantalus trails are closer to the center of Honolulu, but seem as distant, thanks to the lush, undeveloped mountain area they cover. Many trails branch off Tantalus Heights Drive and Round Top Drive, an excellent opportunity to combine bicycling with hiking. For trail information, contact the division of state parks (see Accommodations).

TOUR NO. 16

WINDWARD OAHU
Touring Oahu's Northeast Coast

Distance: 116 miles
Riding time: 3 days
Difficulty: Moderate
Terrain: Easy coastal ride with one 1,000-foot climb
Roads: Well paved, moderately busy roads
Connecting tours: All Oahu rides

By far the most enjoyable and easy ride on Oahu, this tour offers a little of everything Hawaii is famous for: dramatic volcanic ridges, beaches, surf breaks, prime snorkeling bays, missionary churches, and ancient ruins. With easy connections to and from the airport in Honolulu, this tour is one of the easiest to cover within the span of a short vacation. Those with more time can link into other tours on Oahu or neighbor islands, or approach the ride in a more leisurely manner. Cyclists can divide the tour into even shorter segments for maximum time at sights like Hanauma, the Polynesian Cultural Center, or pounding Banzai Pipeline.

This circle tour lends itself to a number of different budget levels and corresponding accommodations. Bed-and-breakfast inns offer convenience and comfort at many points along the route for cyclists with more permissive budgets. Those on a tighter scale can combine camping with one night at hostel-style accommodations on their way around Windward Oahu. Fortunately for them, two secure public parks allow pleasant camping with peace of mind.

Waikiki to Kailua: 28 miles

The first day of this tour rounds Oahu's southeast corner to the Windward Coast, the island's most scenic side. There are only a few climbs along the way, setting the standard for this unchallenging seashore route. Blustery winds are the most likely obstacle along this route, with a chance of headwinds on the approach to Makapuu Point. After that, you can expect crosswinds throughout the windward ride. Although the day's distance is relatively short, you will have a full, fun day including time for snorkeling at popular Hanauma (*bay*).

From your accommodations in the Honolulu area, begin the ride by leaving Waikiki's **east end.** Stay on **Kalakaua Avenue**, the street closest to the beach. When the road splits stay **right** on Kalakaua to pass a series of green parks under the shadow of Diamond Head. After passing a park with a fountain, follow the road as it bends **left,** then

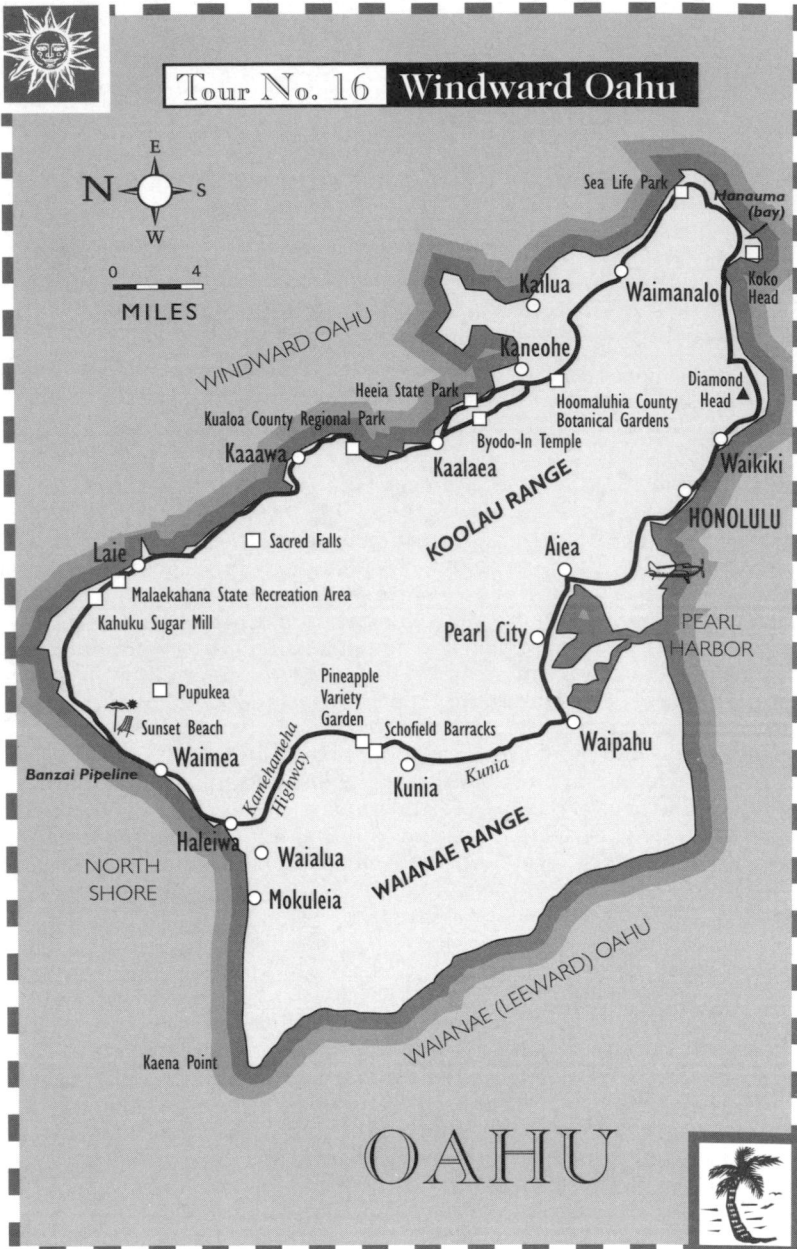

Tour No. 16 **Windward Oahu**

OAHU

turn **right** with signs to Kahala and Diamond Head. Pedal a gradual incline around Diamond Head, where the beautiful coast already contrasts with crowded Waikiki. Far ahead stands distinctive Koko Head, one of the day's recognizable landmarks that beckon you steadily on. When Diamond Head Drive nearly reaches a dead end, turn **left** at the sign for Hanauma on Kealaolu Avenue. This street leads up to **Road 72** (Kalanianaole Highway), which you follow **east (right)**. Unfortunately, this is a busy, noisy road, but as a designated bikeway it also has a wide shoulder.

After 6 mi on this busy road you will reach **Portlock** and the **uphill** climb to **Hanauma**. Shop for lunch supplies for a Hanauma picnic at Foodland, a supermarket on the left at the traffic light at the base of the hill. The **hill** is 0.75 mi long, ascending to the entrance gate to the bay, which lies sheltered below the rise. This climb is the most difficult of the entire tour, which demonstrates how relatively easy the tour really is. If you have been cycling other islands where climbs above 1,000 feet are the name of the game, this will be a breeze. Cyclists just getting rusty muscles rotating again may puff a bit, but the entrance to Hanauma should appear before you gasp your last breath.

Turn **right** and **descend** to the parking area above the bay (13 mi from Waikiki). This high overlook point provides inviting views of the bay with its coral formations showing clearly underwater. Walk your bicycle down the steep **trail** to the beach, a wise safety precaution considering all the pedestrians in the way. Services at Hanauma include snorkel rental, showers, toilets, and refreshment stands. The coral cannot rival the world's best reefs, but bright tropical fish will come face to face with your mask underwater. Before heading into the water, however, take a moment to check out information boards that indicate potential hazards in the bay. Besides snorkeling, you can head to two natural pools along the bay called Witches Brew (located around the right of the bay) and Toilet Bowl (on the left). The latter lives up to its name, flushing bathers around with each good wave. On a good, clear day, neighboring Molokai is visible on the horizon.

Once you have had enough time in Hanauma's waters, **return** to Road 72 to continue the ride. At this point, the shoulder narrows and is squeezed out completely on tight turns of this cliffy area. Backroad cycling it is not, but most traffic runs only as far as Hanauma, and vehicles heading on to Sea Life Park and the Polynesian Cultural Center are courteous enough. Both **lookout points** along the way are worth pausing at. Look for a **blowhole** at the second overlook, with nice views of a sandy strip called (what else) **Sandy Beach**, popular with boogie boarders.

Crazy, confused winds accompany cyclists as they twist through a gap between the rugged hills. The dramatic erosion of these tippy-toes of the Koolau Range reflect Oahu's age, one of the older Hawaiian islands. As you round **Makapuu Point**, another breathtaking lookout offers a vista of the Windward Coast ahead, a fantasy landscape of jagged cliffs and rocky islets. For entertainment, listen to tourists explain sights to each other; you might learn, for example, that Rabbit Island is apparently a bird and rabbit sanctuary (rabbits being anything but in short supply in Hawaii).

Road 72 leads through **Waimanalo** and on to **Kailua**. Kailua, 28 mi from Waikiki, is not a particularly interesting town, but it is a good place to look for indoor accommodations (try local B&Bs) or a supermarket. Those heading downtown can escape traffic by turning right on Keolu Drive (just over 1 mi past a golf course), then follow quieter roads to the town center.

Cyclists aiming for **Kaneohe** or **Hoomaluhia** camping will find it easiest to stay on the highway. When Road 72 comes to a **T**, turn **left** on **Road 61** (still Kalanianaole Highway), then **right** 2 mi later on **Kam Highway** (83) to Kaneohe. Nearly 2 mi after you pass the turnoff to H3, you will reach a shopping area. **Luluku Road** on the left leads up to Hoomaluhia and camping, but first stop by the supermarket on the right (bicycle shop there also). Visitors in search of indoor lodgings may have luck with B&Bs or inexpensive hotels in the Kaneohe area.

Campers must pedal 1 mi up Luluku Road to reach Hoomaluhia County Botanical Gardens' gate and 1 mi more to the Visitor's Center. Hoomaluhia means "make a place of peace and tranquility," a state that has indeed been achieved in this rarely visited park. The 400-acre botanical gardens feature "islands" of land planted with species from each continent in the world. The garden's high "islands" offer terrific views to coastal communities on one side, backed by the sheer vertical lift of the Koolau Mountains.

Hoomaluhia provides cyclists with a delightful opportunity to camp in safety and peace. Campsites are delineated within each of the garden's islands, so just check with the Visitor's Center and select the continent of your choice. Camping is free and secure because the gates are locked each night by the park's resident warden. Call the park

Windward Oahu's sheer cliffs drop to the sea.

(233-7323) ahead of time to check for details and closing days. Mosquitos can come out in force in this high area, so come prepared with repellent.

Kailua to Waimea: 41 miles

This easy cycling day is completely flat with high probability of favorable winds, especially around the island's northeast corner. In a single day, cyclists will progress from eroded cliffs of the Windward Coast to famous surf breaks of the North Shore, taking in a completely new landscape and atmosphere. While Windward Oahu exudes a small-town feeling, the North Shore shows off the more "hippy" character lent to it by surfers and recent imports.

From Hoomaluhia or nearby accommodations, return to the corner of **Kaneohe Bay Drive and Kam Highway** to begin the ride. From that intersection, cyclists can **choose** between continuing straight ahead on Kam Highway (836) for a **quieter coastal ride** past Heeia State Park with its fishpond, **or** following a **busier, inland road** (Kahekili Highway; Road 83) to see a Japanese temple. The coastal route sees few cars, making a more peaceful ride. A line of mangroves marks the obvious outline of **Heeia fishpond**—just look right upon entering the state park. Farther south, you might recognize the shape of Coconut Island, which starred as Gilligan's Island in the television series.

For the **latter option**, turn **left** at the starting intersection. Byodo-In **Temple** is 1.5 mi off the main road (signed left), a serene building set among Japanese gardens where peacocks flash their colors in a reflecting pond. An entrance fee is not always collected at the entry gate. Road 83 is quite busy, but a narrow shoulder helps cyclists along. Either way, both roads meet a few miles south of Kaalaea.

After the **roads merge**, the shoulder fades, but traffic remains at a manageable level. The only exceptions are buses making the run to the Polynesian Cultural Center, but that attraction's late opening time delays the invasion until afternoon (opening 12:30 P.M.).

Past **Kaalaea**, you will round a turn to come upon a beautiful, curving bay with rich tropical colors and views to **Chinaman's Hat**. Vertical cliffs create a stunning backdrop to the distinct islet, and in the foreground small fishing boats float on aquamarine waters—all in all, perhaps the most scenic view of the Windward Coast. Before leaving it all behind, tarry a while in **Kualoa County Regional Park** on the north side of the bay (picnic tables and restrooms there).

A number of tiny communities and small general stores line the road to Laie, a world apart from Honolulu's bustle. Just north of Kualoa, the chimney stack of an old **sugar mill** stands on the left, a testament to past enterprises of this area.

Another bend in the coast brings cyclists to **Kaaawa**, a unique name even in Hawaii, where few words sport three A's in a row. Just sound the name out slowly—Ka'a'awa. The shape of a lion crouches above **Kahana Bay**, a deep cleft in the shoreline. To spot the lion (or any other shape your imagination fancies), look up from the Crouching Lion Inn in **Kaaawa**.

A grove of ironwood trees shelters a county park at the deepest part of the bay. Farther north, you will pass **Punaluu** and the turnoff for **Sacred Falls State Park** (past the 23-mi mark). Sacred Falls is a popular hiking destination, but the long excursion (over 1 hour walking) is rather impractical for cyclists at the midpoint of their ride. The coastal ride offers more beaches and views as consolation, with a few more towns and small historic churches along the way.

Laie is a predominantly Mormon town best known for the **Polynesian Cultural Center** (PCC), one of the top tourist draws in Hawaii. You can't miss spotting PCC for all the flags waving madly around a spraying fountain. Many Pacific islands are represented in replica "villages," usually staffed by natives of that island who demonstrate crafts and traditions.

There are two problems with visiting the center. First, PCC does not open until 12:30 P.M., significantly delaying your progress. Those interested in spending a lot of time there can end the day's ride earlier, by camping in Malaekahana State Park. Second, PCC is registered as non-profit by the Mormon Church, but the admission rivals Disneyland fees. In any case, Laie also has a large supermarket beside the main road, and a gargantuan Mormon Temple can be seen down a long avenue as you pedal out of town.

Malaekahana State Recreation Area is another 2 mi up the road. Cyclists who passed by PCC might be tempted to take a break on the beach here instead or walk to Mokuauia (Goat Island) at low tide. Surf and wind may conspire against your efforts, however, the two elements often raging with impressive force on this exposed windward area. The park allows camping in an enclosed, supervised area 0.75 mi north of the first park entrance. To reserve a site, telephone the park directly at 293-1736.

The last Windward Coast sight along Road 83 is **Kahuku Sugar Mill**, now converted into a shopping mall. Don't get too excited, however: the mall seems to have limited success, offering little of interest besides a convenient post office and a smoothie stand. Putting Kahuku behind, cyclists now make a long, sweeping turn around Oahu's northeast corner from the Windward Coast to the North Shore. Crosswinds turn to tailwinds that breeze cyclists 5 mi to **Turtle Bay**, and soon after, famous North Shore surf breaks. In winter, surf reaches suicidal heights of 30 feet or more, dropping to more tame heights at other times of year.

Sunset Beach is the first of these internationally known surf breaks. Although no signs mark the beach, you can easily recognize it by the parking area and takeout stands across the street with names like Sunset Pizza. Surf aside, the white beaches are nice year-round, each divided by rocky promontories, with views down the North Shore's long curve to Kaena Point far in the distance. Swimmers should be very careful to heed warnings, however, as offshore currents can be treacherously strong.

After Sunset, you will pass **Ehukai Beach County Park** and then world-famous **Banzai Pipeline.** Winter surf draws top-notch surfers who put on incredible displays of balance and skill—or sheer stupidity, depending on your mindset.

Pupukea Beach County Park and a Foodland supermarket signal

Riding the waves on Oahu's North Shore

your arrival in **Waimea** town, a favorite North Shore hangout. Backpackers offers the cheapest indoor accommodations in town in a sprawling hostel/motel-type arrangement with beds in shared (coed) cottages with full kitchens and private singles. The North Shore is lined by B&Bs and a few cheap surfers' hangouts. The nearest parks that permit camping are Haleiwa Beach Park (county) or Kaiaka State Park, both near Haleiwa (neither open consistently).

Once settled in, you can spend time on the beaches or take a short trip to nearby Waimea Falls. For a more demanding side trip, ride uphill past Foodland for 2 mi to reach Puuomahuka Heiau State Monument, a peaceful site with high views over the North Shore.

Waimea to Waikiki: 47 miles

The tour's final day closes the loop around Windward and North Shore Oahu, returning to Honolulu by way of a gradual 1,000-foot climb over the island's agricultural interior. Apart from a handful of fairly interesting sights at the peak of the climb, cyclists can cover the day's distance in a quick, uninterrupted ride.

Begin by continuing **west** along trusty **Kam Highway** (83) from Waimea, a quick 5 coastal mi to **Haleiwa**. The town was named for the frigate birds (*iwa*) that frequent its shores and remains a pleasant area to poke through despite peripheral development. Like Waimea, Haleiwa is a popular place with an interesting blend of old-time tradition and new-age characters. Surf shops dominate the town's main road, although fast-food chains have recently wormed their way in as well.

Beyond Haleiwa, Kam Highway comes to a **traffic circle**, a point to make a few **decisions**. First, cyclists eager to complete a full loop around Oahu can connect directly into Tour No. 17 around Kaena Point and the Waianae (Leeward) Coast. To do so, head straight along the coast for Waialua and Mokuleia. Those heading back into Honolulu can remain on the Kam Highway across the central valley.

Kam Highway begins to climb immediately, with a suitable shoulder until the crest of the climb to compensate for the busy road. During the steady ascent, the road passes sugarcane and then pineapple fields at higher elevations. Dole's processing plant on the right is not open to visitors, but its **Pineapple Pavilion**, a little farther up on the left, sells samples and juices. Soon after, the road comes to a Y intersection, one corner of a large triangle and the summit of the climb. Although cyclists can head straight to follow Kam Highway into Honolulu, that road becomes uncomfortably busy with no shoulder. Instead, turn **right at the Y** toward Schofield Barracks and a quieter alternative road. Dole also maintains a pineapple variety **garden** straight ahead, so detour there first before doubling back for the side road.

In less than 1 mi, turn **left** on an intersecting road (**99**) toward Schofield Barracks. **Schofield** is essentially a town in itself, the heart of the military's obvious presence on Oahu.

From Schofield, follow **Kunia Road** (750) down toward Pearl Harbor instead of returning to Kam Highway (now number 99). Kunia Road is a side route with more shoulder space and far fewer cars, allowing a more relaxing descent to the bustling communities around **Waipahu** and Pearl City. Near the bottom, you will **cross under H1** and soon after turn **left** on **Road 90** (Farrington Highway) toward **Pearl City** and Honolulu.

As Road 90 runs **east** toward **Aiea** and Honolulu, traffic picks up and the shoulder narrows as a number of other roads merge and branch away. Be especially careful at intersections where you must cross lanes of traffic to make left turns. As you near **Pearl Harbor**, Diamond Head's distinctive form becomes visible far in the distance, a beacon drawing you cautiously on through urban traffic.

Near the U.S.S. *Arizona* Memorial and Aloha Stadium, cyclists should bear **right** on a **bike trail** that begins at an **intersection** with McGrew Street. The trail is short but sweet, helping you avoid another tricky left turn through traffic. When the trail ends, cyclists are deposited back on a road with no shoulder, but relief lies just ahead. Soon you will pedal up to the U.S.S. *Arizona* Memorial, after which the main road has a good wide shoulder designated as a bikeway. Follow green BIKEWAY signs up to an intersection with Radford Avenue. At Radford, turn **left** to pedal the opposite sidewalk, **cross** an overpass over a multi-lane highway, and then turn **right** on a wide, separate **bicycle lane**.

This bicycle lane runs by **warehouses** until passing the **airport** and finally ending on **Dillingham Avenue**. Cyclists who pedaled to Waikiki from Honolulu Airport will be back on familiar ground here, repeating their original eastward ride. Rejoin traffic on Dillingham, and in 1 mi, turn **right** at the sign for **Nimitz Highway**, then **left** on that main road (those heading for Sand Island should turn right). For 2 mi, cyclists will relish their own lane while passing through industrial areas.

When the bicycle lane ends at **Fort Street** in the **downtown Honolulu** area, simply continue **straight** along the road. Nimitz becomes Ala Moana Boulevard and enters **Waikiki.** On the way to your lodgings (see Waikiki in the Oahu introduction), keep in mind that most roads in this compact area are one way.

TOUR NO. 17

LEEWARD OAHU
Road and Mountain Biking around Kaena Point

Distance: 99 miles
Riding time: 3 days
Difficulty: Moderate
Terrain: Flat coastal roads, one 1,000-foot climb
Roads: Paved except 5 rough miles around Kaena Point
Connecting tours: All Oahu rides

This tour is only for those dedicated to completing a full circle of Oahu or enthralled by the prospect of a mountain-bike adventure around Kaena Point. A challenging upland route around the point and poor lodgings options on the Leeward Coast create too many distractions for casual cyclists to make the trek worthwhile. Those dedicated to traversing roads less traveled, on the other hand, will have a field day negotiating the obstacles of this ride. A mountain bike is a must for rounding Kaena Point, while road bikers can only follow the tour up to the end of the road on the North Shore.

The first leg of the tour begins innocently enough, with a ride over Oahu's central plateau to beeline for the North Shore. From there, however, road conditions and topography create a far more demanding scenario. In dry periods, the unpaved jeep track around Kaena Point may be pedaled with relative ease, a pleasant ride through a scenic natural area. On the other hand, wet spells turn the trail into a mud bath, creating a trying obstacle for fully loaded mountain bikers. After emerging back on pavement, cyclists are ready to cruise down Oahu's Leeward Coast. The main difficulty there is logistical, a question of locating reliable accommodations. County and state park officials warn visitors against camping in Leeward public parks (see Accommodations), and reasonably priced indoor lodgings can be difficult to come by.

Nevertheless, cyclists who muddle their way past these obstacles will complete the tour feeling satisfied at having seen a worthwhile side of Oahu that few others do. Before setting off, however, take the trouble to plan ahead, a precaution that can smooth out potential wrinkles in your plans. Research the Leeward Coast accommodations situation as well. Those counting on indoor lodgings should not set off without firm reservations because few places permit single-night stays. Campers should only consider Leeward park sites if they travel at least in pairs.

Waikiki to Mokuleia: 43 miles

The first part of this ride winds west through urban Honolulu, a time to exercise patience and caution. You will soon leave the city tangle behind for quieter high ground in Oahu's central valley, which divides the eroded Waianae and Koolau ranges. The ride out of Honolulu is constantly noisy and unpleasant, but not particularly unsafe. Be patient with the knowledge that the greater Honolulu area represents the exception rather than the rule to road conditions, even on this densely populated island.

To begin from Waikiki, follow Ala Moana Boulevard **west**, reversing the bicycle route from the airport. Ala Moana has no bike lane or shoulder, but traffic is bearable if you avoid rush hour. Concentrate and be assertive, claiming a safe space for yourself on the side of the road. Ala Moana becomes Nimitz Highway, which has a **bicycle lane** for 2 mi beyond the downtown area. Just when the lane ends, cyclists should turn **right** up Waiakamilo Avenue, then **left** on Dillingham Boulevard. Another quiet **bicycle lane** begins to the **right** of the point where Dillingham meets **H1**, just past Schuman's Used Cars.

The marked bicycle route runs past the **airport** and then along sidewalks. Signs indicate a **left** to **cross over H1** and then come to a large **intersection** on **Radford Drive**, where BIKE ROUTE signs are cryptic. The designated **bike route** is actually the oncoming lane of the road to the right; therefore **cross the street twice** and **follow the wide shoulder** of that road toward the U.S.S. *Arizona* Memorial in **Pearl Harbor**.

After passing the memorial, you must pedal a **busy road**, following signs for Roads 90 and then 99, Kamehameha ("Kam") Highway. Along this busy road, cyclists must **bear left twice, crossing lanes of traffic**. Once past **Leeward Community College**, Kam Highway turns off to the right, cutting a shorter route to the North Shore. However, that road absorbs most northbound traffic, making for a hairy ride with little shoulder space. Instead, pedal another 4 mi toward Waipahu to access the much quieter Kunia Road.

To reach **Waipahu, do not turn right** on Kam Highway, but go **straight on Road 90** (Farrington Highway). Eventually BIKE ROUTE signs will reappear, leading **right** (inland). Cross **under H1** and continue **straight** on what is now **Kunia Road**, finally reaching quieter ground. You will appreciate the relative peace and wide shoulder of Kunia Road, passing fields of sugarcane and pineapples. The road **climbs** steadily to the top of this central valley. Along the way, you will pass near **Kunia**, a typical plantation town of simple, orderly houses. The settlement reminds modern-day visitors of the not-so-distant days when King Sugar and other agricultural industries dictated nearly every aspect of island life.

Cresting the top of the central rise, you will pass **Schofield Barracks**, a reminder of the military's weighty presence on Oahu (25 percent of the island's land is controlled in some way by the military). At a Y intersection beyond Schofield, you can bear **left for Waialua** for a direct descent to the coast. For a slight detour to points of marginal interest, keep **right for Wahiawa** instead.

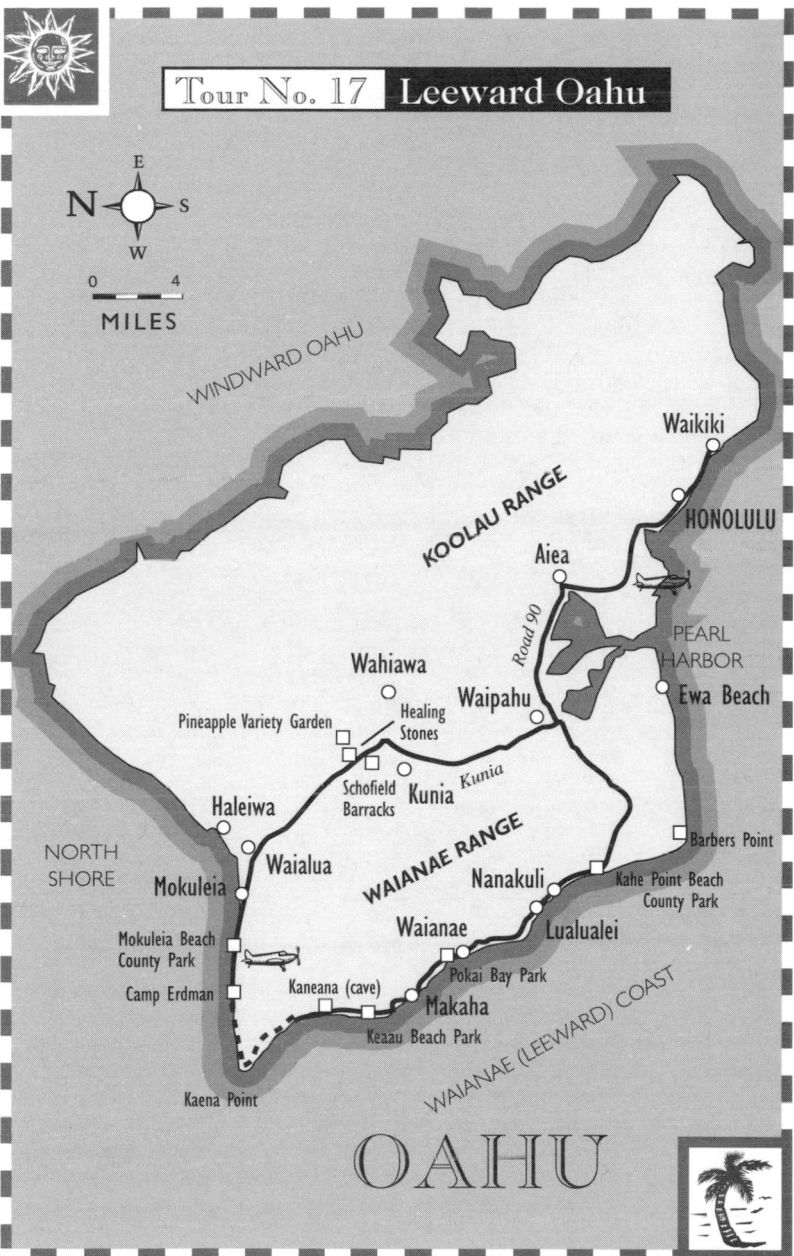

Tour No. 17 — Leeward Oahu

N E S W

0 4
MILES

WINDWARD OAHU

KOOLAU RANGE

Road 90

Waikiki

HONOLULU

Aiea

PEARL HARBOR

Wahiawa

Waipahu

Ewa Beach

Pineapple Variety Garden

Healing Stones

Schofield Barracks

Kunia

Kunia

Haleiwa

WAIANAE RANGE

Nanakuli

Barbers Point

NORTH SHORE

Waialua

Mokuleia

Waianae

Lualualei

Kahe Point Beach County Park

Mokuleia Beach County Park

Camp Erdman

Kaneana (cave)

Pokai Bay Park

Makaha

Keaau Beach Park

WAIANAE (LEEWARD) COAST

Kaena Point

OAHU

For the latter course, take **exit 9** for Kam Highway soon after the right turn, and then go **left for Waialua** (Road 80) at the light. At the **intersection** with California Road, turn **right** for a visit to **Wahiawa Botanical Gardens**. Less than a mile away, the gardens offer twenty-seven acres of peace with many rare and exotic species. Alternatively, a left turn on California Road leads to the **Healing Stones**, an unimpressive collection of rocks (in a cement-block shelter beside the Methodist Church) that believers made pilgrimages to early in this century.

As you continue down **Road 80**, you will pass a supermarket on the left and many fast-food places that have sprung up like weeds around the military bases. Outside town, a slightly more interesting collection of stones can be reached by turning left on a dirt road opposite the turn to Whitmore Village (Road 804). These **Royal Birth Stones** are sheltered within a grove of trees, a pleasant place for a break even if you are not interested in their supernatural powers. Many island chiefs were born at this site, since early Hawaiians believed the children born here would be granted special protection and success.

Just up the road from the Birth Stones is a **triangle** where three roads meet. Bear **left for Waialua** to head for the coast. For one last detour, however, first turn right to visit a modest pineapple variety **garden** that grows along that leg of the triangle. Then put your new identification skills to work as you whoosh by pineapple fields on the **descent** to Waialua.

Outside Waialua stands a snack stand and a jumbled intersection called **Thompson Corner**. Unless you want to visit town or shop for groceries, turn **left** for Mokuleia. After **Waialua**, there are no stores until Makaha, late in the next day's ride. From Thompson Corner, it is 8 mi to Mokuleia campsites. On the way out this remote road, you will pass only a few small ranches and quiet homes. Campers can stop at **Mokuleia Beach County Park**, a nice, grassy spot on the water, or continue to Camp Erdman. After passing the end of **Dillingham Airfield**, be sure to look left for the **waterfall** that cascades down a crack in the impressive cliffs. YMCA's **Camp Erdman** is marked to the **right** soon after the airfield. The site is more expensive than county camping, but Camp Erdman is a more secure site with resident staff and full amenities (call ahead: 637-4615). Cyclists seeking indoor accommodations can try for a B&B in Waialua.

Mokuleia to Nanakuli: 25 miles

Although this leg of the tour is only 25 mi long, that distance can easily require a full day to cover due to the rugged stretch around Oahu's northwestern tip, Kaena Point. Pavement ends only 1 mi past Camp Erdman, from which point a bumpy 5-mi dirt track takes over. The degree of adventure of the ride lies in direct proportion to the amount of recent rainfall. In dry, clear weather, mountain bikes should have a fun time exploring Oahu's least-visited corner. If it has been raining recently, on the other hand, the ride can turn into a miserable walk. After a week-long storm drenched Oahu, for example, it took nearly 4 hours to round Kaena, mostly on foot. Thick mud can clog wheels to the point that they cannot turn, making constant stops

Mountain biking Kaena Point: the agony and the ecstasy

necessary. The moral of the story is do not fight the elements, and pray to the bicycle god for cooperative weather.

Another potential obstacle is washouts in the dirt track, so slow down when rounding blind corners. Riding in pairs or more is a good idea not only for safety but also for help when coming across obstacles like these. The likelihood of having to unload your bike and carry it across or around a washout is high. Remember, it's not just a bicycle tour, it's an adventure!

After you set off down the **dirt track**, you must lift your bike over a knee-high bar at a **roadblock** that keeps jeeps out of the nature preserve (legally open to mountain bikers and hikers). The roadblock should remind cyclists that they must be doubly sensitive in this protected area. **Stay on the trail** at all times to prevent scarring the land or disturbing birds that nest in low brush.

The track is **rocky, then sandy** near **Kaena Point**. **Stones outline the correct trail** around the point, where you may struggle through patches of deep sand. Views from this remote area are raw and humbling, with sharp cliffs unmarked by development of any kind. Even if Kauai is not visible at the time of your visit, a cluster of clouds should give away the neighboring island's position.

Kaena is Oahu's westernmost point and one of the last intact dune ecosystems on the islands. The restricted area protects sand-dune and boulder-slope ecosystems that provide nesting sites for albatross and green turtles. Other visitors include Hawaiian monk seals and humpback whales during the winter breeding season. The State Forestry Department's brochure on Kaena includes an introductory guide with photos of plants and animals. The brochure describes vegetation like *pohinahina*, a colonist plant that keeps sand from blowing away, its flower popular for use in leis. It also explains derivations of some plant names like the *nehe*, named for the rumbling of the sea.

As you round Kaena Point, outstanding views of the arid Waianae Cliffs unfold along the uneven coast, with deeply etched valleys and high eroded peaks above foaming sea waters. This southern leg is easier than the stretch up to the point, because you can now see the light at the end of the tunnel. **Pavement** resumes at a point beneath the large white building visible down the coast.

Swimming and surfing are possible at the beach where pavement begins. As always, be careful when swimming as conditions vary greatly from season to season and even from day to day. The mouth of **Kaneana**, a sacred cave, gapes just 2 mi farther along the road. Native beliefs held that men emerged onto the earth from this cave of Kane, the creation god (*ana* means cave).

Moving farther south, cyclists will gradually re-enter the modern world. **Traffic** picks up as you progress **south**, reaching a crescendo the next day, on Oahu's busy south shore. Unfortunately, cyclists must endure long, shoulderless stretches of road, but at least congestion keeps car speeds down when traffic is high. History buffs might detour 1 mi inland to reconstructed **Kaneaki Heiau** by turning inland on Kipi Drive. To reach the site, one must pass through the gates of Mauna Olu Estates; admission is free but permitted only from 10:00 A.M. to 2:00 P.M. daily except Monday.

Several supermarkets line the main road (Farrington Highway; Road 93) in both **Makaha** and Nanakuli. Towns are not marked as you enter them, so keep track of your distance and position to identify each. If your bike (your gear, your legs, or your entire body) is extremely muddy from the Kaena ride, keep an eye open for a hose at a campground or gas station along the way. For a break from the road, turn into **Pokai Bay Park** in Waianae. At the end of the side road stands shaded Malaea Heiau, a temple dedicated to the dog spirit—just the sort of place for visitors who miss their four-legged friends back home.

Finally you will pass through **Lualualei** and enter **Nanakuli**, which has gas stations and two supermarkets. To reach **Nanakuli Beach County Park**, turn right after the school and basketball court. Camping is permitted in this park, although the Honolulu office and many locals advise against it. Although homeless people live in the park, many are families, which is somewhat reassuring in terms of security concerns, if not societal ones. The camping situation at **Kahe Point Beach County Park**, a few miles south, is no more reassuring.

Cyclists looking for indoor lodgings along the Waianae Coast confront limited options. Unless a B&B service can help, you will have a difficult time finding one-night accommodations (as opposed to weekly rentals). Most hotels and condos cluster around Makaha, a prime winter surfing or summer snorkeling area.

Nanakuli to Waikiki: 31 miles

With two-thirds of this circle tour and the most challenging terrain behind you, you are ready to close the loop back to Honolulu. Few sights mark the last leg of this tour, making it a fairly quick breeze to Pearl Harbor. Progress back through the suburban mess of western Honolulu will be slowed again by traffic, although familiarity with the bikeways helps ease your way.

Simply follow **Farrington Highway** (Road 90) **south** and then **east**, a suitable shoulder making traffic easier to bear. The ride will test how recently your map was compiled, since the entire Barbers Point/Ewa area is undergoing extensive development and construction detours change the situation daily. Your surest course is to remain on Farrington Highway, which becomes a quiet back road itself after H1 branches off. Only upon entering **Waipahu** do cyclists return to more heavily trafficked roads. Many locals pedal along sidewalks to avoid the busy road. Remain patient and alert while faithfully following **signs for Road 90 west**. Designated **bicycle lanes** commence shortly before the U.S.S. *Arizona* Memorial, helping you avoid the worst sections of road in Honolulu itself.

Alternatively, you might be tempted to look for a bicycle trail that runs along an abandoned railroad line along the north shore of Pearl Harbor. The trail consists of hard-packed dirt suitable for road bikes. Although the trail may be tricky to locate, it makes a nice alternative for cyclists who feel nervous on suburban roads.

As you near Aloha Stadium, a short length of **bicycle trail** beginning at the **intersection** of McGrew Street will tease you with an abbreviated taste of peace on a leafy side lane. This lane lets cyclists avoid another hairy left-lane crossover, then deposits them back on the road. After a short, uncomfortable run to the U.S.S. *Arizona* Memorial on the shoulderless road, the **main bicycle route into the city** begins.

Provided you are not in much of a rush, this is a good time to visit the U.S.S. *Arizona* Memorial in Pearl Harbor (see Oahu introduction).

Along **Road 90** near the U.S.S. *Arizona* Memorial BIKE ROUTE signs commence, guiding cyclists as they reverse their original route out of Honolulu. Turn **left** at Radford Street to ride the **sidewalk over H1** and then turn **right** on the continuation of the **bicycle lane**. This handy, now-familiar trail provides safety and relief from traffic as you pass the **airport**, eventually coming to an end on Dillingham Boulevard. Ride straight down Dillingham for 1 mi until the signed **right** turn down to Nimitz Highway. Another 2 mi stretch of designated **bicycle lane** leads downtown, then leaves bikers back on the road. Soon Nimitz Highway becomes **Ala Moana Boulevard**, the main route into **Waikiki**.

Upon closing the circle, you will reap the benefits of returning to a familiar area, knowing exactly which accommodations to head for and how. Back in Waikiki, cyclists can take some time off their wheels to prepare for further adventures on neighbor islands.

ADDITIONAL SUGGESTED RIDES

Diamond Head Day Ride: 8-mile loop from Waikiki

Perhaps the most easily recognized landmark in Honolulu is Diamond Head, the distinctive cone rising at the east end of Waikiki. The cone was formed by a last, late hiccup of volcanic activity on Oahu. During a free morning or afternoon in Honolulu, make time for the great bike/hike trip to Diamond Head for a new perspective or an escape from urban chaos.

Hikers gain unbeatable views from Diamond Head.

To begin the short ride, leave Waikiki by pedaling east toward the zoo and Kapiolani Park. When Kalakaua Avenue, the street paralleling Waikiki Beach, divides in the park, bear left on Monserrat Avenue to curve around Diamond Head (the road becomes Diamond Head Drive). The road's gradual grade helps ease your way uphill, until you reach signs that point right for Diamond Head Crater. To enter the crater itself, you will pedal through a well-lit tunnel, then emerge in sunshine.

A military installation shares space with a public park on the crater floor, but the real attraction lies 560 feet above—the very summit of Diamond Head (called Leahi), 760 feet above sea level. Although signs insist that the hike up requires 1 hour and sturdy shoes, 30 minutes in sandals is more realistic for fit cyclists.

Leahi commands some of the best views on southern Oahu, extending from the long strip of Waikiki to impressive Tantalus and other misty, inland mountains as well as east to Koko Head. Straight down from Diamond Head, you will have bird's-eye views over a lighthouse, sumptuous homes, and offshore windsurfers who hang in the air as they vault off waves. It is a beautiful sight as long as you don't dwell on the fact that in the 1940s only two hotels marked palm-lined Waikiki, now a tangle of skyscrapers.

To return to town, ride **back** through the **tunnel** to the main road. Rather than retracing your original route, however, turn **right** on Diamond Head Drive to complete a circle around Diamond Head. On the way, cyclists will enjoy a nice **downhill** run past the lighthouse and several overlook points where you can walk down to the beach.

Tantalus Day Ride: 9-mile circle

An excellent farewell ride before departing Oahu is a loop up and around Tantalus, above Honolulu. The mountain getaway is accessible via a U-shaped scenic drive comprised of Tantalus Drive, which runs up a western ridge, and Round Top Drive, which circles back down along an eastern ridge. Those pedaling up from Waikiki cannot ascend directly up Pensacola Avenue, which is a southbound one-way road. Instead, ride up Ward Avenue to circle **clockwise** around Punchbowl Crater. Bear **left** on Puowaine Avenue (which turns into Tantalus Drive) instead of making a sharp right up the flag-lined driveway of Punchbowl Cemetery. Ideally, detour into Punchbowl Crater while you are passing by, or combine this outing with a tour of Honolulu's downtown as described in the Oahu introduction. Cyclists will be amazed at how serene and undeveloped the area is despite its proximity to Honolulu's crowded center.

KAUAI
The Garden Isle

Kauai stands out as a gem even within the beautiful tropical chain of Hawaii. Its star attractions, the stunning Na Pali coast and Waimea Canyon—areas many consider worthy of national park distinction—have no parallel in the islands. Kauai is also a well-known center for outdoor activities like kayaking and hiking, attracting and catering to active travelers. The island's attitude, facilities, and natural attributes all make cyclists feel right at home.

No, Kauai is not too good to be true. Other islands also boast of spectacular natural treasures, but many seem to require endless uphill climbs or long treks through remote areas. Kauai, on the other hand, is ringed by a coastal road that allows level seaside riding throughout nearly all the tours. Furthermore, county and state campsites dot the compact island at regular intervals, making Kauai one of the easiest islands to manage on a tight budget. Bed-and-breakfast inns also provide comfort for bicyclists planning a more leisurely trip.

In many ways, Kauai represents the stereotypical Hawaiian paradise in its dramatic scenery and lush natural wonders. Although deforestation and development have left their mark on the small island, Kauai retains much of its native wildlife. For example, Kauai preserves more of its endemic birds than any other island. The island is widely viewed as Hawaii's back-to-nature destination, and its character is indeed more oriented toward outdoor activities and adventure than packaged beach vacations.

Finally, Kauai remains a quiet place with a neighborly attitude. After Hurricane Iniki ravaged the island and left towns without power for weeks, many people pitched in together to restore working order. Huge neighborhood barbecues were common in the first few days when hotels and supermarkets emptied their freezers of steaks and other perishables and hosted giant block parties. Perhaps due to its fringe location along the Hawaiian chain or to its distinct heritage (unlike other islands, Kauai was first settled by Marquesans, not Tahitians), Kauai remains a unique treasure.

Practical Information

Kauai is the northwesternmost and oldest of the principal Hawaiian Islands. The only inhabited island past Kauai in the island chain is little Niihau, a private island not open to visitors. Beyond Niihau, countless islets and atolls stretch another thousand miles across the ocean. Although Kauai's Mount Waialeale is the wettest place on earth, most of the island enjoys fair weather in the typical windward/leeward pattern.

The much-publicized effects of 1992's Hurricane Iniki were severe, but at this time damage is barely in evidence for new visitors. Hurricane damage has no effect on bicycle travel on Kauai at present, except in keeping tourist numbers low and therefore roads more free of traffic. All the main island towns have large supermarkets where you can stock up on supplies, including Lihue, Koloa, Waimea, Kapaa, Princeville, and Hanalei. Most large stores are open from 7:00 A.M. to 9:00 P.M., but some stay open for business as late as 11:00 P.M.

For specific information on Kauai, contact the island's branch of the Hawaiian Visitor's Bureau at Lihue Plaza Building, Suite 207, 3016 Umi Street, Lihue, HI 96766 (telephone 245-3971). To telephone toll-free from the mainland, dial (800) AH-KAUAI. Upon arrival, leaf through the free *Kauai Beach Press* (available around Lihue) for concert listings and schedules of hula shows and farmer's markets, as well as free classes in feather lei making or hula.

Tips for Touring

Kauai is well suited to two-wheeled touring thanks to seaside roads that avoid long climbs over the mountainous interior. A coastal road rings most of the island, although the impassable northwest coast prevents cyclists from completing a full-circle tour. Instead, tourists who pedal out to Waimea Canyon on the south side or Na Pali to the north must eventually backtrack along the same route to Lihue. There are no roads that shortcut through the interior except the rugged Powerline Trail, suitable only for mountain bikes (see Tour No. 20).

Kauai's southwest side is generally dry while the northeast is wetter, but neither side is too extreme since Waialeale seems to suck in most passing rainclouds. Higher elevations like Kokee State Park and the upper part of Powerline Trail are noticeably cool and damp, so be prepared for potentially adverse conditions before setting out for these high points.

Kauai is dotted with bicycle and sports shops that can lend a hand with advice or repairs. Together with the large number and convenient distribution of campsites throughout the island, these factors help smooth potential kinks in your rides around spectacular Kauai.

Airports

Kauai's principal airport in Lihue is serviced by the main interisland lines on a regular basis. To pedal from the airport to town, exit and turn left on Road 51 to Lihue. A right turn into town 1 mi later puts you on Lihue's main drag, Rice Street. A short ride through the center of town leads past a supermarket, banks, parks, and recreation offices, travel agents, and so on (see below).

Princeville Airport on Kauai's north shore is serviced only by Aloha Island Air's eighteen seater planes. This airport offers a good but potentially complicated alternative to backtracking to Lihue after completing the Na Pali tour (Tour No. 18). Technically, bicycles are accepted as baggage, but there is no guarantee that yours will be shipped immediately if the flight is full or heavily loaded. You must remove all gear from your bicycle, turn the handlebars, remove the pedals, and perhaps remove the wheels in order to fit it in the small plane's cargo space.

If the plane is fully booked and there is no cargo space for your bicycle (which gets last priority), it will be sent on the next available flight. Certain flight times are always overbooked while others carry only a handful of passengers, so try to request a less popular time. Hope for either an empty flight or a completely overbooked flight to which all passengers appear. In the latter case, the airline is obligated to pay for a taxi ride to Lihue for you to catch the first available flight, which will be on a large plane that can more easily accommodate bicycles. Basically Princeville Airport provides a no-can-fail proposition, although you may suffer anxiety and delays before actually getting airborne.

Accommodations

Kauai's reputation as a remote, untouristy island does not mean that it lacks a good selection of accommodations. Although damage from Hurricane Iniki caused many facilities to close temporarily, all but a few are back in business. Kauai is one of the easiest Hawaiian islands to tour, both because coastal roads allow fairly level riding and tent sites are available every step of the way for campers.

ROOMS. Lihue is Kauai's gateway town, but most visitors move on to hotels around Poipu or on the north shore near Na Pali. Many new B&Bs have opened across Kauai in recent years, the highest concentration being around Kapaa and Wailua on the east side. The only hostel on Kauai is a poorly run place with the feel of a commune in Kapaa, but at least it is not restricted to accepting only foreigners (see Tour No. 18).

CABINS. Cyclists pedaling up Waimea Canyon and Kokee State Park can reserve a comfortable cabin in Kokee (see Tour No. 19). In the Koloa area north of Poipu, Kahili Mountain Park offers cabins (Box 298, Koloa, HI 96756, telephone 742-9921). Finally, a YMCA camp in Haena also offers bunks in a large cabin as well as camping (see Tour No. 18).

CAMPING. Kauai is one of the best islands for camping-based bicycle touring because it offers many closely spaced sites. The average distance between sites is about 20 mi, although individual sites are closed at times for various reasons. However, an alternate site is never far away, and Kauai campsites are not subject to closeout days like sites on Oahu.

County parks charge a small fee for each person (free for residents), while camping permits for state parks are free. As elsewhere, you must obtain permits specific to sites and dates. When you obtain permits at the Lihue offices, estimate your itinerary as closely as possible but don't worry about altering it a bit along the way. Contact the parks offices at County Parks and Recreation, 4193 Hardy Street, Lihue, HI 96766 (telephone 245-8821) and Division of State Parks, Box 1671, Lihue, HI 96766 (telephone 241-3444).

Park employees check sites often, waking tent occupants early in the morning if they do not display a permit. They generally do not mind if campers switch sites as long as they have paid for the correct number of nights.

A few sites (most notably Lucy Wright Park in Waimea) shelter some homeless people, but security is generally not a problem. "Residents" can be quite nice and friendly to visitors, the overall situation being much more easy-going than on Oahu. As in any campsite, you should still think twice before leaving valuable gear unattended in your tent, but personal safety is generally not an issue on Kauai.

Clockwise from Na Pali, campsites on Kauai include (county parks unless otherwise noted) Na Pali (state), hike-in sites along the Kalalau Trail (state), Haena Beach, Anini Beach, Hanamaulu, Niumalu (near Nawiliwili south of Lihue), Salt Pond, Lucy Wright (Waimea), Polihale (state), and Kokee (state). Polihale is rarely controlled and surfers often camp there for days at a time, but the dirt access road floods at times.

Lihue

Lihue is no great charmer, but the town makes a practical and central gateway for the Garden Isle. At Lihue Airport, a large stand flutters with leaflets advertising B&Bs, hotels, and outdoor activities. Arriving cyclists who pedal to town from the airport will immediately notice the slow pace and easy-going style of Kauai. If you are touring with a companion, park your bike and partner in Lihue's shady central square while you run errands rather than constantly relocking your bicycle around the compact town center. The square has picnic tables on a nice lawn, and everything you need is located within a few blocks.

FOOD AND ACCOMMODATIONS. Campers will find both state and county offices nearby. The state office is on the corner of Hardy and Eiwa streets off the edge of the park (permits and forestry information on the third floor). For county camping permits, follow Hardy Street and head for the parking lot behind the domed building. The Parks and Recreation office occupies the center section of the low, long building behind the dome (just look for the PERMITS sign). For addresses and telephone numbers, see Accommodations above.

There is a supermarket across Eiwa Street from the state building and a few eateries in central Lihue. Cyclists heading immediately west will also pass others in the Kukui Grove Shopping Center on the edge of town.

Lihue has a handful of basic hotels and motels as well as fancier rooms in the huge Westin Kauai Hotel. The nearest park that permits camping is Hanamaulu Beach County Park, but stop to buy supplies in town before setting out to camp there. To reach Hanamaulu Bay, pedal *mauka* along Rice Street and turn right toward Hanalei on Road 56, a busy road with a narrow shoulder. Pass the hospital, go down and up a river gorge, and turn right on Hanamaulu Beach Road. After passing a school, bear right on Hehi Road to reach the park. The site is in a quiet and pretty bay, although the place is a bit spoiled by airport noise and vehicles that drive directly on the beach (making a snooze in the sand an unhealthy proposition). There are a few homeless camps in the park, but it is a secure, quiet site for the most part. Facilities at Hanamaulu include cold showers and toilets.

SIGHTS. Most tourists bypass Lihue in favor of Kauai's few resorts and areas of natural beauty. The only sight of merit in town is the Kauai Museum, if you have the patience to control your outdoor enthusiasm for a time. The museum is located at 4428 Rice Street, near the central square. To visit a typical Hawaiian church with an atypical interior, visit the Old Lutheran Church outside town on Hoomana Road (ride out Rice Street, turn left on Road 50, and look for the road on the right). Immigrants designed their church interior to resemble their quarters aboard the ship that carried them on their voyage to Hawaii.

Along the Way

HIKING. Many hikers rate Na Pali State Park's Kalalau Trail one of the world's premier walks for its stunning beauty and easy accessibility. Kalalau Trail runs 11 mi along the coast, stopping off at three lush valleys marked by waterfalls, ruins, and tiny sand coves. For a handy guide that describes the hike, sights, and practical matters such as water supply and campsites, stop by Lihue's state park office or contact the Department of Land and Natural Resources (3060 Elwa St, Room 306, Lihue, HI 96766; telephone 241-3444). Kalalau trailhead lies at the end of the road past Hanalei, the northwestern terminus of Tour No. 18 (see that tour for information on accommodations and access).

Cyclists who complete the challenging trek up to Waimea Canyon's 4,000-foot rim (Tour No. 19) should not leave without taking the time to explore the area on foot. A number of prime hikes can easily be covered in a morning or by mid-afternoon, allowing enough time for the easy cruise back down to Waimea town at the end of the day. An excellent resource to use before setting out on any hike is Kokee State Park Visitor's Center and Museum. Information on accommodations and facilities in the area is listed in Tour No. 19. For other information, contact the Division of State Parks in Lihue (see Kauai introduction).

All trailheads may be easily reached on foot or by bike from Kokee cabins or campground. For a serious hike, choose between two long loop hikes: one overlooking the Na Pali coast (11 mi on Nualolo and Awa'awapuhi trails) or one following the canyon's rim (7 mi on Kumuwela, Canyon, and Cliff trails).

KAYAKING. One of the most popular outdoor activities on Kauai is kayaking the island's stunning coastline. In fact, kayaking is the only way to reach parts of the island where sheer cliffs prevent overland travel. Many different operators on Kauai offer tours, most of them clustered in Haena, Kapaa, and Poipu. Tours run from 1 to 6 days; longer tours allow more time for side trips on foot to small valleys, waterfalls, and ruins. Prices average $100 a day or more, but the experience should be worth the price if your budget and time frame allow.

The premier kayaking destination of all Hawaii is of course the Na Pali coast. However, the area may be kayaked only between May and September because winter storms create unsafe, rough conditions. Those who visit Kauai in winter can still turn to good kayaking possibilities on the island's south shore. Amateurs without grandiose plans may also rent a kayak for as little as 1 hour on the calm Wailua River (see Tour No. 18).

RIDE TO NA PALI
Lihue to Na Pali State Park

Distance: 43 miles
Riding time: 1 to 2 days
Difficulty: Moderate
Terrain: Rolling coastal hills
Roads: Paved, traffic in sections
Connecting tours: Tour Nos. 19, 20

Kauai, an island of superlative natural beauty, is best known for its stunning Na Pali coast, a line of scalloped, seaside cliffs carved by relentless natural forces. Not only does the scenery of this tour rival the best in Hawaii, but Kauai's seaside roads let the views be appreciated without enduring extreme challenges of terrain. Easy terrain, short daily legs, and the chance to cover a spectacular hiking trail along Na Pali make this tour an excellent choice for novice or easy-going cyclists who are not driven to simply log hundreds of miles. Practical matters like flights to Kauai and accommodations also allow those on strict time schedules to cover this route within a short vacation period or together with other tours.

The first leg of this tour runs only between Lihue, Kauai's gateway town, and Kapaa, an outdoor activities center on the east shore. That short jog accommodates cyclists who wish to incorporate other activities into their trip, such as an afternoon of kayaking on the Wailua River, a boat trip to Fern Grotto, or mountain-bike rides in the surrounding hills. However, those eager to see the north coast's scenery can speed right ahead and visit Kilauea's picturesque lighthouse, camp at Anini's pretty beach, and look out over the flooded taro fields of Hanalei.

Na Pali's sheer cliffs barely allow space for one winding footpath, let alone a road. Therefore cyclists must factor in time to either retrace their tracks back to Lihue or try to catch a flight out of Princeville's small airport (see the Kauai introduction) once their adventures on the north coast come to an end.

Lihue to Kapaa: 9 miles

The ride from Lihue to Kapaa is only 9 mi, leaving cyclists with two options. First, the short day is designed to allow plenty of time for outdoor activities in Wailua and Kapaa, both outdoor centers with plenty of shops and rental equipment. On the other hand, cyclists impatient for the tour's real highlight, the Na Pali coast, can easily push straight on to Kauai's north shore in a single day's ride of about 40 mi, all on

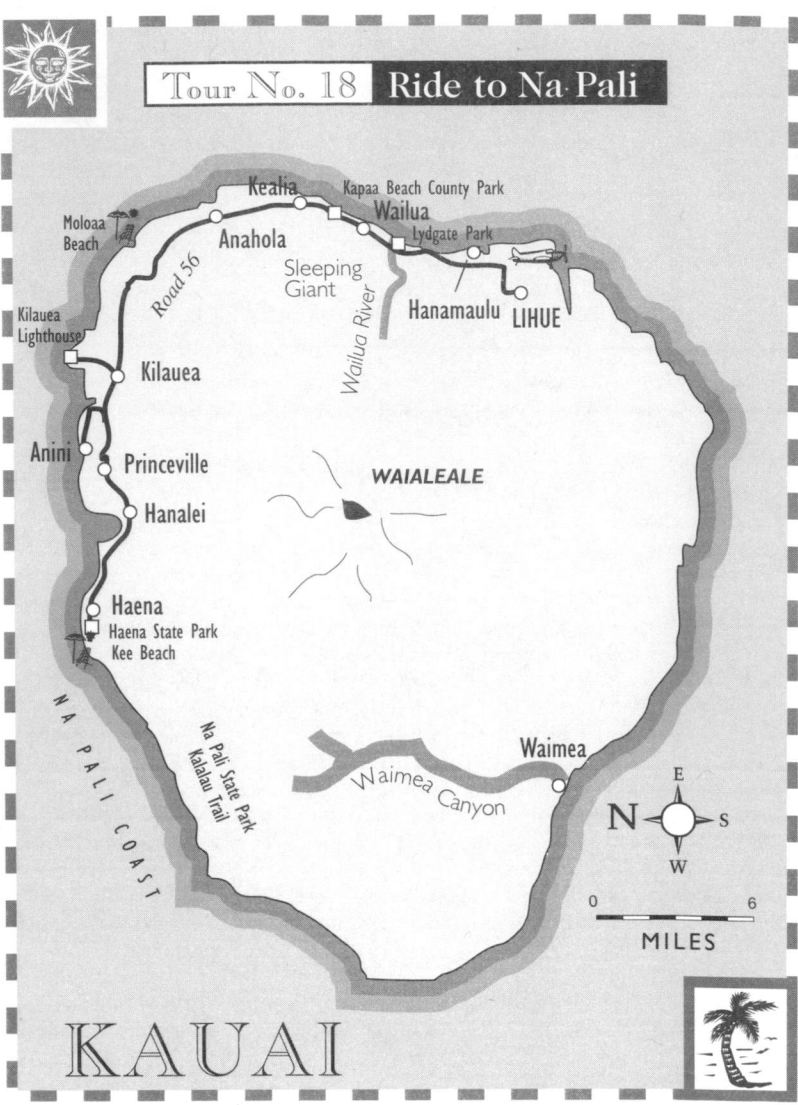

Tour No. 18 Ride to Na·Pali

KAUAI

gently sloping coastal roads. Those who do bypass Wailua's sights have a second chance to visit them on the return trip from Na Pali to Lihue. Campers will have little choice but to move straight ahead, since no parks between Lihue and Anini officially permit tents. Mountain bikers can use a full day in Kapaa to cover trails in Kealia and Sleeping Giant.

Set off up the east coast of Kauai by pedaling **north on Kuhio Highway** (Road 56) toward Hanalei. Unfortunately, this road is uncomfortably busy and fast-paced with only a narrow shoulder until

Kapaa, where traffic thins. Exercise caution on the busy and poorly paved road. In just 5 mi you will come to the town of **Wailua**, a popular stopping point for tourists en route to Na Pali.

The area's top attraction is **Fern Grotto**, but consider shopping for picnic supplies in Wailua either now or after that side trip. Part of its attraction lies in the boat trip necessary to reach the upriver grotto, with the unfortunate side effect of making the trip a somewhat cheesy commercialized venture. Tour boats charge a fee for a cattle-herdlike trip to the "romantic" grotto.

You may be best off foregoing the place in favor of a less crowded, less packaged destination. For example, kayak or canoe rentals make a good alternative for those eager to explore the river on their own. Shop around for a good rental price first, as rates can run quite high. Wailua River is known for its calm waters, perfect for experimenting with an open-shell kayak. You can relax in the river's calm waters, explore tributaries, hike to waterfalls, or explore ruins.

For a cycling **detour**, turn inland on **Road 580** (Kuamoo Road) for 1.5 mi to reach the marked lookout point over **Opaekaa Falls**, another picturesque Hawaiian cascade. Just 0.25 mi from the intersection of 580 and 56 lies a historic temple complex called **Holoholoku Heiau**, once a place of human sacrifice.

Even if you pedal straight by these side attractions, you cannot help but notice the mountain known as **Sleeping Giant**, lying 1 mi north of the junction of Roads 56 and 580. The area is rife with legends of *menehune*, industrious little people who are credited with striking feats and the construction of massive ancient stonework. Islanders from the Marquesas were the first to settle Kauai, only to be overcome by later arrivals from Tahiti, leading many people to postulate that the *menehune* legends owe their origins to the Marquesan legacy. In any case, you will hear of many marvelous and mischievous deeds attributed to *menehunes*, such as the creation of Sleeping Giant. It seems the little people threw stones in an effort to wake the sleeping giant, only to leave him entombed forever.

The ride past Sleeping Giant leads past a long commercial center and into Kapaa's center. **Kapaa** is quite the outdoor center, with three bicycle shops, a dive shop, and several kayak and bicycle rental places.

The Wailua/Kapaa area is chock full of B&Bs, although many require a three-night stay. Budget travelers can head to the Kauai International Hostel in Kapaa instead. Just look for its banner opposite the town beach park from the main road. Your dollars buy a bunk space in a commune-like coed room. Camping is not officially sanctioned in Kapaa's beach park, although locals may look the other way.

Kapaa to Na Pali State Park: 34 miles

Happily, traffic is much lighter beyond Kapaa, leaving you free to enjoy a wide open road and compelling scenery. To continue your interrupted progress from Kapaa, simply remain on **Road 56 north** (Kuhio Highway). Only mountain bikers should bother trying the bike route marked right on Kou Street, a potholed, bumpy dirt track that leads 1.5 mi to **Kealia**, paralleling Road 56.

Kilauea lighthouse illuminates Kauai's north shores.

Road 56 is characterized by gradual slopes that keep you on your toes, cranking steadily up or cruising gently downhill as you round the island's northeast corner. While pedaling around the undeveloped northeast corner of Kauai, look inland for a distinctive mountain rise known as King Kong's profile. About 4 mi north of **Anahola**, mountain bikers can detour off the main way again on Koolau Road. This road is easy to miss, so watch carefully for the sign. If you reach the dairy farm at mile marker 19, you have gone too far. The side road is bouncy and pocked with potholes, but it makes a fun break from the paved road. From Koolau Road, you can also ride a rough side track to rarely visited **Moloaa Beach**.

A good, smooth shoulder hugs Road 56 throughout the ride to Hanalei. Once you turn to ride west along the north shore, you will enjoy beautiful views of the ocean to one side and Kauai's starkly eroded mountains to the other.

Just as you enter **Kilauea**, turn **right** at the sign for Mango Mamma's on **Hooku Road** near the 16-mi mark. After turning right off Road 56, take the first **left**, then go **right** again at the sign for Kilauea **lighthouse**. The photogenic white lighthouse on Kilauea Point is a 1.5-mi ride away. The last section of road may still be closed due to hurricane damage (none of which is evident to the visitor's eye), but even so, you will appreciate the striking view from the overlook point above. The white lighthouse stands sharply against the blue surf, while white wings of birds soaring around the cliffs flash against a blue sky. Birds frequenting the area include redfooted booby and albatross, and visitors often spot porpoises and whales offshore, a designated national wildlife refuge.

To **resume** the westward ride, double back on Kilauea Road and bear right to return to Road 56. Before zooming right along, however, it is worth stopping at Kilauea's small, **lava church** with its unusual lava tombstones. This interesting building lies directly ahead as you turn right from Kilauea Road to return to the main road. Another Kilauea sight is **Guava Kai Plantation**, which offers free samples and tours (located 1 mi *mauka* on Kuawa Road, near the 23-mi marker of Road 56).

After Kilauea, a number of other sights dot the ride to Princeville. Beyond Kilauea, prepare to stop when you see a SCENIC OVERLOOK—100 FEET **sign.** Pull over at a small bridge on the descent before reaching the overlook itself to see a **waterfall** to the **left** of the road. Then stop again at the main overlook point near the bottom of the hill for a tranquil **Kalihiwai Valley** scene where river waters drop off yet another waterfall and wind between lush green banks. From there, well, it is time to negotiate a considerable hill.

At the top of the rise, you can **turn right** for Anini on Kalihiwai Road **or continue straight** ahead for Princeville. The turnoff for Anini is 2 mi west of Kilauea and 12 mi from Haena. Bear **left** on Anini Road from Kalihiwai Road for a 2-mi descent to the beach park. Whether you stop there on this outbound leg of the tour or on the return, campers should try to plan for a night at **Anini**. Anini Beach County Park is one of Kauai's nicest camping spots and also makes a convenient base for those booked on a morning flight from Princeville Airport. Little Anini is more a settlement than a town, with no stores and little commercial development.

Anini's peace and beauty have attracted many wealthy vacationers, who have left their mark in the form of mansionlike vacation homes and the local hot spot, Anini Polo Club. However, the county park remains a homey place with plenty of wide-open space for everyone (including some low-profile homeless). Best of all, the park borders on a

Kilauea's missionary-era lava church

pretty white beach dotted with palms. Just pick the tree of your choice and pitch camp. Then you are free to dip in the rolling waves, beach-comb, and catch nice views back to Kilauea lighthouse in the distance.

Back on Road 56, you can quickly cruise the last few miles to **Princeville**. Although Kauai's north-shore development is not as ex-tensive as that of Poipu, Princeville is a decided rival, with a fancy ho-tel, clubs, and golf courses. For passing cyclists, Princeville's main point of interest is the **Princeville Center,** a mall containing a super-market, travel agents, and a gas station. Hanalei's conveniences are growing, but you might as well stock up here rather than pushing your luck later.

After shopping, return to the road, but almost immediately after pull over to the **left** for a panoramic view of Hanalei's lush valley below and the towering pinnacles of Na Pali ahead. If you have not yet tired of the "recognize the landmark" game, look for the triangular peak called Makana, also known as Bali Hai of the movie *South Pacific*. Natural wetlands and taro fields (wet fields that resemble rice paddies) are be-coming more and more scarce in Hawaii as taro loses its importance. The extensive field system around Hanalei is managed for both agri-cultural yield and as suitable habitat for native waterfowl, preserving a niche for many endangered species and migratory birds, as well as a traditional way of life.

On the way down the sweeping hill to Hanelei, look for a firehouse to catch a sight possible only in Hawaii—a fire engine with a surfboard on the roof. When teased, firemen insist that the board is intended for water rescue, not recreation (yeah, sure). Then cruise down two sharp turns into **Hanalei**, a nice little town centered around but not pander-ing to tourism. Due to its proximity to Na Pali's Kalalau Trail, Hanalei is chock full of outdoor outfitters that include bicycle shops, kayak rentals, and so on. The tidy village center features food places and pic-nic tables on a green lawn, with galleries, craft shops, and a nearby supermarket. Experienced swimmers and snorkelers can enjoy the hid-den cays and coral reef of Hanalei Bay, but conditions there are not re-liably calm.

Even if you do not stop and pay to enter, take note of **Waioli Mis-sion House** as you pedal through Hanalei. One of Kauai's earliest missionaries, William Alexander, arrived in 1837 and established Waioli Huila Church in the now-typical Hawaiian missionary fashion. After that, you can complete your ride to the very end of the road. If you want to delay a bit more, look for a B&B in town or set camp in Hanalei Beach County Park. The last indoor accommodations along the road include a few B&Bs and the YMCA's beachside **Camp Naue**, located near the 8-mi marker (telephone 246-9090). Camp Naue offers bunks in a large, shared cabin (BYO sleeping bag) and tent camping.

During the final 6 mi from Hanalei to Haena, a series of narrow, one-lane **bridges** punctuate the road (called 560 beyond Hanalei), pre-serving the peace of this attractive destination by keeping large tour buses and heavy traffic at bay. **Haena** is not so much a town as a name for a scattered community dotted by many vacation rentals.

From the intersection with Wainiha Powerhouse Road, only 2 mi re-main until you reach Haena Beach County Park, and a final mile to

Only in Hawaii: a fire truck with a surfboard on the roof

the very end of the road at **Na Pali State Park**. This last 6-mi stretch is surrounded by distracting views. Early on, you will take in views by constantly scanning from side to side, rolling by long white beaches with rolling surf. Near the end of the ride, your focus will shift upward as you come right up to the sheared mountain rises of Na Pali (literally, the cliffs). Several caves right off the road offer an alternative angle to crane your neck into.

There is a pay phone in the state park parking lot and at the Hanalei Colony Resort 1 mi east of the **county park.** After passing the resort, you can recognize the county park when you pass a sign that says DIP, indicating a low point in the road that is often flooded to ankle height (or deeper) by a stream. The end of the road lies 1 mi farther, at the 10-mi mark.

Campers have two choices of sites, Haena Beach County Park 1 mi before the end of the road, or directly in Na Pali State Park at the end of the road. Both sites are on the water and offer comparable facilities (cold showers, toilets, drinking water, and picnic tables). Both also require permits secured in advance in Lihue, although the county site charges a small fee while state park camping is free. Obviously, the state park is a more convenient site, although the risk of theft may be greater there since thieves target that site as the obvious choice for hikers absent during the day. This factor may make the county site marginally safer. Both, however, are secure in terms of personal safety.

Congratulations! You have now pedaled yourself into perfect position for a hike in Na Pali State Park on the Kalalau Trail, a cliff- and coast-hugging 11-mi-long venture into uninhabited valleys far beyond the end of the road. Many people consider Na Pali worthy of national park status, so spectacular is its natural beauty. Although many hikers walk the trail daily, few manage more than a fraction of the trail's length, meaning that the farther you go, the more solitude you gain.

Unfortunately, it is impractical for cyclists to undertake a multiday hike. However, a beautiful day hike should satisfy your curiosity and exhaust your sense of the aesthetic—as well as inspire you to return for the full journey. Many visitors cover the first section of the trail to Hanakapiai Valley and its waterfall. Try to obtain a brochure describing Kalalau Trail before setting out (at Lihue's state park office or the Department of Land and Natural Resources, 3060 Eiwa Street, Room 306, Lihue, HI 96766, telephone 241-3444). The Na Pali coast is also the top kayaking destination in Hawaii, and tour operators abound in Hanalei for those interested in gaining a seaborne perspective.

Before setting off on a walk of any proportion, however, you will be happy enough just to preview what lies ahead at the end of this day. You may choose to head for Kee Beach at the Kalalau trailhead to swim or snorkel in the afternoon, for example. Just remember that winter brings rough waters to Kauai's north shore, so assess conditions carefully before leaping in. The ruins of a *heiau* above Kee Beach also makes a good place to explore or let your imagination run wild. On the other hand, you can simply relax at your campsite and watch the evening stars glow more and more brightly as night comes to the Na Pali coast.

TOUR NO. 19

TOURING KAUAI'S WEST END
Lihue to Waimea Canyon

Distance: 124 to 143 miles
Riding time: 4 to 5 days
Difficulty: Challenging
Terrain: Easy coastal terrain until a 15-mile climb up Waimea Canyon
Roads: Well paved
Connecting tour: Tour No. 18

While Kauai's Na Pali coast gets star billing, the south shore boasts its own scenic wonders, with pristine beaches, historic sights, and beautiful nature preserves. This tour visits a typical plantation home of the early 1900s and sugar towns that supported the once-dominant industry. Along the south shore, cyclists can stop to snorkel and watch for spray to kick out of Spouting Horn, a hole in the seaside rocks. However, the tour's prime attraction lies farther east, where Waimea Canyon, "the Grand Canyon of the Pacific," twists a deep gorge through Kauai.

Although most of this tour takes advantage of level coastal roads, the grueling 15-mi ride up along the rim of Waimea Canyon presents a formidable challenge. However, your efforts will be rewarded with a great sense of pride and views in all directions—including up and down. Cyclists who conquer the climb can peer down into the canyon, up over the island's high central mountains, and down again from Kalalau Lookout, a 3,000-foot drop to Na Pali's ribbon of splendor. Finally, this tour of Kauai's west side finishes with a trip to Polihale Beach at the very end of the road.

The same sheer cliffs that force Tour No. 18 to Na Pali to dead-end also cut off the western road at Polihale Beach, requiring cyclists to backtrack to Lihue. Doubling back gives you the opportunity to revisit favorite spots or discover new highlights, however, and the entire distance can be covered in a single day. Cyclists who plan a less strenuous tour can still follow this route, although they must sacrifice the rewarding ride up to Waimea Canyon.

Lihue to Waimea: 23 miles (42 miles with detours)

Tips on accommodations and practical information on the island's principal town are included in the Lihue section of the Kauai introduction. Beginning from Lihue, much of this **westward** ride follows **Road 50** (Kaumualii Highway) toward Waimea. A shoulder that runs most of the way along the relatively busy road helps cyclists begin the ride

Tour No. 19   **Waimea Canyon**
And Kauai's West End

Wailua River

LIHUE

Kilohana
Plantation

Road 50

Poipu Beach

Koloa

Princeville

WAIALEALE

Prince
Kuhio
Park

Lawai

Spouting Horn

Olu Pua Botanical Gardens

Kukuiolono Park

Eleele

McBryde
Sugar Mill

Hanapepe

NA PALI COAST

Puu o Kila Lookout

Salt Pond Beach
County Park

Kalalau
Lookout

Waimea Canyon Dr. Road

Russian fort

Waimea

Kokee State Park
(HQ and museum)

Waimea
Canyon
Lookout

Kokee

Kekaha

Polihale State Park
and Beach

N

E
S
W

Barking Sands Beach

0   6
MILES

KAUAI

safely. Once you pedal past the turnoff for Koloa, traffic to Waimea and the island's west end decreases noticeably.

Not even 2 mi from Lihue, you will arrive at the first of many distractions that can extend this short 23-mi ride into a full day's expedition. Turn right off the "highway" to visit **Kilohana Plantation** (marked). This 1935 manor house and its idyllic grounds offer a glimpse of plantation life in Hawaii's early territorial days, imparting a serene, stately feeling like that of the British Empire in its days of glory. Grazing horses round out the aristocratic scene and now shops,

Kilohana Plantation graces Kauai's southern slopes.

galleries, and a restaurant fill the rooms of the luxurious home (free admission). Passing cyclists can take a moment to sit back in a well-stuffed chair and dream of passing lazy afternoons in comfort like this.

Once your visit to Kilohana is over, **continue** along Road 50. Mountain bikers can take a terribly bumpy **detour** that will add a few miles to the ride but is worthwhile for a break from the busy road and the quiet ride through cane fields. To do so, turn left on Puhi Road at the stop light soon after Kilohana. Ride straight until the T at a stop sign, and turn right twice to parallel a mountain ridge westward. After rattling over bumps and gravel, you will come to a freshly paved section that you must follow back to the main road. Dirt roads continue west from there, but they all dead end at private property after 2 mi.

The **main road** rises gradually here, twisting through a gap in a mountain ridge, the first of several moderately difficult climbs on this day. Headwinds may try to blow you back to Lihue as you pedal west along the coast but rarely pose a serious challenge. Soon after you slip through the gap, you can leave Road 50 behind for a time by turning **left** for Koloa and Poipu through a mahogany tree tunnel (**Road 520**). Although the tree tunnel effect was partially damaged by Hurricane Iniki, you will still marvel at the beauty of the leafy, shaded drive.

Just 3 mi down this road lies the small town of **Koloa**. The best picnic spot short of the coast is the green **park** on the right as you enter town, complete with a monument and some benches. A clump of bushes on that green lawn constitutes an overgrown display of sugarcane varieties marked with badly faded identification signs. Peer deeper into the overgrowth beyond to catch sight of the remains of an 1840s **mill**, a testament to Koloa's role as Kauai's first sugar town. A

Monument commemorating Koloa's sugar plantation workers

monument commemorates all the different ethnic groups who toiled in Koloa's fields, from native hands to Asian and European newcomers.

Overgrown sugar mills and cane are all very well, but hungry, modern-day visitors will be pleased to know that Koloa also has a Big Save supermarket (turn left at the T on Koloa Road). While there, take a look at the Buddhist temple across the street, another testament to the island's immigrant influence.

For a slight **detour** to the island's oldest Catholic church, cruise down Weliweli Road (a right turn off Koloa Road if cycling toward the supermarket), then right on Hapa Road 0.5 mi later. **St. Raphael's Church** stands clear white within black lava walls, another picturesque example of early missionary style. Buildings like St. Raphael's spring to life in the minds of visitors with some background information on the period, especially so for those reading a historical work like Michener's *Hawaii*. Both books and buildings remain rather empty when alone, but together they inspire imaginations to refill them with life of times past.

From the church, return to Weliweli Road. Many side routes that branch off are private cane roads marked NO TRESPASSING. Rather than backtracking directly into town, however, you can add another worthwhile **detour** to the bays of Kauai's south-coast beaches. To do so, pedal **up Weliweli**, then turn **left** on Waikomo, and **left** again on Poipu Road. **Poipu** is a quiet area that is steadily witnessing development as a resort destination.

Near the coast, the road passes a small shopping area with a bicycle shop and then splits. **Keep right** for Prince Kuhio Park and Spouting Horn for a nice seaside cruise that dead ends in 2 mi. The first small bay along the coastal road is **Prince Kuhio Park**, named for the Kauai native who became Hawaii's first delegate to Congress and worked to return lands to native people through the Hawaiian Homesteads Act. Kauai's best snorkeling is found along the coves and inlets of the south shore, and indeed you will see many people floating about to see for themselves. If you are tempted to join in, consider calling it a day and staying at one of the B&Bs along this road. Snorkel rental stands line the road, saving the day for those without their own gear.

The area's main attraction is **Spouting Horn**, a blowhole in the seaside rocks that sprays like a geyser with the help of every strong wave. Spouting Horn sounds and looks like a whale, and lucky bikers may well see the real thing blowing an echoing spray offshore. On a calm day in winter, you have a good chance of spotting whales off Poipu and in waters between Waimea and Niihau. That is, until these amazing animals disappear with a flip of the tail.

From there, you must **backtrack to Koloa**. Local cyclists take advantage of a private back road marked NO TRESPASSING to shortcut west to Numila and Eleele, although it is technically illegal. Officially, you should continue the ride by picking up **Road 530 in Koloa** to rejoin the **main road (50) at Lawai**. This route takes you past two sights that are recommended detours on the return trip to Lihue, **Kukuiolono Park** and **Olu Pua Botanical Gardens** (see Waimea to Lihue day). After a few miles back on the main road, you may **detour** slightly by turning **left** toward **McBryde Sugar Mill (Road 540)** and following a peaceful side road to **Eleele**. The only thing you will miss is a stunning overlook of the Hanapepe River Valley, but you can also catch that sight on the return trip to Lihue.

Campers who wish to shorten the day can turn left off Road 50 in **Hanapepe** for **Salt Pond Beach County Park**, a nicer site than Waimea's Lucy Wright Beach County Park. To reach that site, turn *makai* off Road 50 near the 17-mi marker on Lele Road, then right on Lokokai Road. An advantage of riding on to Waimea, however, is the latter site's proximity to the starting point of the Waimea Canyon ride.

For one last stop before calling it a day, pull over at the Russian fort marked on the left just before Waimea town. Although the "nearly there" instinct may tempt you to forego a tour of the historic site, the fort merits a quick side trip. You can even circle the walls quickly without dismounting if you wish. Although the ruins themselves are fairly indistinct, the site's history as related by informative signs is very interesting. In 1817, a Russian business agent enlisted local help to build Fort Elizabeth, part of an unsuccessful attempt at expansion into the mid-Pacific.

Finally, roll **downhill** and cross a **bridge** into **Waimea**. Lucy Wright Beach County Park is located immediately to the left after the bridge, a convenient if unexciting campsite. The park lies directly off Road 50, but traffic should not be a bother at night. The few homeless people camped in the park are friendly or simply uninterested in newcomers. Ideally, pitch your tent near the beach where outrigger canoe teams practice in the afternoon. Waimea's supermarket is only a short walk away. Like many beach county parks, Lucy Wright sees many weekend day users and hosts the occasional luau that parties into the night—but don't worry, you might even be invited to join in. Facilities at Lucy Wright include cold showers, toilets, water taps, and picnic tables.

Cyclists hoping to find indoor accommodations have only one choice in Waimea, unless a B&B agency can help you with a local reservation. Waimea Plantation Cottages, located on the quiet back streets of town, rents small bungalows (telephone 800-992-4632 or 338-1625 locally).

Guidebooks lead visitors to Menehune Ditch, an unimpressive row of stones 3 mi out of town. To be honest, you are better off unwinding on the beach. The only really worthwhile sight in town, a statue of Captain Cook, stands in a convenient, central location on the main road. The statue commemorates Captain Cook's first landing in what he named the Sandwich Islands in 1778. Although he enjoyed tremendous early success and was well received by natives on Kauai, things eventually took a turn for the worse (the very worst) when Captain Cook was killed on the Big Island in 1779.

From the beach at Lucy Wright Park, you can catch beautiful sunset views of little Niihau on the horizon. Niihau is a privately owned island, a curious anomaly in the modern world. The island's population numbers about 200, and there is no electricity or telephone network. The entire island remains in the hands of a single family that tightly controls visitation (basically by not permitting any) and runs a plantation in the good old-fashioned system of the 1800s (save for a helicopter). Niihau is the only island on which the Hawaiian language still dominates, and indeed the only island that voted against statehood in 1959. This view from Kauai is the nearest most people ever get to the curious island, although some dive trips stop on Lehua Island, a rock beside Niihau. Otherwise you must content yourself to imagine life on the island while soaking in the deep sunset hues from Kauai shores.

Waimea to Waimea Canyon and Kokee State Park: 21 miles

This day is a stunning one, in terms of both views and physical challenge. Waimea Canyon, one of the natural highlights of beautiful Kauai, stretches 14 mi in length and digs 0.5 mi deep. Although it is much smaller than the Grand Canyon to which it is often compared, Waimea is as spectacular in its twisting ribbons of color and sense of vast creation time. The ascent from sea level to nearly 4,000 feet will challenge even the most fit cyclist, a good preview for even more challenging climbs such as Haleakala on Maui. The canyon and overlooks to the Na Pali coast are protected as two adjoining state parks, Waimea Canyon and Kokee.

Two roads climb from the coast along the canyon's west rim. **Waimea Canyon Drive** tackles the ascent directly from Waimea town, but that steep road can be tricky to locate. Instead, local cyclists follow **Kokee Road,** which originates in **Kekaha**, 4 mi west of Waimea. Although this route adds 5 mi to the ride (4 of them flat), Kokee Road allows a far more gradual approach, a healthier option for your grinding knees. Ideally, cyclists can round out the tour by ascending via Kokee Road and returning along Canyon Drive to catch the different views from each.

Most cyclists can complete the ride up Waimea Canyon as a day trip with a long ride up in the morning (about 4 hours). This schedule allows for lunch and a look around the canyon, then a quick, easy return to the coast. On the other hand, it is a shame to work so hard to visit an area only to flee away. Ideally, plan on spending the night in the campground or state park cabins in Kokee for more time to appreciate the unique canyon and beautiful Kalalau overlooks. Road bikers can hike in Kokee and Waimea Canyon, while mountain bikers can explore jeep trails. Those counting on indoor accommodations should reserve a cabin well in advance. All cyclists must bring supplies from Waimea, as facilities at both parks are limited to one early-closing restaurant and a snack bar.

To pedal up via Kokee Road, follow signs for Waimea Canyon along **Road 50 west** to Kekaha, a quick 4 mi ride. Turn **right** at the sign for **Kekaha** and ride straight to the center of town, passing the town's huge sugar mill. Another sign for Waimea Canyon indicates the beginning of Kokee Road, a **right** turn. Ready or not, here you go! The climb begins almost immediately. The road all the way to Kokee and Kalalau Lookout is well paved, suitable for both road and mountain bikes.

From Kekaha to the point where Kokee Road and Waimea Canyon Drive meet is 7 mi of gradual to steep uphill, passing expansive fields of sugarcane. Gaining elevation, you will also attain tremendous views of the coast, Niihau, and little Lehua Island in the distance. The climb begins in earnest at the first sharp **hairpin** turn. Plan on taking a few short breaks on less challenging sections along the way. Quick cyclists can calculate 3 hours (including breaks) to reach Waimea Canyon Lookout, and those who like to take their time might need 4 hours. At Waimea's upper elevation, temperatures can be 15 degrees cooler than at the coast, so keep a jacket handy when you pull over.

One can only flip through gears for so long before reaching the last. A seasoned cyclist with good gear strategy will have a much easier ride up, so take the following advice to heart. I routinely pass men much stronger than myself on long mountain ascents thanks to good gear strategy. Do not run through your gears and simply remain in your last granny gear for the rest of the ride up. Click into the second-to-last gear and relax as much as possible on the not-so-nasty sections, granting your pumping legs some relief by being able to click back again when tackling the next, more difficult section.

Bear **left** at the **intersection** with Waimea Canyon Drive near the 7-mi marker (a good flattish spot for a break). From this point, take solace in the fact that the climb becomes more gradual and eventually reaches nearly level stretches. At the 9-mi mark, you will even cruise a short **downhill** before reaching 3,000 feet between the 9- and 10-mi marks. Waimea Canyon Lookout lies just 4 mi from the intersection of the roads.

Hooray! You made it! (Nearly: Kokee remains a bit higher up). **Waimea Canyon Lookout** may be full of tour buses throughout the day, but it is still a lovely spot and perfect for a well-deserved picnic.

Hardy cyclists can enjoy the view from Waimea Canyon Lookout.

There are toilets at the lookout, but drinking water is not available until Kokee State Park. The only elements that detract from the lookout's splendor are hoards of tourists that periodically engulf it and flightseeing helicopters that buzz through the canyon.

Soon, however, the crowds thin and helicopters are replaced by graceful white terns that soar soundlessly through the canyon. Goats that roam the canyon are cute and amazingly nimble, although they may ultimately spoil Waimea Canyon as destructive, introduced animals that outcompete native species and cause terrible erosion. At this high elevation near Kauai's wet interior, there is good potential for gray skies, but clear views into the canyon are almost assured since clouds tend to hover at rim height.

From the lookout, only 5 mi remain until Kokee State Park, where both the campground and cabins are located. Count on a few last climbs and descents as the road rolls along smooth pavement to Kokee. On the way, be sure to pull over at **Puuhinahina Lookout**, another excellent vantage point over the canyon. From there, a short trail leads to **Niihau Lookout** for a mountaintop view of the intriguing island. Finally, you will roll over the boundary into **Kokee State Park**, the day's challenge overcome. Onlookers may even cheer your achievement as you pull into park headquarters, a nice reward for your efforts. If the park information booth is closed, pedal over to Kokee Museum (open 10:00 A.M. to 4:00 P.M. daily). No matter what your interests, Kokee Museum is an essential stop with exhibits on natural and cultural history, an excellent selection of books, and helpful staff. Pick up a free map handout or splurge for a more detailed hiking guide to the state park trail system. Although Kokee is officially a separate park from Waimea Canyon, the two are closely run and their trails intertwine.

Kokee Lodge, a privately run operation beside the museum, has a restaurant, snacks, and pay phone, and operates the concession on park cabins. Their comfortable cabins can accommodate up to twelve people. The Lodge recommends six months advance reservations, although last-minute cancellations create some openings. Cabins come fully furnished with a refrigerator, stove, linens, and hot-water showers. Address inquiries to Kokee Lodge, P.O. Box 819, Waimea, Kauai, HI 96796 (telephone 335-6061).

Campers will find nice grassy sites just down the road from the museum (permits should be secured in advance at any state office), scattered across a hill behind the main restroom building. The campsite has cold, indoor showers as well as faucets and tables at each site. The water is fine for drinking, but taps should run for a few minutes to clear first. Wild roosters never cease crowing in the area, however, bringing to mind tempting recipes for a nice dinner of coq au vin.

The nature trail behind the museum can be covered in only 15 minutes with the help of a self-guiding tour pamphlet. The short walk offers an excellent introduction to local flora as it describes species variety, niche evolution, native uses of plants, and problems with introduced species. Generally, introduced species outnumber natives in Kokee, due to tremendous deforestation brought about by the chaos of sandalwood trade and cattle ranching. Aerial seeding efforts in the 1920s and 1930s introduced many new species to the area, so that most of Kokee's present-day forest does not reflect its original condition. A few native patches do remain, and this hike will help you recognize and appreciate those all the more.

Side Ride to Kalalau Lookout: 3 miles

An excursion not to be missed is the ride out to Kalalau Lookout from Kokee. Unfortunately, it is a wildly **hilly and steep** 3 mi, mostly up on the way out, and more downhill on the return. At least cyclists can console themselves that the road is well paved all the way, with the exception of a few treacherous potholes at the base of severe dips.

Rustic campground in Kokee State Park

Your best chance to catch a clear view lies in the early morning or late afternoon, also coinciding with the best time to avoid most tourists. Simply continue outward along the same road **through Kokee** until you reach the lookout parking area.

Although you will be tempted to try, no photo can adequately capture the spectacular Kalalau view. From a height of 4,000 feet, the cliffs (literally, Na Pali) sheer straight off into the sea, towering over verdant valleys accessible only by sea.

A **right** turn at **Kalalau Lookout** leads 1 more steeply rolling mi to the very end of the road and **Puu o Kila Lookout**. The view from this point is only slightly different, so you might skip it if you are truly exhausted. On the other hand, even a small difference in angle is enough to create new patterns of shadow and light across the eroded cliff faces. The trail into **Alakai Swamp** also begins from this point. Even if you are not planning to slog through Alakai's mud, Puu o Kila's high vantage point offers superior views across central Kauai to Mount Waialeale, the wettest place on earth.

Kokee State Park and Waimea Canyon to Waimea: 17 miles

Before zooming directly back down to Waimea town, consider a day hike in or around the canyon. Trails like Canyon Trail and Cliff Trail lead right up to the very edge of the canyon, while Nualolo Cliff Trail offers adventurous hikers views over the Na Pali cliffs and the sea. For more information and a hiking map, inquire at Kokee State Park Headquarters or the Kokee Museum.

Calculate about 1 hour for the 17-mi **downhill** cruise to Waimea via **Waimea Canyon Drive**. You might choose to spend the morning hiking or biking in the high reaches of the parks and cruise downhill in the afternoon, or plan for a relaxing day by descending early and spending time in Waimea or getting a head start back to Lihue. Another practical option includes descending early enough to spend the afternoon pedaling out to Polihale Beach. Campers can choose to leave their gear at a base in Waimea or pedal everything out to Polihale, camping in more scenic but less developed sites of the state park there.

Waimea Canyon Drive is a more open, scenic route than Kokee Road, tempting cyclists to pull over often for a photo or simply to soak in more views. This road **traces the canyon's lowering rim** for its entire length toward the sea, making a final swoop down into Waimea over **two hairpin turns**. The road ends on back roads of Waimea, from which point you can turn left and then right to return to **Waimea** center and **Road 50**.

Waimea to Polihale State Park: 16 miles each way

To complete your tour of Kauai's west end, ride out to the end of the road and Polihale State Park, where cliffs meet the sea and prevent any further progress by land. Simply follow **Road 50 west**, which has a good shoulder until **Kekaha**. After that point, traffic is so quiet that cyclists will have most of the road to themselves, although a headwind might put up some resistance. The entire ride is flat and quick, although the last few miles over a rough dirt road may slow progress. Bring a picnic and plenty of water from Waimea before heading out, since Polihale offers no services at all.

On the way, you will pass the Pacific Missile Range military installation at **Barking Sands**. Those who are determined to test if the beach really barks can detour there by stopping at the military gate for a pass. The installation serves as the main radar/intelligence station for the entire Pacific. On a more benign level, equipment there also collects and records humpback whale songs.

Past Barking Sands, a sign indicates the **left** turn for Polihale State Park. The last stretch to Polihale Beach is perhaps the bumpiest 5 mi on Kauai, a **dirt road** that tough road bikes might be able to handle. The first mile is the worst, with no escape from ripplelike bumps. Just keep your tongue tucked safely out of range of your rattling teeth. A mountain bike is obviously best for this ride, but Polihale is worth seeing even with a rattling road bike.

At a **large tree** 4 mi along the dirt road, **bear left** to reach the only reliably safe, sheltered swimming spot along this coast, otherwise considered unsafe due to powerful currents. **Bearing right at the tree** along the main track brings you to the end of the road and the main beach access point. Locals boast that Polihale is the longest white sand beach in all Hawaii, as it stretches all the way to Kekaha. Then again, folks on Molokai claim their Papohaku Beach takes top honors. Either way, you will be wowed by the blazing white sands of Polihale, the turquoise swells rolling in, and the towering cliffs that shear off the corner of the island.

Camping at **Polihale State Park** is free with a permit obtained in Lihue or another state park office. Facilities at Polihale include drinking water, day-use shelters, and picnic tables (no showers). Just claim your own patch of shade and relax. High winter surf attracts a number of surfers who often remain to camp overnight (rangers rarely head out to Polihale to check for camping permits). One surfer spotted me sweaty and hot from biking and immediately offered me an ice-cold drink, instantly shattering my stereotype of self-absorbed surfer dudes.

Polihale camping brings you miles away from lights and traffic, leaving you alone with the waves, stars, and views of cliffs outlined in moonlight. It is easy to sit here at what feels like the end of the world and entertain thoughts large and small. There are also two *heiau* ruins in the area, but both are difficult to reach through thick, tangling scrub. Weekends bring more visitors to Polihale, including some annoying all-terrain vehicles that buzz around the beach, so try to time your visit for midweek. When you are ready to depart, simply reverse your route to Waimea.

Waimea to Lihue: 28 miles

Cyclists have no option but to **reverse** their **original route** to Lihue via **Road 50** (Kaumualii Highway), this time with a tailwind and fewer detours. Lihue lies 28 mi away, including a 3-mi detour to Kukuiolono Park, one of two sights passed on the westward leg. Returning cyclists have the chance to catch these and others they might have missed on the way out, lending fresh interest to familiar territory.

After passing through **Hanapepe**, cyclists can choose to either stay along the busier, **main road or turn right for Road 540 and McBryde Mill**. This detour offers close views of the working sugar refinery and cane fields, but also involves a 1-mi uphill back up to Road 50 (which also climbs, but not as drastically). The long, gradual hill may seem endless, but you should be ready for anything after conquering Waimea Canyon. Upon rejoining Road 50, a sign points left to **Olu Pua Botanical Gardens**, another possible detour. Unless you are a real botany buff, however, you will be satisfied by Kukuiolono Park farther ahead, by turning right (east) on the main road.

From this point, the main road has a wide shoulder all the way to Lihue. For a nice break, turn **right** on Papalina Road in **Kalaheo** to visit **Kukuiolono Park**. The only unpleasant aspect of the park is its hilltop location, which requires a 1.5-mi uphill **detour**. After laboring **up** Papalina Road, cyclists will **descend** briefly, then make a **sharp right** to pass **under** the park's stone archway. The pretty park's golf course and serene Japanese gardens create a pleasant picnic setting despite the uphill ride.

Eventually, resume **eastward** progress back on **Road 50,** this time subtracting the Koloa detour. After a few more gradual uphills, you will soon pull into **Lihue**. Since this day covers only 28 mi, those continuing on to the Na Pali tour (Tour No. 18) can get a head start by continuing directly on to Wailua or Kapaa. Cyclists finished with their Kauai explorations should have plenty of time to catch an afternoon flight or relax around town until departing the next day.

POWERLINE TRAIL
Mountain Biking

Distance: 14 miles
Riding time: Day ride
Difficulty: Challenging
Terrain: Steady climb to Kauai's interior
Trail: Very rough jeep road
Connecting tour: Tour No. 18

Kauai's Powerline Trail, a rough, 14-mi jeep road, cuts over Kauai's central mountains, challenging mountain bikers to penetrate those tantalizing heights. Few venture up this remote inland trail, built in the 1930s when a new powerline was installed between Wailua and Princeville. Although the trail is wide, its surface calls for a mountain bike or at least a sturdy hybrid with suitable tires.

Miles of unlimited trail and rewarding sights like waterfalls and Mount Waialeale reward those willing to explore this remote path. In addition, Powerline also allows access into Kauai's high, wet interior, where few trails and no roads dare lead.

Bikers heading for Powerline Trail have several options in terms of lodgings. They can make a base at either end of the ride (such as camping at Anini Beach or Kapaa's hostel or a B&B), ride the entire trail, and circle back to base camp by way of the coastal "highway," Road 56. Those hoping to put in less mileage can simply sweat up to the trail's high point, then turn around and cruise back down to their starting point.

In any case, you are in for a full, tiring day of adventure. Count on being entirely self-sufficient on the remote ride, with tools, first aid, a lunch, and plenty of water. Although Kauai's highest elevation is only 5,000 feet and Powerline Trail barely rises above 2,000 feet, its high point can still feel quite cool and damp. Pack a light windbreaker to ensure a comfortable picnic break and warmth on the swift, windy descent.

Riding Powerline Trail

To begin the ride from the north, **pedal inland** from Road 56 at Pooku Stables. The stables lie west of the 27 mi mark, east of Princeville and 4 mi west of Kilauea. A paved road runs inland for 1.5 mi, passing the stables and a few ranch houses. No signs mark the way, but Powerline Trail is the only dirt road that runs south here. When the **pavement ends**, simply ride **straight** ahead on the **dirt track**.

For the most part, Powerline Trail is as wide and open as a one-lane road but takes on the character of doubletrack or even singletrack in

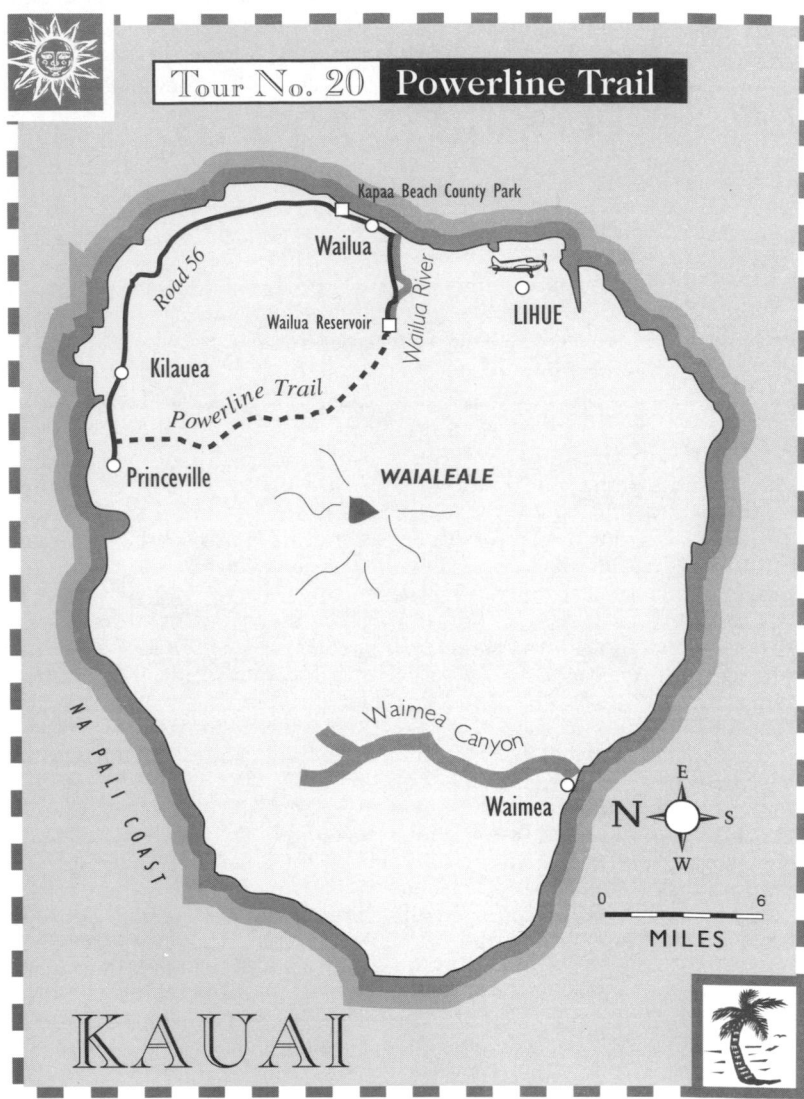

Tour No. 20 Powerline Trail

Kapaa Beach County Park

Wailua

Road 56

Wailua Reservoir

Wailua River

LIHUE

Kilauea

Powerline Trail

WAIALEALE

Princeville

NA PALI COAST

Waimea Canyon

Waimea

N E S W

0 6
MILES

KAUAI

places where most of the trail is simply too rough to negotiate. The effect is that of an obstacle course that requires constant attention and, of course, exertion on the way uphill. The trail's worst conditions come in its first 5 mi, where deep tire troughs and a section of low boulders demand a carefully chosen route. After that, smoother dirt and grass make for easier cycling, although the incline becomes more challenging.

Powerline Trail reaches its peak 8 mi from the end of the pavement, at an obvious **cleft** between two sharp hilltops that stand like guard towers above a fortress gateway. Pause there to soak in views of Wailua Valley and the flatlands of the east coast as well as the craggy north shore. Mount Waialeale rises to the southwest, its slopes dark from moisture (the wettest place on earth with an annual average of 451 inches of rain).

From there, the trail **dips** sharply, then **ascends** for the last time to roll over a second high point. Finally, Powerline Trail descends to **Wailua Reservoir**, looking out over the irrigated lowlands of Wailua Valley, an area sheltered by sharp ridgelines. You will come away from Powerline Trail weary but satisfied with a good day of biking and views of Kauai's natural gardens from a fresh angle.

Mists cling to the high slopes surrounding Powerline Trail.

APPENDIX

BICYCLE SHOPS BY ISLAND

S = service and repairs
R = rentals
T = guided tours offered

Hawaii

B&L Bike and Sports (S), Kona Industrial Area, Kailua-Kona. Tel. 329-3309.

The Bike Shop (S), 258 Kam Avenue, Hilo. Tel. 935-7588.

C&S Cycle and Surf (S), Waimea. Tel. 885-5005.

Competitive Edge Triathalon Center (S,R), Waimea Center. Tel. 885-2115.

Dave's Bike and Triathalon Shop (S,R), 75-5467 Kaiwi Street, Kailua-Kona. Tel. 329-4522.

Hawaiian Pedals Limited (R), Kona Inn Shopping Village, Kailua-Kona. Tel. 329-2294. Also Waikoloa. Tel. 883-0131.

Hilo Bike Hub (S), 318 E. Kawili, Hilo. Tel. 961-4452.

Mauna Kea Mountain Bikes (R,T), Kamuela (Waimea). Tel. 885-2091.

Mid Pacific Wheels (S,R), 1133 Manono Street, Hilo. Tel. 935-6211.

Maui

Barefoot's Cashback Tours (T), 834 Front Street, Lahaina. Tel. 667-5011.

Bridget Bike Rentals (R), 360 Front Street, Lahaina. Tel. 661-7337.

The Bike Shop (S), 111 Hana Highway (near airport), Kahului. Tel. 877-5848.

Chris' Bike Adventures (T), Kahului. Tel. 871-2453.

Cruiser Bob's (R,T), Paia, 96779. Tel. 579-8444.

Fun Bike Rentals (S,R), 193 Lahainaluna Road, Lahaina. Tel. 661-3053.

The Island Biker (S,R), Kahului Shopping Center, Kahului. Tel. 877-7744.

Kukui Activity Center (R), Kukui Mall, Kihei. Tel. 875-1151.

Lahaina Cyclery (S), 3600 Lower Honoapiilani Road, Napili. Tel. 669-1351.

Maui Downhill (T), 199 Dairy Road, Kahului. Tel. 871-2155.

Lahaina Cyclery (S), 3600 Lower Honoapiilani Road, Napili. Tel. 669-1351.

Maui Mountain Bike Adventures (T), Napili. Tel. 669-1169.

Maui Mountain Cruisers (T), 220 Lalo Place, Kahului. Tel. 871-6014.

Mountain Riders (T), Wailuku. Tel. 242-9739.

Molokai

There are no bicycle shops on Molokai. Fun Hogs at Kaluakoi Resort in Papohaku rents mountain bikes, but the business is just a shack by the beach with unpredictable hours and services. Unless you have firm arrangements, do not count on it.

Fun Hogs, P.O. Box 424, Hoolehua. Tel. 552-2555, ext. 7570.

Lanai

There are no bicycle shops on Lanai, but The Lodge at Koele rents mountain bikes with solid "English" tires.

The Lodge at Koele, Box 774, Lanai City. Tel. (800) 321-4666; 565-7300 locally.

Oahu

Bicycle Works/Island Spokery (S), 46-216 Kahuhipa (across from City Mall), Kaneohe. Tel. 247-5200.

The Bike Factory Sports Shop (S,R), 1695 Kapiolani Boulevard, Honolulu. Tel. 946-8927, 942-7655 for rentals.

The Bike Shop (S), Hawaii Kai Shopping Center. Tel. 396-6342. Also: 98-019 Kam Highway, Aiea. Tel. 487-3615. Also: Windward City Shopping Mall, Kaneohe. Tel. 235-8722. Also: 1149 S. King Street, Honolulu. Tel. 596-0588.

The Bike Way (S), 250 Ward Avenue, Honolulu. Tel. 591-8817.

Blue Sky Rentals and Sports Center (R), 1920 Ala Moana Boulevard, Honolulu. Tel. 947-0101.

Economy Cyclery Inc. (S), 28 Oneawa, Kailua. Tel. 261-1197.

Eki Cyclery (S), 1603 Dillingham Boulevard, Honolulu. Tel. 847-2005.

Fantasy Cycles (S,R), 66-134 Kam Highway, Haleiwa. Tel. 637-3221.

Hawaiian Island Creations Bike and Surf (S), Pearlridge Center, Aiea. Tel. 483-6704.

In Shape Bicycle and Skate Shop (S), 95-1249 Meheula Parkway, Mililani. Tel. 623-6343.

Island Triathalon and Bike (S,R), 569 Kapahulu Avenue, Honolulu. Tel. 732-7227. Also, Hickam, Tel. 422-5188 and Schofield, Tel. 624-2349.

Kailua Bike Shop (S), 354 Hahani, Pearlridge-Aiea. Tel. 266-6730.

McCully Bicycle and Sporting Goods (S), 2124 S. King Street, Honolulu. Tel. 955-6329. Also, 94-320 Depot Road, Waipahu. Tel. 671-4091.

Royal Hawaiian Bicycle Rental (R), 333 Royal Hawaiian Avenue, Waikiki. Tel. 924-7511.

Two Wheel Ventures (R), 1982 Kalakaua Avenue, Honolulu. Tel. 943-0223.

University Cyclery (S), 1728 Kapiolani Boulevard, Honolulu. Tel. 944-9884.

Kauai

Bicycle John (S,R), 3148 Oihana Bay 15, Lihue. Tel. 245-7579.
Bicycles Kauai (S), 1379 Kuhio Highway, Kapaa. Tel. 822-3315.
Bike Island Style (S), Hanalei. Tel. 826-7907.
Dan's Sports Shop (S), Kukui Grove Center, Lihue. Tel. 246-0151.
Kauai Downhill (T), PO Box 3322, Lihue. Tel. 245-1774.
Outfitters Kauai (T), 2827A Poipu Road, Poipu. Tel. 742-9667.
Pedal and Paddle (R), Hanalei. Tel. 826-9069.

BED AND BREAKFAST BOOKING AGENCIES

AA Paradise Network Maui (Maui only), P.O. Box 171, Paia
96779. Tel. (800) 942-2242 or 579-8500.
All Islands B&B, 823 Kainui Drive, Oahu. Tel. (800) 542-0344
or 263-2342.
B&B Hawaii (Kauai base; all islands), P.O. Box 449, Kapaa
96746. Tel. (800) 733-1632 or 822-7771.
B&B Honolulu, 3242 Kaohinani Drive, Honolulu 96817 (all
islands). Tel. (800) 288-4666.
Becky's B&B, Naalehu, Big Island. Tel. 929-9690.
Go Native–Hawaii (all islands), P.O. Box 11418, Hilo 96721.
Tel. 935-4178.
Hawaii's Best B&Bs, Box 563, Kamuela 96743 (all islands).
Tel. 885-0550.
My Island B&B (Big Island only; no fee, 36 homes), Box 100,
Volcano, 96785. Tel. 967-7110.
Volcano Reservations (all islands; no fee), P.O. Box 998,
Volcano 96785. Tel. 967-7244.

INDEX